THE ROLE OF GOVERNMENT IN THE UNITED STATES

Practice and Theory

Edited by
Robert E. Cleary

A Report of a Conference
at the
College of Public and International Affairs
of
The American University

Washington, D.C.
March 2-3, 1984

UNIVERSITY
PRESS OF
AMERICA

LANHAM • NEW YORK • LONDON

Copyright © 1985 by

University Press of America,® Inc.

4720 Boston Way
Lanham. MD 20706

3 Henrietta Street
London WC2E 8LU England

Library of Congress Cataloging in Publication Data
Main entry under title:

The Role of government in the United States.

"A report of a conference at the College of Public
and International Affairs of the American University,
Washington, D.C., March 2-3, 1984."
    1. United States—Politics and government—1971-
Congresses. I. Cleary, Robert E. (Robert Edward),
1932-   . II. American University (Washington, D.C.)
College of Public and International Affairs.
JK271.R538   1985   320.973   85-13337
  ISBN 0-8191-4798-2 (alk. paper)
  ISBN 0-8191-4799-0 (pbk. : alk. paper)

THE ROLE OF GOVERNMENT IN THE UNITED STATES

Table of Contents

INTRODUCTION:

THE ROLE OF GOVERNMENT IN THE UNITED STATES:

THE NEXT FIFTY YEARS

Introduction: Robert E. Cleary, Dean, College of Public and International Affairs, The American University

Welcoming remarks: Richard Berendzen, President, The American University

Speaker: Honorable Richard Bolling

THE ROLE OF GOVERNMENT

IN THE UNITED STATES

Robert E. Cleary

What are the best ways for American government to further the goal of a "truly fair society," a society in which everyone will have "a life of opportunity, a fair shot at sharing with others, a life with a future?" How does the government attempt to preserve individual opportunity and choice in the face of an increasingly complex society?

And there is a host of more specific, related policy questions. Should the federal government endeavor, for example, to insure that every individual or family has a minimum level of income? Which public functions are national responsibilities, which belong to the states, and which are shared? Should the death penalty for capital crimes be abolished? Should the furtherance of international competition be a conscious goal of United States trade policy? Should the government foster cultural interdependence among nations as a fundamental aim of its international policies?

These were some of the public policy issues discussed when the College of Public and International Affairs celebrated fifty years of public affairs education at The American University in 1984-85. To inaugurate its anniversary celebration, the College sponsored a special two-day conference on March 2 and 3, 1984. The theme of the conference was "The Role of Government in the United States: The Next Fifty Years."

Those of us who specialize in the study of public affairs do so in part because of a realization that the key issues affecting our society's life and well-being are decided in public forums by public servants. We hope that we can, at least in a small way, improve the nature and quality of this public decision-making. As Frederick C. Mosher noted a few years ago:

> As in our culture in the past and in a good many other civilizations, the nature and quality of the public service depend principally upon the system of education. Almost all of our future public administrators will be college graduates, and within two or three decades a majority of them will probably have graduate degrees. Rising proportions of public administrators are returning to graduate schools for refresher courses, mid-career training, and higher degrees. These trends suggest that university faculties will have growing responsibility

for preparing and for developing public servants both in their technical specialties and in the broader social fields with which their professions interact.[1]

It was with this perspective that a School of Public Affairs was established at The American University in 1934, charged with the responsibility for organizing public affairs education programs that emphasized the resources and needs of the nation's capital. The School was made a college in 1972, and today it enrolls over 2200 students, compared to the 80 students registered in the School in 1934.

At the March 3, 1934 ceremony marking the School's founding, President Franklin D. Roosevelt proclaimed its mission as follows:

Among the universities of the land American is yet young, but you have a great future--a great opportunity for initiative, for constructive thinking, for practical idealism, and for national service....It is a good thing for our American life that this University should be situated in the capital of the country. It is good in the opportunity which it gives to higher education to come into a more intimate understanding of the practical problems of what we call government.

Arthur S. Flemming, an American University alumnus who later became Secretary of Health, Education, and Welfare and still later Chairman of the U.S. Civil Rights Commission, was appointed the School's first director. He developed a curriculum, described as radical at the time, centering on public affairs education programs that maximized the value of the School's location in the nation's capital.

The College of Public and International Affairs continues to emphasize this mission. In 1984, over 1250 undergraduates and nearly 1000 graduate students, representing diverse geographical, ethnic, and cultural backgrounds, participated in its programs. The College had 90 full-time faculty members, including nationally recognized scholars in a variety of fields, the largest number of political scientists and specialists in public administration of any faculty in the nation, and numerous individuals distinguished by their public service records. Its adjunct faculty of over 100 public affairs practitioners included a number of eminent government officials. Over 14,000 people were graduates of its programs, with the majority still residing in the Washington metropolitan area and many serving in federal, state, or local government.

The four teaching units of the College--the School of Government and Public Administration, the School of

International Service, the School of Justice, and the Center for Technology and Administration--offer programs in political science, public administration, international relations, development management, justice studies, computer systems applications, and the technology of management. Applying the best academic scholarship to the practical issues of governmental organization, process, and public service, these programs offer virtually unparalleled opportunities for the study of public affairs and preparation for public service. This potential derives from a combination of several factors: a full-time faculty deeply interested in both teaching and research, supplemented by eminent practitioners who have special insights into public affairs education and the practical functioning of government; location in a city which serves as the seat of national government and which has one of the largest concentrations of international agencies and organizations in the world; a unique arrangement of schools and programs that encompass a variety of specializations in public affairs education; a philosophy of education that recognizes the value of a liberal arts education for students specializing in public affairs; and a commitment to students and to learning, reflected in an emphasis on small classes, a carefully organized professional counseling system, and an overall availability of faculty to students.

In a commencement address to the 1982 graduates of the College of Public and International Affairs, Arthur Flemming recalled his first commencement as director of the public affairs school. "As I participated in that particular commencement, I had some hopes and some dreams as far as that particular school was concerned, as far as the university was concerned. And, I am delighted that I have been privileged to live long enough that I can say that under the leadership of those who now have responsibility for the work of this great university, I have been able to see many of those hopes and dreams realized." Dr. Flemming's conclusion is supported by the high rankings of CPIA programs in recent national surveys.

The School of Government and Public Administration's public administration program rated among the leading programs in the United States according to surveys published by the Public Administration Review.[2] The National Association of Schools of Public Affairs and Administration included SGPA's MPA program among the nation's first to conform with NASPAA's standards for professional master's programs. SGPA's Key Executive program was the first non-federal program to be certified by the U.S. Office of Personnel Management as an alternative to OPM's own Executive Development Seminar. The SGPA and the School of International Service doctoral programs were named by The American University Senate Graduate Studies Committee as two of the three AU doctoral programs that should be selected for distinctive treatment by the University. SIS has been highly ranked nationally on the quality of its international relations program according to surveys reported at annual meetings of the International Studies Association. Similarly, the School of Justice has been highly rated among schools of criminal justice for the quality of its faculty and its program reputation.

Given The American University's continuing involvement with public affairs education over the past half century and, even more importantly, given our accomplishments over the years, it seemed fitting to celebrate our fiftieth anniversary by analyzing major issues of public policy in the fields represented by the teaching units of the College of Public and International Affairs, in the hope that we will advance the understanding of these issues as well as their implications for the public affairs curriculum. Accordingly, the March 1984 fiftieth anniversary conference brought together some 160 distinguished public officials, scholars, and leaders from business and other groups to discuss government in the United States from differing perspectives. With the exception of three plenary sessions, the conference consisted of small-group, specialized panels in which each participant took part in deliberations for one and one-half days. This volume is a report of the proceedings.

The opening session of the conference was a plenary one featuring a presentation by former Congressman Richard Bolling. Representative Bolling called for a reorganization of the American governmental system to engender a more careful allocation of public tasks and responsibilities. He declared that Americans with different goals and perspectives must work together to improve our system of government in order to direct our efforts toward achieving a "truly fair society," a society in which everybody will have "a life of opportunity, a fair shot at sharing with others, a life with a future." He asked colleges and universities to join with public officials and leaders to accomplish this laudable goal.

Congressman Bolling's presentation was followed by a plenary session on "Federal, State, Local Relations: The Next Fifty Years." Elmer B. Staats, former Comptroller General of the United States, chaired a panel composed of Wayne F. Anderson, Secretary of Administration and Finance, Commonwealth of Virginia; Manuel Deese, City Manager, Richmond, Virginia; Parris Glendening, County Executive, Prince Georges County, Maryland; and Mark Keane, former executive director of the International City Management Association. Bernard Ross, Director of Public Administration at The American University, and Richard Higgins of the School of Government and Public Administration faculty, served as rapporteurs.

Financial considerations were uppermost in the minds of the panelists in this discussion. However, structural and functional changes in state and local governments--within the context of their appropriate federal roles--also received considerable attention. As one participant expressed it, intergovernmental relations are "federal-money driven," with state and local roles substantially determined by policy and financial developments at the federal level. The panelists concluded that the major intergovernmental issue for the next few years will be the clarification of structures and financing for public functions.

The opening sesssions were followed by panels which explored the following topics: "The Public Sector: Responsibility and Accountability," "Science, Technology, and Government, Harnessing the Technological Revolution for the Public Good," "Social Justice: Beyond Criminal Justice," and "The American Democracy in the Global Community: U.S. Foreign and National Security Policy."

The panels on "The Public Sector," organized by AU's School of Government and Public Administration, reflected the breadth of focus that is the mission of this School. Throughout its history, SGPA has consistently received national and international recognition for the quality of its instruction, its faculty and scholarship, and the quality of its graduates in political science, public administration, and policy analysis.

From the days of the ancient Greeks it has been recognized that one cannot be considered to be truly educated until he or she understands the nature of the institutions by which that person is governed, the philosophical foundation of the government system, and the nature of its public policies. Thus, the study of the political system has always been included among the liberal arts--liberal in the sense that they liberate individuals by building an understanding of themselves in relation to their society, to their state, and to governments that exceed national boundaries.

There were two panels that dealt with the Public Sector. The first one--"Confidence in Government"--was chaired by the Honorable John W. Macy Jr., former Chairman of the U.S. Civil Service Commission. The keynote paper, written for this panel by Chester Newland of George Mason University on "Decades of Disaffection: Conditions for Confidence in Government," is included in this volume. Four notable individuals responded to this provocative paper: Patricia Florestano of the University of Maryland and President of the American Society for Public Administration; A. Lee Fritschler and Charles Levine from the Brookings Institution; and Dwight Waldo, Syracuse University professor emeritus and former editor of the Public Administration Review. Some twenty other academics and public servants joined these respondents in a wide-ranging discussion of the topic. Howard McCurdy, from the School of Government and Public

Administration faculty, served as rapporteur for the panel. His report on the discussion is included in this book as an introduction to the Newland paper.

Dr. Newland, after examining the recent decline of confidence in government in the United States, argued that it is essential for political leaders to combine values of civic duty and public service if the country is to enhance the quality of its political leadership. A recovery of confidence depends in part on a renewed devotion to the fundamental ideals of representative democracy, equality, and ethical conduct by government leaders. The conference participants expressed optimism that this can be accomplished through a careful examination of past successes, from which we can charter courses for the future.

The second panel on "The Public Sector" discussed a paper written by Nelson Polsby of the University of California at Berkeley on "The Role of Government in Providing for the General Welfare." Stuart Eizenstat, former domestic policy advisor to President Jimmy Carter, and John Svahn, Assistant to President Ronald Reagan, were the respondents. Dorothy B. James, Dean of the School of Government and Public Administration, chaired the discussion in which a number of other academics and public servants took part.

Dr. Polsby propounded the theme that both the public and private sectors are intimately involved in providing for general welfare. He stated that, as a nation, our "general welfare" has improved dramatically over the last fifty years, even though the popular perception has been to the contrary.

The panel discussion focused on the responsibility of the polity for providing for the general welfare versus what people should do in their own self-interest. The panelists concluded that it is exceedingly difficult to develop a definitive statement about the government's role in this context because of the absence of national values and any consensus on the subject.

Former Congresswoman Martha Keys, in a prepared reaction paper, pointed out that while the general perception is that welfare is "relief" for the poor, in actuality 80% of welfare programs benefit the middle class. She argued that one cannot look at social policy without examining the tax structure and its role in policy. "The tax structure and the 345 billion dollars of federal tax expenditures is very much a part of social policy," Representative Keys declared, and "the direct beneficiaries of these social policies are certainly middle class."

Dr. Polsby's paper, Representative Keys' comments, and a rapporteurial summary of the discussion by Michael Hansen of the School of Government and Public Administration faculty, are included in this volume.

The fiftieth anniversary program panels on Science, Technology, and Government were organized by AU's Center for Technology and Administration. Today's revolution in computer-based information systems has dramatically changed American society, its politics, and the nature of its public services. For more than twenty-five years, the Center for Technology and Administration has focused on the study of the applications of technologically-based information systems to public-sector organizational and policy issues. CTA chose to explore two topics in this area for the Public Affairs-50 conference: "Science, Technology, and International Competition," and "Science, Technology, and Government: Regulation of Private Enterprise."

Science and technology have caused major changes in society in recent years. While these changes have generally been beneficial, they have also precipitated certain adverse impacts on health and safety, to the environment, and to organizational infrastructures. Consequently, the federal government has increasingly been called upon to participate both in international competition and as a general regulator. At the same time, federal tax incentives, financing, and regulatory, patent, and antitrust policies often impede the ability of the private sector to utilize technology to improve the quality of life.

Louis Tornatsky of the National Science Foundation chaired the international competition panel: John Holmfeld, Committee on Science and Technology, U.S. Department of Commerce; Bruce Merrifield, Assistant Secretary, U.S. Department of Commerce; Walter Plosila, Deputy Secretary for Technology and Policy Development, Commonwealth of Pennsylvania; and Ronnie Straw of the Communication Workers of America. Nanette Levinson of the Center for Technology and Administration faculty served as rapporteur. Her report of the discussion appears in this volume.

The panelists expressed concern for strengthening the U.S. science and technology base in support of international competition. Participants proposed altering the science and technology infrastructure, to include the establishment of a Department of International Trade and Industry, modification of U.S. antitrust laws, and changes in federal funding for research which would include applied research.

The "Science, Technology, and Government: Regulation of Private Enterprise" panel, chaired by William Rowe of the Center for Technology and Administration, discussed three sub-topics: "Implications of Regulation in Controlling Adverse Impact of

Scientific and Technological Innovation," "The Impact of Standards and Regulation on Technical Innovation," and "The Alternatives, Supplements, and Institutional Arrangements for Efficient Regulation." Marilyn Bracken, Vice President of the Environmental Testing and Certification Corporation, was the rapporteur. Her summary of these discussions is included in this volume.

The federal government's involvement in the regulatory process has been seen as the solution or at least a control mechanism for a wide variety of science or technology-related problems. Participants in this discussion agreed that some degree of regulation is frequently necessary on these matters. But the group concluded that the regulatory process, with its accompanying layers and time delays, often impacts adversely on the ability of business and industry to use technological advances to improve productivity or even the quality of life in society. The panel concluded that there is a real need for continuing critical examination of the regulatory process.

Under the heading of "Social Justice: Beyond Criminal Justice," The American University's School of Justice organized two panels: "Integrity in Justice Institutions" and "Punishment in a Just Society." These topics describe important interests of the School of Justice faculty, but they represent only a small share of the varied research conducted by the School's faculty. Had more time been available, panels might have been organized on the history of penal codes dating back to Hammurabi, tracing and comparing them to the American Law Institute's Model Penal Code; on systems of justice in democratic and totalitarian societies, with special emphasis on the United States and the Soviet Union; on the debate surrounding the defense of insanity; on victims and their role in the judicial process; on the formulation of a rational and effective policy vis-a-vis the use and distribution of drugs; and on issues of justice for immigrants and natives in the formulation of U.S. immigration policy. These topics describe some of the current research interests of the School of Justice faculty.

The panel on "Integrity in Justice Institutions" focused on perceptions of corruption by officials in justice agencies. It included presentations by James Q. Wilson, Henry Lee Shattuck Professor of Government at Harvard University; Patrick Murphy, former Police Commissioner of New York City and President of the Police Foundation; and Edward Codelia, a former New York City narcotics detective who is currently Associate Director of the Prison Fellowship. Dean Rita Simon of the School of Justice chaired the panel. James Fyfe of the School faculty serverd as rapporteur. Dr. Wilson's remarks are reproduced in this volume, along with Dr. Fyfe's summary of the discussion.

The panel concluded that members of the public need to be educated regarding the negative consequences of corruption in the justice system in order to help deter efforts to corrupt officials. Due process requirements and resource shortages may make it difficult for even efficiently-run, honest agencies to act effectively against offenders. The necessity for maintaining a high level of public confidence in justice agencies dictates that administrators carefully explain the limits of their authority.

Members of the panel did feel, however, that corruption and other forms of official misconduct are likely to decrease as agencies become increasingly pluralistic and more representative of the various constituents and interests they serve. The entry of greater numbers of females and minorities into justice agencies is likely to increase public confidence that government is open rather that simply a reflection of one set of values imposed upon a diverse population.

The second justice panel focused on the issue of punishment and its role in society. Adam Bedau, Professor of Philosophy at Tufts University, gave a formal presentation on "Punishment in a Just Society," which is reproduced in full in this volume. William Hemple from the Probation Office of the U.S. District Court of the District of Columbia, and Jeffrey Reiman of the School of Justice served as respondents. Dr. Reiman also chaired the panel, while Ronald Weiner of the School faculty served as rapporteur. His summary statement appears in this book.

Dr. Bedau's thesis was that society has moved from harsh and destructive modes of punishment (with the exception of the death penalty) to more productive modes of punishment. He argued that we should not aim at the elimination of punishment, however, as that would be worse for society than policies which inflict restrictive forms of punishment on wrongdoers. The panel concluded that law and punishment must continually be examined in the light of social justice. There is a need for a reasoned defense of the justice system, but this must go hand in hand with efforts to rectify injustice whenever it is found.

AU's School of International Service organized the discussion on "The American Democracy in the Global Community: U.S. Foreign and National Security Policy," focusing on two perspectives--the legislative branch and the executive branch. These panels represented one of the many areas of expertise in the School of International Service. Founded in 1958, SIS--with a special emphasis on service--has established itself as a leader among American institutions, preparing young women and men for both careers abroad and citizen participation at home.

While international relations as a field of study merges several disciplines, the core is always politics. SIS is concerned with many aspects of the field, including world order, international development, regional studies, international communication, and policymaking. It was this last area of international relations that comprised the contribution by the School of International Service to the fiftieth anniversary convocation; SIS predicated its addresses and deliberations upon those constitutional provisions dealing with responsibility for foreign policy and the common defense.

Sven Groennings, Director of the Fund for the Improvement of Post-Secondary Education, was the featured speaker on the panel dealing with the executive branch and U.S. foreign and national security policy. Richard Arndt of the United States Information Agency; Charles Maynes, editor of Foreign Policy; Robert Beckman of the School of International Service; and Duncan Clarke (chair) of the School of International Service formed the panel on this topic. Joseph Bock of the School of International Service served as rapporteur. Dr. Groennings' presentation and Mr. Bock's summary are included in this volume.

Dr. Groennings propounded the concept of an international education triad composed of international exchange programs, technical and development assistance, and foreign language and area studies. He compared this educational triad with the strategic nuclear triad, which aims to instill fear in order to enhance deterrence. The educational triad, according to Groennings, cultivates understanding, which in turn enhances cooperation and mitigates misperceptions among nations. This panel concluded that there is a deep need for the educational triad to cultivate awareness of the growing interdependencies of the modern world.

Former Senator and Ambassador Gale McGee was the featured speaker on the panel which discussed the role of Congress in foreign policy. He was joined by Willard Berry, Executive Director of the Coalition for Employment Through Exports; Stanley Heginbotham of the Congressional Research Service; and William Olson, Dean of the School of International Service. The panel was chaired by Stephen Cohen of the School of International Service, and Ernest Plock of SIS served as rapporteur. The McGee paper and Plock summary appear in this volume.

The legislative panel noted that in recent years there have been sharp divergencies in the United States over the goals of American foreign policy. At the same time, a more active Congressional role in the foreign policy process has introduced new complications in foreign policy formulation. Moreover, the growing independence of individual legislators and the decline of discipline in Congress hamper the legislature's ability to respond in a timely and unified fashion to pressing international events. The panel concluded that overall there has been a significant deterioration in the executive-legislative relationship, accompanied by a noticeable decline in public confidence in the federal government's ability to carry out a coherent foreign policy.

In the closing plenary session of the conference, Elliot L. Richardson made a compelling plea for a sustained effort by the governed as well as the governors to preserve personal opportunity and choice even as government and society grow more complicated in the years to come. Ambassador Richardson drew attention to the probable future results of such phenomena as population growth, environmental pollution, and the increasing complexity of transportation and distribution systems. He called for the careful use of technology to improve the utilization and manipulation of interrelated masses of data so as "to make sure that government intervention is as precise as possible and causes the minimum, optimum effect." He argued that "the role of the federal government in the next fifty years is going to depend to a large degree on the extent to which during the next fifty years we the people remain committed to a society in which our participation in its ultimate choices is an end in itself."

This was a fitting finale to the formal portion of the convocation, and was followed by a closing luncheon, co-sponsored by the National Academy of Public Administration, during which Arthur Flemming was honored for his contributions to public service. The conference ended with The American University's public commitment to publish a report on its discussions and to explore implications for the future roles and tasks of government as well as for the university and college curricula that prepare government administrators and leaders.

This volume constitutes the conference report. A review of the materials included herein indicates that certain themes occurred and reoccurred in the discussion. The main themes involved:

* The roles and functions of government, including: sub-roles and sub-functions;
  issues of intra- and intergovernmental relationships;
  the relationship of the governed to the government;
  benefit/cost questions; and
  allowing for (and even expediting) change.

* Confidence in government, including:
  the performance of government;
  the nature of governmental regulation;

the importance of integrity and the role of law in government decision-making;
the need for equity;
the centrality of justice; and
the nature of public service.

* The nature of governmental decision-making, including:
the utility of a consensual process; and
the importance of cooperative decision-making.

Of these themes, confidence in government was the most pervasive, with members of virtually every panel noting a lack of public confidence in the ability of government officials and procedures to resolve major problems in their areas of concern. However, a number of other major themes reappear in different situations as well. This fact should not be surprising. There are certain fundamental issues in the American polity, and it is to be expected that they will be present in different forms and under varying circumstances. Thus, the issue of confidence in government is clearly related to the growing complexity of American society and the resultant increasing difficulty for the governors as well as the governed in understanding the relationships inherent in a democracy, the requirements of constitutionalism, and the actions of government.

This volume includes the papers that were written for the anniversary conference, as well as interpretative papers specially prepared by rapporteurs in every panel after the conference. An interpretative paper opens each volume section relating to a particular rapporteur's panel assignment(s). More than an introduction or a summary, these substantive pieces attempt to outline the thrust of the argument presented by the main speaker/panel(s); emphasize the key issues; summarize areas of agreement and disagreement; identify new ideas (especially those on the "cutting edge"); stress themes or sub-themes where they occur; summarize proposals for action, research and/or progress; and define implications for government, public service, education, and/or university curricula.

A great many people are owed thanks for their work on and participation in our fiftieth anniversary convocation. The American University certainly owes a debt to all the conference participants (see Appendix III at the end of this volume for a complete list). More particulary, the panel chairs, those who gave papers, reactors, and rapporteurs did yeoman work, as did Professor Bernard Rosen of the School of Government and Public Administration, Professor William Cromwell of the School of International Service, Ms. Prudence Hoppin of the Center for Technology and Administration, and the entire staff of the Dean's Office. Finally, I hereby acknowledge the major assistance provided by the members of the Distinguished

Advisory Committee for Public-Affairs-50: Arthur S. Flemming (chair), Alan L. Dean, Earl H. DeLong, Ernest Griffith, John W. Macy Jr., Elmer B. Staats, and Richard W. Van Wagenen. Without their help this conference would not have occurred.

NOTES

1. Frederick C. Mosher, Democracy and the Public Service (New York: Oxford University Press, 1968), 219.

2. David R. Morgan and Kenneth E. Meier, "Reputation and Productivity of Public Administration/Affairs Programs," Public Administration Review 42 (March /April 1982): 171-73; William C. Adams, "Reputation, Size, and Student Success in Public Administration/Affairs Programs," Public Administration Review 43 (September/October 1983): 443-46.

THE ROLE OF GOVERNMENT IN THE UNITED STATES:

THE NEXT FIFTY YEARS

Richard Bolling

This paper attempts to give some perspective on where we are in our government and in our society. It will briefly outline where we are and how we can do something about it, because I think that we are again in one of those crises that comes so often in American history.

The history of this country is endlessly fascinating. We live in a world in which we are enormously interdependent, but at the same time enormously responsible. We all understand how complex this world is and how difficult it is to do any of the things that we must do as a leading nation--the leading nation of what I still call the Free World.

We made the transition to world leadership during 1940-1942 --before that we had been completely isolationist, irresponsible, rather proud of having wrecked the League of Nations, but completely unaware of what was even then our dependence on the world and its dependence on us.

The next 20 years or so, probably for the world and certainly for the United States, brought greater changes for more people than ever before in the history of man. Opportunity for people in this country--available only to a privileged few--became accessible to many residents. I know of no society that in so short a time had such a high degree of success in improving the lives of millions. This achievement involved a very complicated and little understood society and economy, a society which has never appeared to be governable and has been so varied that it is occasionally said that--albeit an exaggeration--there are more differences between the regions of the United States than there are between France and Germany.

Our society has changed enormously. We have just emerged from the worst recession since the Great Depression. But 70% of our people maintained a lifestyle which, if not affluent, was nearly affluent throughout that time. This is markedly different from the condition of the country 50 years ago. We face more change in the next 50 years, and we face it with new and rapidly developing technologies, but I would like first to point out some aspects of the past that are important.

Our country has always achieved its success through coalitions of the unlike, those who disagreed on many matters, including some fundamentals. The Revolutionary War was led by people who had violent differences of opinion, and who came from diverse regions. To oversimplify the matter, it was the alliance of New England and the Southern colonies that made the Revolution possible--a coalition of the unlike. When they began to disagree so strongly that they were unable to reconcile their differences, we had the bloodiest war to date--the War Between the States, as it is called in some areas; the Civil War, in other areas; the War of the Rebellions, according to the history books. This war served as the transition from warfare that was relatively limited in its number of casualties, to that which is almost endless in its casualties. Today weapons are limitless in their ability to destroy the world.

There have been two fascinating eras in this country which, in retrospect, could not be described as successful in achieving their objectives: the Wilson era and the Roosevelt era. We did not come out of the Depression because of the New Deal. We did come out of it because of the war and a very complicated set of events that gave the American people unprecedented opportunity.

Many of today's problems stem from changes which have made life better for individuals while complicating society as a whole. Currently, we are confronted with the same difficulties we had in the late 1940s--our alliances are slipping; troubles with our allies are just as great. While no longer poverty-stricken, our allies have strong opinions and the natural desire to exercise independent judgment. And we have a whole new group of nations that seek to find a way of government that will enable survival. This last group appears to have two goals, the same goals that we sought when our nation was born: freedom and opportunity. They especially seek the equal opportunity that will allow them to obtain "the good things in life."

We have not been skillful in dealing with the developing nations. In fact, we have made the same mistake often made in the past: applying a program that worked in one kind of country to other countries, where it ended up a failure.

We also have a basic dilemma insofar as there is a lack of communication among countries. This dearth of discussion may be in part the fault of the academic community. It is certainly, in a major way, the fault of the political community, and the world economic situation. We must find realistic solutions quickly, and many of the necessary ideas are going to have to come from those who dedicate their lives to seeking truth.

During the last 20 years we have allowed ourselves to develop a situation where we have seldom been able to participate in policymaking at the political level. I have watched the House of Representatives and various Presidents struggle to deal with our fundamental problems, some of which have seemed so intractable that we have tended to forget them. For example, we are the only nation on earth that does not have a national welfare system. The implications for chaos in this area are monumental. We have more than 50 state-based welfare systems, which has resulted in a divisive, problematic situation. When we debate with our allies, they are not aware of that complex and uneven system and cannot comprehend our lack of real fairness to the poor.

We have allowed our governments to get out of hand, to become confused and confusing so that we have, to a great degree, lost the support of the people. It is not simply because of Watergate and Korea-gate and other scandals that we face this dilemma--it is due to the day-to-day difficulty of transacting business with different governments, the administrative confusion, and the bewildering number of programs, even very good programs, that we have in place.

The solution is obvious, but very difficult. When I first entered Congress in 1949, the working relationship between business, labor, and academia was incredibly strong. It was amazing to watch the great men of industry, business, labor, and academia work together on common international programs, programs like the Marshall Plan that made it possible for us to help the developed nations rebuild themselves. In contrast, many domestic programs, such as those proposed by the Hoover Commission and the Employment Act of 1946, accomplished little except the expression of ideas and establishment of institutions.

Today's complexity is much worse than that which existed in 1946. We must be willing to look at all levels of government if we are to achieve one government that the people of the country look to with pleasure and with satisfaction. We must reorganize our governments.

Finally, we must make this a truly fair society. If it is not a fair society, it will not be a stable society. And if it is not a stable society, we will not be able to have the kinds of programs necessary to survive in this world. Society will not even be capable of functioning to the advantage of the very rich. We must have peace and stability at home as well as in the world. To come full circle, unless the society is fair, there is no possibility of stability, peace, and justice.

We have made enormous strides toward making this a more just society. We have improved civil rights, education, health, and housing, all the fundamentals that make it possible for a mother to look at her newborn baby and say, "This child is

-17-

going to have a chance. It's a healthy child and it's going to have a chance."

Now we have to find a way to give everybody a life of opportunity, a life with a future. At the minimum, we have to ensure that everybody has food, housing, education, opportunity--in other words, full employment.

A number of people argue that achieving full employment is impossible, but this has been said about very many things. In 1955, when we started work on the first civil rights bill to become law, it was "absolutely clear" that there was nothing to be done about civil rights--there was no way to get it through the Senate. The same was said about education, about health, about legislative reorganization, about foreign policy, about defense policy. Yet improvements came in all these areas.

I believe there is a solution to unemployment, and I believe it is a solution in which the universities can play a major role. It will involve building a much more orderly set of governments in the next 50 years. We will achieve our goals through a political process not unlike that which we now have, but it must be perfected.

The electoral system must be improved. It is ridiculous to allow small states, albeit of great importance and significance on their own, to determine, or at least to dominate, the outcomes in the Presidential nominating process.

The role of money in Congressional politics must be modified. While money is a necessary element in politics, we must also determine how to make the media equally available to all candidates. Money can be an insidious force unless there is a counterbalancing influence. Even the very best legislative system in a democracy is enormously fragile. It does not take the subversion of many members of a committee--probably only 5% to 10%--in order to destroy that committee's effectiveness. The democratic process has to have incomparable purity--and that is achievable. I spent enough time in Congress and was sufficiently experienced to have a sound notion of what kinds of people come to Congress. The wrong types will continue to come to Congress if we do not limit the power of money in politics.

Academics can do enormous good if they will seriously and objectively study the problems of money and politics. We need to see that our people regain their faith in government. They are not going to regain that faith unless political leaders live up to their demands to a degree, which in turn involves on the part of politicians more openness, more frankness, and an effort to serve, not just to be reelected.

Politicians can behave differently than they do now vis-a-vis the media. We have not, as a society, absorbed television yet, and we need to do that. We have to assimilate it in such a way that it is not our master, that it cannot create situations where electoral outcomes are determined or greatly influenced by television. I count on the people who think for a living to help us find ways to realize this. And as solutions are developed, we have to implement them through the political process.

This country has always worked through what I have called the "coalitions of the unlike." We have striven for a rather simple goal: results. The coalitions of the unlike have joined in this fashion: they disagree on the solutions for a series of problems; they recognize their disagreement and the resulting deadlock, which derives from the country's complexity, its cultural mix, the confusion that exists among governments; and they bring themselves together. And as they coalesce, these groups create an atmosphere in which the politicians, the knowledgeable, and the public servants see that there is a new opportunity. For example, it wasn't General Marshall or Dean Acheson or President Truman who passed the Marshall Plan. It was the Committee for the Marshall Plan, which was comprised of disparate citizen groups and their leaders who united in the face of an emergency and said, "We must come up with a political compromise that is viable in this society and in this world."

It was precisely the same with the first Hoover Commission. The history of the Commission is fascinating because the key element was the coalition of the unlike. Approximately 70% of the first Hoover Commission's recommended legislation on the improvement of government passed through the Congress. During the time that I served in Congress, I watched those recommendations and who lobbied for them. The lobbyists came, in effect, from disparate sectors of society--they were coalitions of the unlike, who came from different regions, had different businesses, had participated in different institutions.

I am convinced, after having worked in Congress for a very long time, that the only way in which important work is accomplished in this country is by joining seemingly ill-matched people and making them understand what Franklin said: "If we don't hang together, we'll hang separately."

Academia and schools like this one have a significant role to play. That is the reason I retired from Congress; it was not ill health, nor displeasure with the institution. I remain convinced that ideas and their expression in a practical form, along with their implementation in the democratic process, are the most crucial areas of responsibility.

Federal, State, Local Relations:

The Next Fifty Years

Chair: The Honorable Elmer B. Staats, The Truman Foundation

Panel Members: Wayne F. Anderson, State of Virginia
Manuel Deese, Richmond, Virginia
Parris Glendening, Prince George's County,
Maryland
Mark Keane, Former Executive Director,
International City Management Association

Rapporteurs: Bernard Ross
Richard G. Higgins Jr.
The American University

Summary of Discussion

Section I

Recently, structural and functional (service) reforms at the state and local levels have been developed to cope with the increasingly turbulent financial environment. These issues can not be discussed, however, without reference to the appropriate federal role in these matters. Intergovernmental relations are often based on financial considerations, and state (as well as local) roles are partially determined by reactions to policy and economic developments at the federal level.

State and local governments are not passive actors--they are taking necessary steps to deal with their revenue and expenditure obligations. What is in question in the current "sorting out" process is which functional activities should be assigned to what level and how these activities should be financed and provided. A financial, structural, and functional breakdown is the most appropriate way to summarize the issues and policy options discussed in this section.

A) Financial Issues

1. The greatest single determinant of the financial future of government revenue at all levels (federal, state, and local) is the condition of the domestic economy. Recent national recessions and regional economic declines in the Northeast and industrial Midwest have revealed how dependent the intergovernmental system is on a growing economy.

2. In areas of substantial federal grant reductions, it is expected that the states' willingness and ability to step in as fiscal partners for their local governments will be tested.

3. State and local officials have been forced, in many instances by citizen-inspired tax limitations, to secure non-tax revenue from "public-pricing" mechanisms such as user charges and fees for services.

4. In addition, government officials will increasingly become "entrepreneurs" and "brokers" who secure private sector financial assistance for public sector projects and services.

B) Structual Issues

1. The states are indeed becoming the "key actors" in the intergovernmental system. After more than twenty years of reform in constitutional, executive, legislative, and judicial

systems and processes, states' capacity to deal with both administrative/political and fiscal challenges is "unparalleled."

2. In a related developement of the past decade, cities are likely to become more dependent on state governments.

3. Over the past two decades, state governments have made great strides in improving their tax structures (incomes and sales) and the management of state revenue systems. The flexibility and capacity of state revenue systems--in light of both economic limitations and recessionary pressures--have been put to severe tests in recent years.

4. It is unlikely that structural reorganization will occur on a large scale at the local government level. Functional consolidations and shared service arrangements, as well as the establishment of special districts on the sub-state and sub-county levels, are likely to continue to increase.

C) Functional Service Issues

1. Governments at all levels are facing hard choices about which services are essential. Many new services must either pay their own way or face elimination. The feasibility of allowing the private sector to provide these services is receiving serious attention.

2. The federal government alone remains capable of handling basic income maintenance responsibilities. States are expected to concentrate their efforts in three major service areas:

- education,
- economic development; and
- infrastructure maintenance.

3. It is anticipated that states will be able to assume a greater portion of local education costs, but most other local services will remain local responsibilities, both financially and administratively.

Conclusion

While the most serious financial adjustments for states and cities have probably already been made, the intergovernmental system is still involved in a realignment of functions and finances. While it is too early to depict the final result of that process, it is clear that federal and state-local spenders have "gone their separate ways." Current economic and political trends suggest it is most unlikely that we will return to the intergovernmental system of the 1960s and early 1970s in the near future, if ever.

Financial Issues

Until recently, developments in intergovernmental relations generally moved forward in the traditional, incremental fashion. There were differences of opinion among federal, state, and local government policymakers that had to be "ironed-out," usually in favor of federal interests; the academic community has never agreed upon a single vision of intergovernmental relations or its parent, federalism. But in comparison to the stormy seas of the 1980s, the first two hundred years of federal, state, and local relations were smooth sailing.

There have been a number of major developments which the Advisory Commission on Intergovernmental Relations (ACIR) has labelled "de facto new federalism." This, in the words of John Shannon, is not the "nice, neat, and orderly sorting out process that political scientists and reformers yearn for."[1] There have been a number of major changes in our intergovernmental environment in recent years--changing social values, changing political and policy preferences, and major oscillations in economic conditions. All these transformations converge when one considers the hostile fiscal environment currently faced by policymakers, particularly at the state and local level.

Before considering specific financial developments, it is appropriate to summarize the recent history of fiscal federalism, once again borrowing from John Shannon of the ACIR:

The new fiscally austere federalism can best be understood by comparing it to affluent old federalism which began at the end of the Korean War and ended in 1978--the year of the Russian invasion of Afghanistan and the California taxpayer revolt.

* Old federalism was characterized by steadily increasing state-local dependence on federal aid as the nation increasingly looked to Washington to set the domestic agenda. New Federalism is marked by steadily decreasing state-local reliance on federal aid dollars as the country increasingly looks first to the localities and then to the states to handle domestic issues.

* Old federalism was intrusive in character--a steadily growing number of federal aid "strings" and conditions were designed to alter state and local budgetary priorities and to race state and local fiscal

-23-

engines. New federalism is becoming increasingly extrusive in character--the federal government is pulling aid funds and tax resources from state and local governments to strengthen the financing of its own national programs.

*   Old federalism represented a continuous but unplanned advance into areas that had heretofore been the exclusive province of state and local governments. New federalism represents a continuous but unplanned retreat from federal positions staked out during the "Great Society" era.

*   Old federalism resolved the political and fiscal doubts in favor of social equity concerns, domestic public sector growth, and defense contraction. New federalism resolves the doubts in favor of economic development, defense expansion, and domestic public sector containment.[2]

The key issue underlying Shannon's observations is that federal policymakers, on the one hand, and state and local officials, on the other, are increasingly going their separate ways--both in terms of spending priorities (expenditures) and financial resources (revenues). The following observation reinforces that point.

While state and local policymakers cut budgets and raised taxes in 1983, their counterparts in the federal government continued to increase spending and to reduce taxes. Consequently, state and local budget problems created by the recession were contained, while the federal deficit continued to grow at record peace-time levels.

The enormity of the 1983 federal budget deficit of $195 billion is underscored by a stunning comparison--it is about $25 billion larger than the total 1983 tax collections of all state governments combined.[3]

Public opinion polls are beginning to reveal that the citizenry views each level of government (federal, state, and local) in very different lights. The central finding of the 1984 Public Opinion Poll on Government and Taxes conducted by ACIR is that the public believes it receives more for its money from local governments and, for the first time, more from state governments than it does from the federal government. Previously, the federal level had never finished third in the survey, which dates back to March 1972; in 1984 the local and state levels received their highest support levels to date (35% and 27% respectively).[4] While there has not yet been a comprehensive analysis of these findings, ACIR has offered two early explanations of this phenomenon:

> In a period of high and continuing deficits, part of the sharp decline in public support for the federal government can be attributed to recent publicity highlighting wasteful spending in the federal government, such as reported by the Grace Commission. The increase in public support for state and local governments may also reflect public perceptions that states and local governments are doing a far better job of getting their budget acts together than has the federal government. In striking contrast to the massive federal deficits, states and local governments appear to have done whatever it took to avoid deficits during the severe 82-83 recession, including cutting back spending and raising taxes.[5]

While it would be difficult to quibble with the impact of events such as the Grace Commission inquiry concerning public opinion on governmental effectiveness, particularly at the federal level, the focus here will be on financial adjustments at state and local levels--the second explanation given by ACIR for the unprecedented high public support for state and local governments.

Several points should be made before a discussing these financial adjustments. First, while economic considerations are uppermost in the minds of public officials, they are also focusing considerable attention on the appropriate form of government structure and the potential for non-traditional modes of service delivery. Second, intergovernmental relations have always been driven by fiscal interests, and state and local roles are at least partially determined by reactions to federal policy and financial developments. This is not meant to suggest that state and local governments are totally passive actors--they are taking the necessary steps to deal with their revenue and expenditure obligations. What is in question is the "sorting out" process referred to previously, namely which activities should be assigned to what level and how they should be financed and provided.

Federal Level

The essence of the "de facto new federalism" mentioned earlier is that federal spending will increasingly be devoted to strictly national programs--defense, social security, Medicare, and interest payments on a $1.5 trillion national debt. The combined forces of fiscal stringency and the conservative attitude toward government spending which took hold in the late 1970s virtually guarantee lower levels of federal spending for domestic purposes, particularly in the grant-in-aid programs. Two federal fiscal developments in recent years provide some rays of sunshine in an otherwise gloomy forecast:

1) The most drastic federal aid reductions have apparently already been made and the level of federal assistance to state and local governments overall has leveled off.

2) The Administration's fiscal policy measures have contributed to an improvement in the national economic condition, which has strengthened, or at least halted, the deterioration of most state economies.

State Level

The state level financial picture has resembled a roller coaster in recent years. After tremendous expansion in the use of income and sales taxation in the 1960s and early 1970s, the tax revolt period[6] (1978-1980) brought a sharp contraction in state tax powers. To the casual observer, the period of tax increases that followed (1981-1983) might have suggested that the tax revolt was over. In 1983, 38 states raised tax revenues, while only three states did not significantly increase taxes in 1981-1983 (Georgia, Texas, and Hawaii).[7]

A close look at the situation suggests that major state tax increases in a post-Proposition 13 era is more indicative of fiscal desperation than a sign that big spenders are once again in office. A report from the National Conference of State Legislatures echoes this theme:

This year's tax increases (1983) do not imply that the spirit of the Tax Revolt is dead. The Tax Revolt was very successful in reducing state tax burdens, perhaps too successful. Most states made significant tax reductions in 1978, 1979, and 1980 and refrained from raising taxes substantially in 1981 and 1982. As a result, state taxes fell from 7% of personal income in fiscal year 1978 to 6.5% in 1982. When a long and deep recession and federal aid reductions followed these tax cuts, state fiscal conditions deteriorated very seriously. This year's tax increases should be seen as a means of repairing the damage to state fiscal systems caused by past tax cuts, the recession, and federal aid reductions.[8]

During this time period most states were combining tax increases with major reductions in expenditures; for example, in 1983 across-the-board cuts were made in 27 states, and 37 states made selected program cuts. In addition, personnel reductions were imposed in 20 states and hiring limits enforced in 37 states.⁹ Further evidence of austerity at the state level became clear when most of the tax increases were used for expenditures that had been previously postponed and to rebuild depleted fund balances.

The continuing reduction by states of personal income or general sales taxes must be viewed as a response to the popular conservative view that a fund surplus is a sign of irresponsibility. A potential problem could develop quickly for these states as well as others if the national economic recovery either slows down or reverses itself.

To round out the picture on the state level financial front, several other developments should be noted:

*   the tax revolt fever is not dead, demonstrated by the fact that eight states are considering changing their existing tax and expenditure lids;

*   in addition, six states are considering new taxing and spending limits; and

*   to guard against another recession, more than 20 states have established revenue stabilization ("rainy day") funds. While the specific features of these funds vary from state to state, they are all founded on the notion that the states will be forced to weather the next recession without help from the federal government. The funds receive revenue in the "good years," which can be used to finance services in years when revenue collections are less than normal.

Local Level

The financial picture at the local government level, while not quite as volatile as the state scene, is still characterized by austerity measures. Local officials have been forced by citizen-inspired tax limitations to secure non-tax revenue from public pricing mechanisms such as user charges and fees for services. In some jurisdictions charges and fees raise more revenue than the property tax. Moreover, local officials, particularly in major urban areas, have become entrepreneurs and brokers who secure private sector financial assistance for major public works and economic development projects. In many instances this is the only avenue available for local capital investment due to federal fund withdrawals and reductions in state fiscal resources for local purposes.

The basic message from the largest U.S. cities is that the worst of the fiscal stress is over. They could, however, easily find themselves in a more precarious position than the states if the economy took a sudden downturn. In its annual survey of the nation's cities, the National League of Cities found that austerity measures have been widespread and that cautious optimism and current and future fiscal conditions prevailed.[10]

The Joint Economic Committee (JEC) survey of city fiscal conditions corroborated the basic findings of the NLC study. But one new finding regarding the fiscal problems of medium-sized cities is cause for some alarm:

> This year's survey found a continuing high proportion of cities with operating deficits. This is particularly serious for two reasons. First, for some cities the current budget stress marks another chapter in the prolonged saga of strained budgets, forcing a difficult choice between raising taxes or cutting services in a depressed economy. In addition, for the first time, there is a large increase in the number and proportion of medium and large cities with operating deficits. In the past, the largest proportion of deficits was in the largest-city category.[11]

Local governments in general and cities in particular are striving to heed the call for revenue diversification, which in local terms translates into "anything but property taxes." The realities are that any new revenue discoveries will by necessity be coupled with expenditure reductions in most service categories. Where spending is increased, it is likely to be in areas where expenditures have been postponed over the past several years (similar to state level behavior). The growing concerns of economic development (the infrastructure issue) and educational expenditures will probably absorb any new fiscal resources. As expected, the "going it alone" revenue situation has not been easy for local governments in the 1980s.

Some hope for relief lies in two directions:

1) Recently some states have been able to assist the localities in the two areas mentioned, economic development and education. However, it is unlikely that the states have either the capacity or willingness to assist in other functions.

2) Over the past year the municipal bond market has treated state and local borrowers somewhat more favorably than in recent years. This is in part due to improvements in local government management. If the economy continues to improve and local government borrowers maintain their prudent judgment, the high

costs of borrowing in the 1978-82 period are unlikely to return.

SECTION III

The Changing Nature of State Government

The changing image of state government was enhanced by four factors: 1) the move of the National Governors' Conference to Washington, 2) reapportionment, 3) the growth of metropolitan areas, and 4) the creation of Departments of Community Affairs in state governments.

In 1967 the National Governors' Conference (now the National Governors' Association, or NGA) moved its headquarters to Washington, D.C. This move promoted greater visibility of the governors in the policymaking centers of government and created the appearance that the states were represented in Washington, prepared to take a more active role in issues that directly affected them. The new offices of the NGA established better communication links with influential Members of Congress and government agencies, and monitored key legislative and administrative actions on a daily basis. The NGA was not only able to impart the views of top state officials to federal government leaders, but it was now in a better position to notify appropriate state officials of the federal government's actions and to mobolize these officials to take steps, when necessary.

Reapportionment has been a key issue in intergovernmental relations; as a result of the reapportionment cases, many states began to view their metropolitan areas in a different light. The growing power of suburbia became a political reality to many elected state officials.

The third factor--the growth of metropolitan areas--also followed from the reapportionment cases. Once the state legislatures were reconstituted, the legislators could more accurately assess the real problems of metropolitan areas. Besides a lack of financial resources, it was clear that administrative and geographical problems also existed. The political fragmentation in most large metropolitan areas made it virtually impossible for any coordinated planning or program implementation to take place. Councils of Government, which many hoped would solve this problem, remained voluntary organizations with limited powers. Consequently the states began to look more closely at their metropolitan areas.

One of the techniques employed by the states to monitor and to assist their cities was the creation of a state office or department of community affairs. More than half the states have opened these offices, with most of them located in the executive branch, some with Cabinet status. The Community Affairs Offices have organized resources and coordinated programs that have dealt with city problems. As these offices developed, they also began to serve as a vital link between the funding agencies in Washington and the local officials in city hall.

The federal grant system continued to grow and the states began to play a pivotal role as the key financial intermediary in all but a few programs. Many large federal programs required states to channel funds to local governments, while other programs required state fiscal contributions or administrative oversight.

Each of these factors helped to increase the visibility of the states as actors in the intergovernmental system. However, forces were also at work within the states to help them modernize their governmental structure in order to meet the political and administrative challenges of the last half of the twentieth century. A look at some of these changes helps in understanding how far the states have come in the past twenty years.[12]

Major constitutional reform emerged from the drafting and adoption of new constitutions. Whereas no new state constitutions were adopted between 1921-1945, during the 1960s and 1970s eleven states adopted new constitutions. Over 40 states modernized their existing constitutions, while several others revised or rewrote important articles. In summarizing the constitutional changes, ACIR wrote:

> Present day constitutions conform more closely to the principles of brevity and simplicity. In general, the substantially revised or rewritten documents included provisions to strengthen the executive powers of the governor, to unify the court system, to improve legislative capability for local governments. Further, they contain reasonable amendment or revision processes urged by reformers for many years.[13]

Governors and the Executive Office

One of the most serious weaknesses in state government was the failure to provide for strong executive leadership. The constraints placed upon executive power included two-year terms, low salaries, limitations on re-election, lack of control over the budget, weak appointment and reorganization powers, and too many independently elected state officials.

The states have corrected many of these deficiencies. Only four states still have two-year terms for their governors--a

zeable decrease from 1960, when 16 states had two-year terms.
milarly, only five states bar their governors from re-election,
ereby reducing the lame duck liabilities of the elected state
ficials and giving the governor more control over the executive
anch through the exercise of his/her appointive powers.

In addition, governor's salaries have been raised from a
dian of $16,000 in 1960 to $50,000 in 1980. Governors have
so been give greater powers to reorganize the executive branch
government. In half the states, departments and agencies
ve been overhauled and clearer lines of authority and
sponsibility have been established. This, in turn, has helped
reduce overlapping and duplication.

Finally, almost all governors have been given greater budget
thority. They are authorized to prepare and to present the
nual budget, as well as to monitor expenditures--similar to the
dget authority of the President of the United States.

ate Legislatures

The 1960s and 1970s also produced dramatic changes in the
ate legislatures. Perhaps the most dramatic reforms have
curred in how and when the legislature conducts its business.
y 1980 three-fourths of the state legislatures met annually and,
the 14 states which met biannually, several were called into
ecial session by their governors on a regular basis. In the
rly 1960s only 20 state legislatures met annually. This change
s allowed the states to remain current with the rapidly
anging pace of events in American political, social, and
onomic life. A number of states, though, still limit the
gislative session to 60 days or less.

The state legislatures also took steps to professionalize their
erations. In 1960 few states had full-time professional staff
r their key committees. By 1980 36 states had implemented
is reform in both houses, making it much easier for members
be briefed on changing aspects of the budget or legislation.
w committee members could also be quickly provided with
dates by the professional staff.

The legislatures have also opened many more of their
mmittee meetings to the public and have begun to record roll
ll votes. At the same time, a number of states have passed
nflict of interest laws, while others have greatly strengthened
eir lobbying laws by tightening up their regulations on
gistration and disclosure of lobbying activities.

In another reform movement, spurred by the apparent
crease in corruption on the state level, the legislatures began

to pass laws on campaign financing and ethics in government These actions not only helped to identify illegal activities, bu they went far towards improving the public image of stat government and particularly state legislatures.

The state legislatures have also become more involved i both the auditing and the oversight functions of government Today, over 20 legislatures are responsible for auditing stat programs. Over three-fourths of the state legislatures ar accountable for the appropriation of federal funds which com into the state. This almost doubles the number of state reporting such an obligation in 1975.[14]

Judicial System

By the 1960s the state court systems had become the focu of considerable criticism. Confusion, delay, and lack of accurat information impeded the flow of justice. The ensuing refor movement in the 1960s was highlighted by revamped systems i California, Colorado, Illinois, Michigan, Nebraska, New Mexico New York, Oklahoma, and Alabama. This reform continue through the 1970s. Most of the initiatives occurred in the are of court administration and management. The state courts wer integrated so that cases could be processed fairly an expeditiously, and accurate information was available to al concerned. Judicial selection procedures were standardized and in many cases, depoliticized. Full-time professional staff wer hired to administer the caseload and oversee record-keeping an paperwork. Over 80 percent of the states established effectiv machinery to discipline and, if necessary, remove incompeten judges.

CONCLUSION

The history of federal, state, and local relations has alway been characterized by a complex weave of political, economic and administrative issues and events. The most recent chapte in that history has been characterized as a major reform perio in terms of both structures and finances at the state level National economic developments and changing policy agenda associated with the "new federalism" (post-1978 variety) hav triggered a restructuring of finances at local levels as well. I appears that the federal government, on the one hand, and th state and local governments, on the other hand, are truly "goin, their separate ways" financially and functionally.

The key questions asked by most intergovernmental relation observers (officials and researchers alike) are: 1) Have w completely shed the cooperative federalism mantle, where nationa finances and standards are seen as the "carrot and stick" o intergovernmental policy development?; and 2) Can the newl eformed states meet the challenge of forming greater partnerships with local government and the private sector which appears to have been thrust upon them?

The answers to these questions will in large measure determine the future course of intergovernmental relations over the remainder of this century.

NOTES

1. Advisory Commission on Intergovernmental Relations, "De Facto New Federalism or a 'Sorting Out' of Sorts," Testimony o Dr. John Shannon before the Subcommittee on Intergovernmenta Relations of the U.S. Conference of Mayors (Philadelphia, PA June 15, 1984).

2. Ibid.

3. Advisory Commission on Intergovernmental Relations Significant Features of Fiscal Federalism, 1982-83 Editio (Washington, D.C.: Advisory Committee on Intergovernmenta Relations, 1984), 1.

4. Advisory Commission on Intergovernmental Relations "Public Opinion 1984," News Release, July 1, 1984. The specifi question asked of the respondent was "From which level o government do you feel you get the most for you money--Federal, State, or Local?" In May 1984, 24% chos "Federal," 35% picked "Local," 27% selected "State," and 14 reponded "Don't Know."

5. Ibid.

6. In this period no new taxes were adopted and there wer only eight instances of tax increases and 54 instances of ta decreases. See ACIR, Significant Features of Fiscal Federalism 53.

7. Ibid.

8. Steven D. Gold and Karen M. Benker, "State Budge Actions in 1983," (Denver, Colorado: National Conference o State Legislatures, September 7, 1983), 1.

9. National Governors' Association and the Nationa Association of State Budget Officers, Fiscal Survey of the State 1983 (Washington, D.C.: The National Governor's Conference 1984).

10. Frances Viscount, "City Fiscal Conditions and Outlook fo Fiscal 1984: Resourcefulness vs. Resources" (National League o Cities, December 1983).

11. Joint Economic Committee, U.S. Congress, "Trends in th Fiscal Conditions of Cities: 1981-83" (Washington, D.C., 1983).

12. For a discussion of these changes, see State and Loca Roles in the Federal System (Washington: Advisory Commissio

on Intergovernmental Relations, 1981).   Also see The State of the States in 1974:   Responsive Government for the Seventies (Washington, D.C.:   The National Governors' Conference, 1974).

13.   In Brief: State and Local Roles in the Federal System (Washington, D.C.:   Advisory Commission on Intergovernmental Relations, 1981), 5.

14.   The Intergovernmental Grant System as Seen by Local, State, and Federal Officials (Washington, D.C.:   Advisory Commission on Intergovernmental Relations, 1977), 101.   For a discussion of one of the more interesting court cases on this subject, see A. Lee Fritschler and Bernard H. Ross, Business Regulation and Government Decision-Making (Boston, Massachusetts: Little, Brown and Co., 1980), 126-128.

Part I: The Public Sector: Responsibility and Accountability

A. Confidence in Government

Chair: Honorable John W. Macy Jr.,
        former chairman, U.S. Civil Service Commission

Presentation by: Chester A. Newland, George Mason University

Respondents: Patricia Florestano, University of Maryland
              A. Lee Fritschler, The Brookings Institute
              Charles Levine, The Brookings Institutue
              Dwight Waldo, Emeritus, Syracuse University

Rapporteur: Howard McCurdy, The American University

CONFIDENCE IN GOVERNMENT

Howard E. McCurdy

Public confidence in American government fell sharply in the sixteen years between the enlargement of the American presence in Vietnam and the hostage crisis in Iran. This followed a period during which the public had expressed great trust in the American government and its leaders. In a series of national public opinion polls taken between 1958 and 1964, three-fourths of the persons sampled expressed "trust" in government. A decline set in during 1965 and reached such proportions that by 1980 pollsters could find only one-fourth of the public still willing to say that they trusted "the government in Washington to do what is right most of the time."[1]

While these figures seem rather straightforward, the depth and significance of the confidence problem is not. Some persons interpret the figures as signs of fundamental discontent within the American political system, as a crisis in confidence that can be relieved by nothing less than major political change. At the opposite extreme, others see only the traditional American tendency to praise the system while regarding with suspicion the people who are thrust forward to run it. This latter point of view often leads to the conclusion that the problem, to the extent that a problem exists at all, is a product of political rhetoric and will be ameliorated as soon as politicians stop bad-mouthing the government.

Between these two views lie the interpretation represented in the paper prepared by Chester Newland, the keynote for this panel. Newland believes that the confidence problem is real, deep-seated, and capable of triggering fundamental constitutional change. At the same time, he does not think that fundamental change is necessary. The cause of the problem, Newland argues, can be traced to poor governmental performance and can therefore be corrected by improving performance and the public sense of civic accomplishment. The panel on "Confidence in Government" addressed the causes and consequences of the confidence problem. Chester Newland presented the lead paper, which is reproduced here. Dwight Waldo, Charles Levine, Patricia Florestano and A. Lee Fritschler delivered formal responses, while John Macy chaired the panel. In all, 28 academics and practitioners participated in the discussion which followed. This paper reviews the different perspectives on the confidence problem and the proceedings of the panel.

Politics and Performance

The questions posed in public opinion surveys suggest that the public perceives both problems of integrity and problems of performance in American government. Politicians quickly picked up these trends in public opinion; before public confidence had dropped fifteen points from its 1964 high, a major presidential candidate was running on an anti-governmental platform. Other candidates soon learned the political advantages to be gained in running against the government, particularly in focusing public discontent on the non-elected branch, the bureaucracy. But in spite of the attempts by politicians to deflect public discontent toward the bureaucracy, the public remained dissatisfied with the government in general as well as with other American institutions, including a number in the private sector. This left many commentators--including members of the panel--wondering whether the discontent had reached such levels that the public was prepared to consider major constitutional changes and revisions in mainstream policy. At the same time, doubters and cynics wondered whether the "crisis in confidence" was anything more than a phoney issue drummed up by politicians at election time, useful for campaign rhetoric but incapable of providing real momentum for fundamentally new directions in government policy.

The first dimension of the confidence problem is suggested by the word "trust." Pollsters from the University of Michigan Center for Political Studies asked, in a general way, "How much of the time do you think you can trust the government in Washington to do what is right--just about always, most of the time, or only some of the time?"[2] The dwindling rate of approval suggests that Americans in increasing numbers became cynical about the moral principles of people who held high office, not a surprising result in light of the confessions and convictions amassed during the 1970s.

Two follow-up questions bear this out. The pollsters asked respondents whether the government is "run by a few big interests looking out for themselves" and whether the people "running the government are a little crooked." Public response to the question on trust in general moved from a disapproval rating of 22% in 1964 to a disapproval rating of 74% in 1980. The follow-up questions showed similar trends. The number of people who felt that the government was "run by a few big intersts" climbed from 31% to 77%; those who felt that "quite a lot" of the people running the government were "a little crooked" climbed from 28% to 45%.

Two other follow-up questions posed in the polls suggest not only that the public found its leaders lacking in virtue but that it also found its government to be lacking in competence. The pollsters asked whether "people in government waste a lot of the money we pay in taxes" and whether "the people running the government are smart people who usually know what they are doing?" In 1964, only 27% of the people sampled thought that public officials did not know what they were doing; by 1978 this had climbed to 51%. While 46% of the respondents thought that public officials wasted "a lot" of their money in 1964, by 1980 fully 78% agreed with this statement.

Almost as soon as the decline in confidence began, politicians recognized the advantages in exploiting it for political gain. In the race for the Presidency in 1968, independent candidate George Wallace won 13.5% of the popular vote and 46 electoral votes, the largest electoral total for a third-party non-incumbent since John Breckinridge won 72 electoral votes for secession in 1860. According to pollster Patrick Caddell, it became apparent that many Americans were prepared to cast their votes for any "fresh face" who promised change--regardless of whether the candidate was liberal or conservative. ("If you appeared to be a fresh face, that would attract Wallaceites."[3]) The "fresh face" theory led to another historic first in American government--the successive unseating of two incumbent Presidents by a disgruntled public. By 1980 the public, which expressed such high confidence just sixteen years earlier, apparently had come to believe that the government could neither win wars nor whip inflation, and that its aptitude for making blunders was matched only by its appetite for consuming ever larger shares of the national wealth.

In 1960, when John Kennedy ran for the Presidency, he challenged young people to look to government for a career or a term of service. He established agencies to serve as vehicles for the ensuing enthusiasm. By the 1980 election, with only 25% of the public expressing confidence in American government, candidate Ronald Reagan ran on a platform of getting government "off of our backs and out of our pocketbooks." In the prior election Jimmy Carter had criticized the government as a "horrible bureaucratic mess...disorganized, wasteful, has no purpose, and its policies...are incomprehensible or devised by special interest groups with little regard for the welfare of the average citizen."[4] Neither candidate praised public service as a worthy career. To suggest reforms, Reagan invited business men and women to come to Washington and look at executive branch activities "as if the agencies being studied were companies they might wish to buy or take over."[5]

The bureaucracy proved to be an inspiring target for politicians seeking to translate confidence crises into political gain. Compared to the Congress, the bureaucracy was not organized well enough nor did it have sufficient access to the media to respond effectively to attacks. In contrast to the

Office of the President--which was also malfunctioning--attacks on the bureaucracy did not run the risk of confronting a reservoir of public sympathy for the institution. And compared to organizations in the private sector, the objects of attack during earlier eras of discontent, the federal bureaucracy was not a source of large campaign contributions that might be frightened off by campaign rhetoric.

Nevertheless, all of these institutions were experiencing slides in public confidence similar in degree to those facing the public service. By 1979, expressions of "a great deal of confidence" in various public and private American institutions stood at the following lows: the executive branch, 17%; Congress, 18%; the military, 29%; big business, 18%; organized labor, 10%; organized religion, 20%; the medical establishment, 30%, down from 73% thirteen years earlier.

By mid-1984, state legislatures had come within two states of a call for a constitutional convention. Technically, the call was for a Constitutional amendment requiring Congress and the executive to balance the federal budget; but once a constitutional convention is called, it may meet for any purpose. The last time that the states called for a convention for the "sole and express purpose" of amending the existing document, the delegates threw out the Articles of Confederation and created the Constitution of the United States.

It is not unrealistic to view the performance of government as a constitutional problem, one that requires fundamental changes in practices or policies for which there has previously been a high level of approval. In this light, the above mentioned opinion polls can be interpreted as a beneficial indicator that the public understands the limits of governmental power and "the need for lowered expectations." The American government certainly has less influence over events than it did in the closing months of World War II, when it produced a much larger proportion of the world's gross domestic product and could still demand unconditional surrender from its enemies.

Although many of the panel were prepared to include constitutional dimensions in the confidence problem, few were prepared to acknowledge constitutional change as a solution. A majority of the participants--including some who espoused the constitutional interpretation--thought that political solutions would answer the problem. Concerned with the tendency of politicians to "whip the public service" for short-term electoral gain, these participants wanted to increase the risks and decrease the benefits of employing what has been viewed by politicians as a relatively cheap but effective campaign technique. Certain participants went so far as to treat confidence strictly as a political issue, rooted in campaign management, generated by politicians and the press, and reflecting no deep-seated desire to restructure the political game. In short, a number of panelists believed that any crisis of confidence was a phoney issue.

A Phoney Crisis?

Chester Newland begins his paper by reviewing the dimensions and indicators of loss in confidence. Focusing only on the survey research data--that is, the general drop in "trust" from 76 to 25%--it is not clear that the confidence crisis rests, to use Arthur Miller's words, in "widespread, basic discontent and political alienation."[6] It is equally plausible that the "confidence problem" is a phoney crisis, manufactured by the press, by pollsters, and by interest groups for whom the "crisis" provides a convenient pretext for enhancing their own personal power.

Ben Wattenberg proposes a similar argument in his 1974 analysis, The Real America. He bases his conclusion on two sets of contradictory data from public opinion polls and other sources. Wattenberg does not contest the University of Michigan survey research data which shows that trust in American government is plummeting. He simply stacks that data up against the equally plausible evidence which shows that Americans are doing better and are happier about their own lives. Wattenberg's analysis was regrettably published prior to the Carter-Reagan recession of 1980, when pessimism did finally penetrate the faith of Americans in their own future.

Newland can neither base his case for a "confidence crisis" on a public opinion poll nor on a single Presidential speech. President Carter delivered such a speech on July 15, 1979, an apocalyptic statement fashioned largely by pollster Patrick Caddell. It is noteworthy that Carter's decision to address the nation on the confidence crisis was opposed by both his chief domestic adviser, Stuart Eizenstat, and by then-Vice President Walter Mondale, who called both the speech and its principal author "crazy." Following the speech and subsequent events, Carter's popularity plummeted to a 19% approval rating. This helped to convince Ronald Reagan and his advisers of the necessity of projecting an aura of Presidential optimism even in the face of disaster. As of late 1983, public "trust" in government had climbed 21 points to 46%, suggesting a shallow trust problem that might be corrected through image building, patriotism, and public relations.

If the confidence crisis is phoney, it should not carry over into opinions about basic American policies. Public discontent should be counterbalanced by a continuing consensus on the basic role of government in society and on constitutional practices such as public election methods. People might generally rant and rave about elected politicians--but they should also express fundamental agreement with the central policies of the American system.

Newland cites two studies, one based on opinion data and the other on newspaper content, which suggest that confidence crises extend to government policies. A 1974 analysis, as well as another in 1979, were published in the American Political Science Review. The 1974 analysis, as its authors report, shows widespread "dissatisfaction with the policy alternatives that have been offered as solutions to contemporary problems."[7] Politicians, the authors go on to say, will find the task of formulating alternative policies increasingly difficult because of the divisiveness accompanying public dissatisfaction:

> The findings strongly suggest, moreover, that policy alternatives more acceptable to the total population will be exceedingly difficult to discover in the future because of the existing degree of polarization.[8]

Other indicators, such as voter participation and citizen contact with government, are less convincing. The analysis suggests, however, that the confidence crisis penetrates the historic support for the "American system" as a whole.

Fundamental Change

Having suggested that the confidence crisis is real, that it extends to policies as well as to personalities, Newland returns to the middle ground to construct his solution. Had the government and the individuals leading it during the 1970s not performed so poorly, he suggests, public dissatisfaction would not be so deep. Even though dissatisfaction with governmental performance may lead to dissatisfaction with centrist policies, it is not essential to change policy radically or to rewrite the constitution in order to win back public support. It may only be necessary to improve performance.

Newland offers an analysis of the 1980 election as evidence. Reagan and his conservative supporters might wish to see in their 51% majority (Carter got 41%, Anderson 7%) a "mandate" for new directions in government policy, but the polling data does not seem to support that view. Reagan was elected, Newland says, because of "pervasive dissatisfaction with (Carter's) first-term performance and doubt about his personal competence as a political leader." The 1980 election, says Newland, signaled public desire for a strong Presidency, not "a sharp change in policies." In short, Newland concludes, people want effective leadership. Reagan and his supporters, however, attempted to interpret their winning margin as a mandate for fundamental change. Public opinion research, Newland argues, suggests that any attempt to change the fundamental direction of government will polarize an electorate for whom policy dissatisfaction is already a source of alienation.

Few of the panel participants objected to Newland's analysis of factors contributing to the disastrous performance of American government in the 1970s. Newland catalogues an impressive list. It includes: a series of negative elections that propelled people with poor leadership capabilities into high office, the media's preoccupation with portraying failure, a long series of negative audits and investigations, and the single interst group politics of the period. The decline in public confidence began shortly after the assassination of John Kennedy, continued through the war in Vietnam (the longest in American history), accelerated with the Watergate scandals (and President Gerald Ford's pardon of Richard Nixon, an act which is generally said to have cost him the 1976 election), and reached its nadir during the hostage crisis in Tehran, when the government was unable to free the captives.

In Newland's view, the same forces which pushed the country toward its crisis of confidence are now being used to promote constitutional reforms that would significantly weaken the government. As part of the general assault on government, the public service has been singled out as a target for special change. Newland cites two lines of thought as illustrations. "Public choice" theory, which has provided the academic justification for a variety of conservative reforms, treats bureaucratic power as the primary source of public discontent. In fact, empirical studies show that bureaucratic power is only one of a number of factors contributing to the growth of government; but the bureaucracy has nevertheless proved to be a popular target, even among social scientists. Newland chides the bureaucracy-blamers for being "unrealistic," yet admits that they speak to an appreciative audience.

Newland also cites academic efforts to discredit the politics-administration dichtomy. The belief that "technical" administration could be divorced from "political" policymaking has always had a mythical quality about it, but then myths often serve useful purposes. For over 60 years, following the passage of the Pendleton Act, reformers used the myth to justify an independent, technically competent public service. Academics attacked this as inaccurate (bureaucrats did make policy) and undesirable (bureaucrats should make policy). Politicians apparently listened, but in a way that academics had not fully anticipated. If bureaucrats make policy, politicians observed, and policymaking is a poltical function, then control of the bureaucracy becomes an important political objective.

The upshot of this is Newland's now famous observation that political candidates intend to "politicize and deinstitutionalize" the public service.[9] They intend to do so, moreover, in the name of restoring confidence in American government. Newland makes a very convincing case--here and elsewhere--that such a "return to spoils" is underway. What is more interesting in his suggestion that such a movement will further erode government performance in the name of improving it. The capture of the bureaucracy for short-term political gain will probably diffuse its technical capacity for effective administration. This not only would lead to new crises in performance, but could also fuel the popular disatisfaction with the government policy that results from it.

Civic Duty

Newland believes, along with most of the other panel members, that professional opinion among public leaders must be mobilized to repel the notion that confidence can be restored by destroying the public service. At the same time, he says, measures must be taken to improve government performance. Newland thinks that both goals can be reached through the restoration of what he calls "civic duty."

In analyzing upswings in public confidence during the past 20 years, Newland isolates two motivating events. Initially, people start to feel "better off." It then jells, says Newland, when leaders follow this up with expressions of optimism and appeals to civic pride. He believes that long-term recovery of confidence would have to build upon this mood in three ways. First, government leaders need to proclaim their devotion to the ideal of public service as the most fundamental exercise of citizenship. This expression would need to be accompanied, in the second instance, by demostrations of civic confidence--trust in government--by national leaders. Finally, the general public must come to believe that they participate effectively in the governance process, not only when they vote, but when they participate in "private" affairs such as commerce, religion, education, and charity.

The Politics of Pillorying

Newland's call for a return to civic duty did not strike the panelists as a particularly promising method for restoring confidence, but they were more than willing to join Newland in his attack on politicians who ridicule and politicize the public service in the name of re-establishing faith in government.

As an example of "bureaucratic reform" rhetoric used as a device to change the course of government, the panel discussed the so-called "Grace Commission" report. Issued in 1983 by industrialist J. Peter Grace and a staff of some 2,000 business men and women, the report ostensibly sought to improve the management of government through busines-like methods. Grace announced that $424.4 billion could be saved over the following three years by the adoption of "management reforms." In fact, on closer inspection, the report reveals not only that many of the figures were manufactured but, more important, many of them represented savings that could be achieved by enacting conservative programs rather than "improving management."

When a leading academic sought a professional opinion on the report, he was warned that a high-ranking official had told one potential author that "anyone in government informed enough to write about the Grace Commission would also 'be smart' enough not to do so."[10] Professionals apparently felt that a criticism of the report would lead to repercussions that would damage their careers--a consequence, given the depth of anti-government feeling in the country, which they could not neutralize by appealing for public sympathy.

The participants discussed various responses to counter assaults on the public service. All agreed that such assaults had transgressed the point at which professionals could respond through academic journals. Most agreed that it was futile to try to change the attitudes of the general public, given the strength of their skepticism and hostility toward the bureaucracy. Instead, most agreed that national leaders could be convinced of the long-range dangers of using anti-government rhetoric to weaken the powers of the state.

Improving Performance

In the long run, the restoration of confidence in American government will depend in large part upon the ability of career professionals to help improve the performance of government. Effectiveness is the issue. Too often, the government assumes a task that it cannot accomplish, as was the case in Vietnam and in domestic programs like the War on Poverty.

The panelists agreed that the professional community could contribute to governmental performance in a number of ways, such as by restoring an understanding of the principles of good management. Professional experts can advise politicians on ways to strengthen administrative management in government agencies. There is a fine line between such recommendations and lobbying, as politicians can treat such contributions as just another effort on behalf of public employees. Moreover, these experts do not possess a clear understanding of the factors that contribute to governmental performance. The participants felt that there is a need for more research on the factors that contribute to program success.

It is difficult however, to study program success when one is not sure which programs are successful. While there has been considerable research on public perceptions of government, very little has been written on confidence within government. How, for example, do public executives view the performance of various government programs? What means do legislators use to assess program success or failure? How do business managers who spend short terms of service in government view the contribution of the public administration movement to program success?

As Elliot Richardson pointed out in his address to the conference, it is widely believed among people with managerial experience that governmental performance remains hard to measure because public programs have no "bottom line." But, he added the behavior of mutual insurance company executives--who do not work for profit--differs unappreciably from those in privately owned insurance companies. Each respond to societal notions of performance that involve something more than profit. There have been no significant studies done on perceptions of performance within non-profit and government organizations, with the result that the public service tends to be judged by business analogues that do not fit or, worse yet, economic models that carry ideological baggage. A number of participants felt that attitudes about performance within government was an area deserving much more attention by both political scientists and public administrators.

In the meantime, the public continues to perceive the government as ineffective and unproductive. People are told that government agencies possess few incentives to keep overhead costs as low as possible, especially when compared to business firms, which must hold down costs of production to survive in a competitive market. The tendency of the government to overestimate revenues and underestimate costs is well known by people who follow trends in governmental management. As students, future public executives learn that public officials are consitutionally incapable of dealing with long-term problems and that the political system allows interest groups to push through programs that benefit only a small sector of society while taxing the rest.

A very telling comment was made at the end of the conference by P.B. Akridge, a young executive with I.B.M. Throughout the conference the discussions had been dominated by persons who had served in, or at least were familiar with, the "golden age" of public adminsitration. Akridge asked how it was possible to trumpet the virtues of the public service, much less to devote great energy toward improving its performance, when career possibilities for young people were now so slim. Fewer jobs are opening up in the public service, he said, and the ones that do exist are neither particularly exciting nor close to the centers of decision and power. In the so-called "golden era," professional public administrators shared power with political executives. As politicians took those jobs away from "professionals," there was little motivation for talented young people to make a long-term commitment to improving the quality of public service. The new generation, he implied, views the future of the public service much differently than do the reformers who remember the growth and good government era.

NOTES

1.   Figures for the earlier years can be found in the article by Arthur H. Miller, "Political Issues and Trust in Government: 1964-1970," American Political Science Review 68 (September 1974): 951-972. Data on the later years must be retrieved from a variety of sources: Arthur Miller, "Is Confidence Rebounding?" Public Opinion 6 (June-July 1983): 16-20; "Opinion Roundup," Public Opinion 7 (February-March 1984): 29; and Warren E. Miller, Arthur H. Miller, and Edward J. Schneider, American National Election Studies Data Sourcebook: 1952-1978 (Cambridge: Harvard University Press, 1980), 170-71, 251, & 255-68.

2.   Miller, "Political Issues and Trust in Government: 1964-1970," 952.

3.   Sidney Blumenthal, The Permanent Campaign (New York: Touchstone Books, 1982), 49.

4.   As quoted in James MacGregor Burns, J.W. Peltason, and Thomas E. Cronin, Government by the People (Englewood Cliffs, NJ: Prentice-Hall, 1981), 417-18.

5.   Charles T. Goodsell, "The Grace Commission," Public Administration Review 44 (May-June 1984): 198.

6.   Miller, "Political Issues and Trust in Government: 1964-1970," 951.

7.   Ibid., 970.

8.   Ibid., 970.

9.   Chester A. Newland, "The Reagan Presidency," Public Administration Review 43 (January-February 1983): 1-21.

10.   Goodsell, "The Grace Commission," 196.

DECADES OF DISAFFECTION,

CONDITIONS FOR CONFIDENCE IN GOVERNMENT

Chester A. Newland

Unprecedented declines in public confidence in American national government occurred during the 1960s and 1970s. High or moderate trust in government, one aspect of confidence, was expressed by over three-fourths of the people polled in 1958, but by only one-fourth in 1980. In 1964, three-fourths of the persons sampled indicated "trust," but a steady decline then set in, with a trend reversal occurring in 1982.[1] Polls showed similar declines from 1964 to 1980 in equity, efficiency, and personal efficacy or governmental responsiveness.

Public disaffection and its causes and consequences are principal topics of this analysis, along with their flip side, citizen confidence in government. Confidence within the federal government--the less measured relationships within the branches and among politicians and the bureaucracy--is also examined. Intergovernmental and political party relationships and the judiciary are only briefly noted, although they are highly relevant to the topic.

The first part of the paper discusses dimensions of citizen disaffection and related research on confidence indicators. Second, the probable causes of diminished confidence are examined, focusing on governmental performance; conditions commonly associated with personal, organizational, and civic confidence are also discussed. The third part of the paper deals with issues concerning institutions and the constitutional rules of the game as they relate to confidence in the governmental and political system.

I. DIMENSIONS AND INDICATORS OF DISAFFECTION

Three points in time most clearly reveal the dimensions of the public disaffection regarding American national government: (1) major popular and scholarly publications in 1974 on public opinion; (2) President Carter's Crisis of Confidence speech of July 15, 1979; and (3) President Reagan's Renewal of Confidence agenda of 1981. Those examples are examined in the first part of the paper. Highlights of research on indicators of citizen disaffection are then reviewed. Finally, needs for research on confidence in government among political and career officials are noted.

Highlights of Disaffection and Confidence

From 1964 to 1974 the percentage of citizens who expressed high or moderate trust of government plummeted from 76% to 37%. Pollsters tracked the steady decline to 1972 and the drastic drop during the next two post-Watergate years. Commentators regularly probed causes and possible cures.

The 1974 Alarms   Two publications in 1974 marked that year as a high point of concern over the growing disaffection: Ben J. Wattenberg's popularized and optimistic analysis, The Real America, and Arthur H. Miller's scholarly alarm in the American Political Science Review, with an extended critique by Jack Citrin and a forceful rejoinder.

Ben Wattenberg's 1974 analysis stressed two contradictory findings from census, polling, and other "hard" data: improved personal conditions and self confidence among a new "Massive Majority Middle Class," and "pessimistic conventional wisdom." He found that polls showed "Americans say their own lives are fine. And they say that America is in trouble."[2] Extensive data were chronicled to support the thesis that "there was great and healthy change in the United States since 1960--on almost every measurable front."[3] Wattenberg cited evidence of "progress, growth, and success" in employment and working conditions, fringe benefits, financial security, income, housing, personal property, education, health, and progress of blacks.

Despite such indicators, Wattenberg found that America had become dominated by a rhetoric of "crisis, failure, guilt." He then sought to answer the question, "If everything is so good, how come everything is so bad?"[4] He attributed the problem to a "tribe of people with a cause," "freelance naysayers."[5] That critique of causes of disaffection is discussed in the second part of this analysis.

Arthur H. Miller of the University of Michigan, using survey studies conducted by the University's Center for Political Studies, sounded an alarm in 1974 of the sort that bothered Wattenberg. Miller warned that "A democratic political system cannot survive for long without the support of a majority of its citizens."[6] He concluded:

A situation of widespread, basic discontent and political alienation exists in the U.S. today. Support for this contention can readily be found in the daily reports of the mass media, in an examination of recent political events--witness the substantial support for George Wallace in both the 1968 election and the 1972 primaries--and in the 1972 political campaign rhetoric.

But, more convincingly, it is also found in national survey data.[7]

Miller focused on two disaffection indicators: political trust and efficacy. He found high levels of cynicism and political alienation toward "the government in Washington."

Miller studied several position issues: racial integration, Vietnam, urban unrest, campus riots, pollution, and health insurance. He also examined what was then predominantly a valence issue, inflation. He found "a great deal of conflict," and concluded that a majority of Americans did not prefer a centrist policy alternative on these issues, contrary to the 1971 conclusions by Richard Scammon and Ben Wattenberg.[8] Miller significantly reasoned that public disaffection stemmed from "great dissatisfaction with the policies of both parties."

Jack Citrin of the University of California, Berkeley, has taken issue with Miller's belief that centrist policies accounted for disaffection. On the contrary, he argues, "the performance of political officeholders and institutions determines their legitimacy."[9] These different theories about the causes of decline in public confidence are discussed later. Here, it is important that Citrin and Miller agreed on "the sharp increase in political cynicism among the American public."[10]

Carter's Crisis of Confidence Speech   In the summer of 1979, malaise overtook President Carter. On July 15, he delivered a Sunday night homily to the nation. The focal point of the three-part lecture was designed to inspire Americans to raise themselves from what the President termed a "crisis of confidence." Still playing an outsider to the government, Carter described the situation in apocalyptic terms: "It is a crisis that strikes at the very heart and soul and spirit of our national will....The symptoms of this crisis...are all around us....Washington, D.C. has become an island. The gap between our citizens and our government has never been so wide....We simply must have faith in each other....Restoring that faith and that confidence to America is now the most important task we face."[11]

That speech captured the country's worried mood, particularly coming four weeks into the 1979 summer gas panic. But it did not inspire hope. Two days after the address, without advising the Speaker of the House or others outside his Georgia circle of advisors, the President requested resignations from his entire Cabinet in order to ease the firing of three of them. The President's already low approval rating plummeted to 19% by September.

Although disastrously sandwiched between the gas panic and the Cabinet "slaughter," the Carter speech was the determined product of a lengthy decision process. The President's pollster, Patrick Caddell, had long worried about Carter's declining popularity. Reading the same survey results as Wattenberg and Miller, plus others, he concluded that the peril was great. He met on the matter in April with Mrs. Carter, and by April 23 he had prepared an "Apocalypse Now" memo. For the President's eyes only, Caddell's memo began as follows:

America is a nation deep in crisis. Unlike civil war or depression, this crisis, nearly invisible, is unique from those that previously have engaged Americans in their history. Psychological more than material, it is a crisis of confidence marked by a dwindling faith in the future....This crisis is not your fault as President. It is the natural result of historical forces and events which have been in motion for twenty years. This crisis threatens the political and social fabric of the nation....Everywhere there is a grouping tentative swirl of discussion among the most intelligent elites from many fields over these matters....one out of three Americans see their own lives going straight downhill....[It] is a psychological crisis of the first order.[12]

Economic advisor Stuart Eizenstat and Vice President Walter Mondale attempted to dissuade Carter from what the Vice President termed "a Jonathan Edwards condemnation of the people," according to the author Theodore H. White. They would rather have seen the President give a speech on the oil problem. But the pollster, Caddell, won with statistics; and the result was a Presidential speech of unparalleled, deep despair.

Reagan's Images of Optimism   Reagan is an inveterate optimist, by all reports. Lawrence Barrett's insider portrait of[13] Reagan in the White House, Gambling With History, alludes to the President's characteristic search for "the pony" with evident accuracy. That positive personality trait has also been strategically buttressed by Reagan's advisers, during the campaign and as President.

Reagan's pollster, Richard Wirthlin, studied many of the same survey results as did Wattenberg, Miller, Caddell, and others. His assessment of conditions was similar to Miller's and Caddell's analyses; his recommendations differed from the advice given Carter. Wirthlin's 1980 assessment of the confidence problem was as follows:

From 1973 to 1980 fewer than 20 percent of the country felt the nation was on the "right track." Seventy-five out of every hundred Americans thought the country was misdirected and in disarray....

The shattering of traditional confidence in America in the last twenty years stems from an erosion in the expectation that, given an abundant environment and an adequate amount of time, the individual with sufficient diligence and ingenuity would achieve a measure of economic security and a reasonably comfortable lifestyle....The lack of confidence in...American value structure relates directly to the American Presidency.[14]

Wirthlin advised Reagan that a consistently affirmative image of leadership--with a focus on the public's personal economic concerns--was the formula for success.

As President, Reagan forcefully asserted his sustained agenda of limited government, encouraged self-governance, and unswervingly concentrated on the "Economic Recovery Program" during his first year. In his March, 1981 budget message and revisions, Reagan presented the four initial objectives of his strategic plan, focusing on the confidence problem:

1. Breaking the cycle of negative expectations.
2. Revitalizing economic growth.
3. Renewing optimism and confidence.
4. Rekindling the nation's entrepreneurial instincts and creativity.

Correlated with those aims were the following four initial policy priorities:

1. Substantial reduction of federal expenditures.
2. Significant reduction in federal tax rates.
3. Prudent relief of federal regulatory burdens.
4. Consistent monetary policy.

Implementation of the 1981 Economic Recovery Program was immediately followed by the deepest economic downturn since the Great Depression, with amelioration in mid-1983 and 1984. The President's image of confidence was, however, consistently sustained.[15]

In addition to his personal optimism and stategically-oriented staff support, Reagan brought to the confidence problem unprecedented media experience, which he fully deployed. Between 1980 and 1982 respondents with high or moderate trust of government increased from 25% to 33%, the first upturn in two decades. However, according to that survey, trust and other indicators of confidence in government remained dramatically low--less than half of the 1964 level.

Indicators of Public Disaffection or Confidence

Assessment of disaffection or confidence in government requires indicators of several factors. The three examples above show how data has been used extensively and at powerful levels to study public confidence in the national government. Surveys have not been widely used, however, to assess confidence within government, a crucial but neglected subject. Polls have surveyed public confidence in performance, but sometimes with inadequate discrimination or balance between pretested position issues (which at a given time tend toward polarization) and valence issues (which indicate more general tendencies at a given time).[16] Performance assessments may discriminate between opinion about events, general policy, and officials, but the impressively documented work--and disagreement--of Arthur Miller and Jack Citrin, noted earlier, demonstrates limits in doing that. Beyond those three performance elements, indicators are needed of confidence in institutions and underlying constitutional norms. Often, those are not distinguished from other performance factors, though surveys and elections studies are useful to discern them. Attitudes on efficacy may be particularly relevant indicators.

Further examples of uses of and conclusions from opinion polling are discussed in later parts of this analysis. Before probing causes of disaffection and confidence more specifically however, four other commonly used indicators besides opinion polls warrant comment. Also, possible indicators of confidence and disaffection within government must be noted.

Content Analysis, Multiple Measures, and Case Studies The media, identified by Ben Wattenberg as one culprit responsible for the disaffection in recent decades, must be considered in this study. Wattenberg's analysis was more anecdotal (albeit extensive and well-documented) on that subject than on most others. Content analysis of newspapers combined with survey data has been done on the confidence problem, however, and more such media research is needed. Arthur Miller, Edie Goldenberg, and Lutz Erbring published research in the American Political Science Review in 1979 on "Type-Set Politics: Impacts of Newspapers on Public Confidence"[17]--a study exceptional among scholarly survey analyses in that it used a mix of polling data and other direct research measures and tested more than one explanation in the same analysis. Content analysis of 94 newspapers disclosed primarily neutral or positive reporting, but where negative criticism in reporting was found it affected feelings of trust, not efficacy. The authors posited "a structural explanation of inefficacy as a result of accumulating distrust, where policy dissatisfaction, rather than dislike of incumbent leaders, acts as the main determinant of cynicism." That conclusion reaffirmed Miller's 1974 position, noted earlier, and contradicted Jack Citrin's view. In the authors' 1979 model, they concluded that "media criticism serves as a 'mediator' of political realities which eventually, although indirectly, affects political malaise."[19]

Two other recent reports on media impact help to distinguish differences between opinions on personalities and parties from those on policies. Martin P. Wattenberg reported on impacts of the change in American newspapers from strict partisan identification to independence in recent decades. Coupled with television's tendency to focus on personalities rather than parties (except for conventions), this development has contributed to the declining salience of political parties and heightened visibility of a few political personalities.[20] The usual view of the media's influences on a specific policy--by reporting, thereby impacting public opinion and policymakers--was contradicted in a case study published by Public Opinion Quarterly in 1983. Several Northwestern University professors reported what is commonly observed in Washington: media policy influence derived less from an aroused public than from "active collaboration between the investigative journalists and officials of the U.S. Senate Permanent Subcommittee on Investigations."[21]

Elections Studies Elections are classic democratic measures of public opinion, of course. In addition, several types of elections studies have been used to discern public confidence. Political volatility--the recent series of one-term Presidents--has been researched during the decades of disaffection in terms that continue to fit a classic genre.[22] Judging from continued disagreement over the comparative weights assigned to policy issues and candidates as causes of disaffection, illustrated by the Miller-Citrin disagreement, these studies do not meet the needs for understanding.

If multiple indicators are employed, understanding may be improved, even given the risk of less precise science and some experience-based conjecture (commonly called "current history"). For example, by the end of 1983, the Washington Post-ABC News Poll indicated heightened popular anticipation of the 1984 election, increased polarization around economic policies based on income levels, and related polarization for and against Reagan.[23] Looking back at the 1960s and 1970s, while polarization of the sort found by Miller was dominant, there was widepread agreement that the parties and candidates were Tweedledee/Tweedledum. Reagan's performance, by contrast, has apparently convinced people, according to a December, 1983 poll, that the President and the party do make a difference. Consequently, 1984 began as a year of highly consistent polarization around issues, the incumbent and, generally, the parties, based to a high degree on socioeconomic status. The question of whether those attitudes depend more on perceptions of general economic conditions or direct personal experience is answered differently in research findings. The 1983 polling data reported in the Washington Post would indicate attitudes are based on perceptions of personal economic self-interest. But research reported in 1981 by Donald R. Kender of Yale University indicated that "In evaluating the President, citizens seem to pay principal attention to the nation's economic predicament, and comparatively little to their own."[24]

Election participation patterns have also been studied with reference to feelings of efficacy as an indicator of confidence. Voter turnout in presidential elections declined from an all time high of 63% in 1960 to 53% in 1980. In off-year congressional elections it declined from a high of 45% in 1962 and 1966 to 36% in 1974, 1978, and 1982. A scholarly analysis of those trends (until 1980) by Paul R. Abramson and John H. Aldrich, using Michigan's SRC-CPS data, concluded that the declining participation of the 1960s-1970s could be attributed to the combined impact of two attitudinal trends: "the weakening of party identification and declining beliefs about government responsiveness, that is, lowered feelings of 'external' political efficacy."[25]

The low voter turnouts in 1974, 1978, and 1982 were second lowest to the 33% of 1942. This edged up to 37% in 1946 and then climbed to the all-time high of 45% in 1962 and 1966.[26] Those statistics could perhaps be as indicative of disinterest, consent, or other factors, as of disaffection. The lows during World War II, for example, are not commonly attributed to disaffection.

Citizens Contacting Government   Research about citizen-initiated contact of government provides yet another indicator of confidence, particularly of a sense of efficacy. The distinguished 1963 assessment by Gabriel Almond and Sidney Verba, The Civic Culture,[27] was a forerunner of many behavioral studies of citizen participation and confidence. A 1972 book by Sidney Verba and Norman Nie, Participation in America: Political Democracy and Social Equality,[28] particularly generated useful followup research because they found that, unlike other forms of citizen participation, there is no correlation between contacting and socioeconomic status. Subsequent research yielded vastly conflicting findings--contacting of government by citizens and socioeconomic status are positively, negatively, parabolically, or negligibly related.[29] In short, more research is needed.

Social Indicators   The final category noted here is the growing literature that examines several variables longitudinally rather than positing a single global indicator. Following the important 1969 classic, Toward a Social Report, prepared under the guidance of Alice Rivlin and Wilbur Cohen and released by HEW (HHS) in the closing days of the Johnson Administration, the United States Government published three reports, the most recent of which, Social Indicators III, was released in 1981.[30] Four issues of The Annals of the American Academy of Political and Social Science have dealt with the subject, the most recent one in 1981.[31] Civil disobedience has been neglected in such reports, although studies of riots done during the 1960s were related to social indicators research. Civic culture generally has not been a principal focus of federal reports on social indicators, but they nonetheless reflect importantly on public institutions and their performance. The research needs to be bridged, as in the pioneering work by Almond and Verba, for an understanding of confidence and disaffection. In that respect, the dominance of the Social Indicators movement since 1968, upheld by economists and related policy analysts, and the separation of political analysts from those efforts has not been constructive.

Indicators of Confidence Within Government

With respect to confidence in government, some of the potentially best informed elites--people within government--have been largely ignored by pollsters and others. Surveys of career employees, particularly of Senior Executive Service members, are common, but these usually pertain to issues of employee interests such as compensation or job security.

Two types of potentially useful research related to confidence in government are noted here: (1) attitudes and morale of officials as indicators of malaise or satisfaction, and (2) system performance, in terms of short and long term responsiblity.

Officials' Attitudes   Three examples suggest potentially useful research, now largely neglected, on attitudes of knowledgeable participants in government.

First, how is confidence in government efficiency related to decisions by key officials to leave or continue in office? In 1984, for example, Texas Senator John Tower's frustration with Congress as an institution contributed to his unexpected decision not to seek reelection. Another example from the 1970s, when the confidence issue was heavily affecting Congress, was Congressman David Henderson's decision not to seek reelection after he had ascended to the Chair of the House Post Office and Civil Service Committee. Again, frustration with single-interest politics and non-collaborative processes contributed to the departure of an exceptionally respected leader in his prime. While difficult to assess, this dimension of disaffection is sufficiently serious to warrant study.

Second, to what extent is popular confidence a factor in officials' political decisions? A familiar example is the 1968 decision of Lyndon Johnson not to seek or accept renomination. Popular media wisdom of the time and now the generally accepted version of history is that he was driven from office because of Vietnam and related disorders. But strong evidence exists that even prior to the 1964 election Mrs. Johnson and the President considered a single term as the longest that he could serve due to health and other considerations. Johnson in 1964 seriously "did not believe he should accept the nomination."[32] On August 25, 1964, Mrs. Johnson wrote him a letter, originally drafted on her steno pad, encouraging him to run again.[33] Whatever the causes involved in Johnson's decision were, did the media's projection that he was driven from office contribute further to the decline of confidence in government? To understand confidence problems, is it important to know whether in fact the media version or Mrs. Johnson's was correct and also to understand the impact on public confidence of the media's assumptions? Such knowledge is probably of sufficient importance to warrant more scholarly and popular attention.

A third, larger source of potential knowledge may be attitudes of key political and career officials on the efficiency of policies, institutions, and the organizations they serve. Is confidence in the United States government high or low at the key interfaces of top political and career leadership? Some research on relationships at those levels is noted later, but there have been no general studies on the large issue of confidence in government among such officials.

System Performance In addition to studies of attitudes and the morale of key officials as indicators of confidence within government, more general system performance analysis is needed. Several such studies of management and of specific institutions exist, and some of those are highlighted in subsequent parts of this paper.[34] Longitudinal policy studies tend to focus on single areas or issues; social indicators aggregate around selected topics; generally there is only limited research on linkages.

Assessments are also needed of "if, how, and why" government deals generally with the short term at what may be unacceptable long term costs, i.e., the accumulation of causes of disaffection. For example, was the equanimity of the 1950s caused by a deferral of crucial matters, and did that contribute to the turmoil of the 1960s? Or, did Great Society promises raise expectations well beyond achievable levels, leading to disillusionment in the 1970s? Did short terms of political appointees in the early 1970s and limited competence of officals diminish the government's capacities? Or, is government underfunding in the 1980s buying current satisfaction for middle

nd upper level taxpayers at acceptable future costs? Are those
olitical issues beyond objective research? What is the state of
aith in a science of politics and government?

In short, what is known and what can be known about
auses of disaffection and confidence in government? What has
een learned from existing experience and research? What else
eeds to be known? That is the subject of the next section of
his paper.

II. CAUSES OF PUBLIC CONFIDENCE AND DISAFFECTION

Three broad topics are examined here with respect to causes
f public disaffection and confidence in government. First,
hree sets of governmental performance factors are discussed:
vents, officials, and policies and their implementation. Second,
here is an examination of a preoccupation with failure. The
hird set of factors studied include conditions associated with
onfidence in private and personal affairs, and their relevance to
he United States government. Confidence issues more
pecifically related to political/governmental institutions and the
onstitutional system are examined in Part III.

overnmental Performance Factors

The superbly documented polling analyses by Miller and
itrin, cited earlier, demonstrated the difficulties and hazards in
rawing firm conclusions about causes of disaffection. But when
uch opinion analyses are combined with experience reflected in
olitical and media studies and histories, the three categories of
overnmental performance factors listed above appear highly
elevant to disaffection. Key events stand out prominently with
he hindsight of history, if not always in polls of the moment.
herefore, they are noted here first, not necessarily as the most
nportant, but as the most obvious of three crucially important
ets of causes.

Events as Causes and Effects   Six events or clusters of
vents of the 1960s and 1970s stand out as causes, with at least
wo of them equally constituting effects of disaffection:
ssassinations; Vietnam divisiveness; urban riots, drug and
rime cultures, and turmoil in universities; Watergate; the
ribbling disclosures of corruption, as in Abscam; and the
ranian hostage situation.

It is hard to escape the connection between the malaise of
ne 1960s and the assassination of President Kennedy on
[ovember 22, 1963; of Martin Luther King on April 4, 1968; and
f Robert Kennedy on June 5, 1968, as he led in California in
he primary campaign. In virtually all the polls, the public
ood began to decline early in 1964; the drop accelerated after

1968. The biographies, memoirs, and histories of the time relate the impact far better than did the polls. A telling example: Senator Mike Mansfield, the reflective history teacher, arrived to confer with the President at 7 a.m., the morning after Robert Kennedy was shot. His first comment: "What is happening to our country?"[35] Fifteen hectic hours later, Mrs. Johnson reflected: "All day long I heard this cacophony over and over--the reactions of people questioned. What is our country coming to? What is happening to us? Are we a sick society?[36]

Vietnam and its controversy was a second major problem. The disaffection was wholly unparalleled, polarizing opinion, increasing the alienation felt by opponents and supporters of the war.

Four sets of problems also polarized public opinion. While distinct, they tended to cluster in reinforcing impacts: urban riots, largely racially and economically oriented; drug dependency, associated for a brief while with countercultures; crime, newly visible as a pervasive subculture; and university turmoil.

Those three sets of events, the assassinations, Vietnam divisions, and social turmoil, contributed to general social malaise. Nonetheless, opinion surveys showed that confidence in government slightly rebounded between 1970 and 1972. For blacks, trust continued to decline during that Nixon period, but for whites it increased slightly. During the Johnson period, blacks had been more trusting than whites; people with earnings below $5,000 were more trusting than those with over $15,000; and manual workers were more trusting than business people. All those attitudes reversed in 1970 and 1972, with an overall marginal increase.

Then came Watergate. The popular trust index fell from 53% to 37% from 1972 to 1974, more than double any previous two-year decline. Watergate prompted introspection within government circles about underlying deficiencies in the political system. The National Academy of Public Administration (NAPA) in March, 1974, issued a report which observed: "Watergate damaged the image of the public service, which already had been suffering from a decline in public confidence for several years. It represents not only an aberration, but, perhaps more important for those concerned with America's future, a culmination of converging trends developing and gathering over the post World War II decades. The focusing of attention on the abuses associated with Watergate now lays the ground for much needed reexamination and reform."[37] NAPA criticized the monolithic Presidency, declining Congressional influence over the bureaucracy, and other institutional faults considered in Part III of this analysis.

Following Watergate, disclosures of corruption in the federal government became a major media feature when Abscam hit. The Iranian hostage situation capped the series of blows to public confidence, with Walter Cronkite counting the days and months of American incapacity. Trust in the national government continued to slide to an all-time low of 25% in 1980.

Officials and Disaffection   Could anyone provide leadership in the midst of these events? Leadership in Congress and in the Executive Branch was seriously eroded during the 1960s and 970s. Events left the Democratic Party in massive disarray in 968--"the party that would need a generation to come back" had returned after only four years. In 1972, McGovern lost in a reversal of 1964. Then Watergate helped to elect Carter, whose big loss four years later helped to elect Reagan. The period was characterized by a series of negative elections, resulting partly from initially high expectations of Presidents, followed by disillusion when they failed to meet those standards--a persistent popularity/disapproval cycle.[38]

Two Presidents (Lyndon Johnson and Gerald Ford) inherited the office and led as experienced Washington craftsmen, political professionals who knew the territory but who lacked other leadership images. Ford was eagerly portrayed by the media as a bumbling mediocrity. Two later Presidents (Jimmy Carter and Ronald Reagan) were outsiders to Washington and successfully cultivated that image. Alan K. (Scotty) Campbell described that quality of Carter's leadership: "When I was...director of the Office of Personnel Management, I frequently heard from career people who wanted to know why the President was not saying nicer things about them. The trouble was the political advisors round the President, who argued that it was bad politics to do so."[39]   Based on his series of Presidential elections studies from 956 to 1980, writer Theodore H. White concluded that, by 1980, forces outside Carter or Reagan had significantly shaped that election. White commented that "Public affairs had gone off the track, almost as if the country had lost its way into the future. There was no sense of coherence in government; it did not respond; it could not manage. Nor was it the fault of the Carter administration alone, or the Nixon administration, or the Johnson administration. It went much farther back than any of the seven national campaigns I had covered."[40]   White found that America in 1980 was "in search of itself."

Public attitudes in 1980 were surveyed more extensively than ever before by the University of Michigan's Center for Political Studies under the auspices of the National Election Studies NES) project. In a detailed analysis of the 1980 NES data, Gregory B. Markus of Michigan concluded that the public was searching for competent political leadership, not a change in policy directions. Markus concluded that "the data clearly indicate that Carter's loss can be attributed to pervasive dissatisfaction with his first-term performance, and doubt about his personal competence as a political leader."[41]

Two qualities of the 1980 candidates were important in public attitudes: integrity, important for Reagan but not a concern about Carter; and competence, the crucial negative for Carter. Policy differences were not the decisive factor. However, the electorate did not ignore issues. Rather, a retrospective verdict was rendered on "whether or not the incumbent had performed satisfactorily on important issues marking his first term in office."[42]

<u>Performance as a Confidence Factor</u>   Governmental performance was a major factor in the 1980 election according to the NES data, but that issue focused mostly on Carter as incompetent. Public attitudes were tracked for a full year on four policy performance areas: inflation, unemployment, Iranian hostages, and the energy problem. Respondents expressed negative opinions of Carter's past performance. Markus also studied NES data on four policy matters: inflation/unemployment, domestic services, defense spending, and detente. He concluded:

> The results are unambiguous. First, political ideology had no effect whatsoever on the election outcome. Further, Reagan's positions on important domestic and foreign policy matters gained him only one percentage point over Carter, an advantage that was more than countered by the prevailing Democratic bias in the distribution of partisan attachments. There is thus no evidence to support the argument that Reagan's victory represented a mandate for either his ideological posture or his policy intentions.[43]

In short, in 1980 people generally wanted effective leadership. Reagan could, however, interpret the election almost as an open mandate.

The Reagan Administration chose to pursue a mandate for major changes which would potentially result in socioeconomic polarization. The Reagan agenda of limited government (distinguishing governance and government) was based on reduced inflation and taxes, appealing to those with high and middle incomes--the new "Massive Majority Middle Class" referred to by Ben Wattenberg. This formula polarized the unemployed and the poor, who could be outvoted in subsequent elections.

Foreign affairs policy, except for the Iranian hostage issue, was inconsequential in the 1980 election. Some defense enhancement was supported by 1980 opinion polls, but not at the ost of drastically reduced domestic program spending. When nly moderate defense and welfare tradeoffs proved possible, Reagan [44] accepted a classic political alternative: massive deficits.

The initial Reagan interpretation of his mandate included regulatory reform, substantially achieved, with the exception of several legislative failures. An initial central element of Reagan's agenda was state-centered federalism, largely unsuccessful except for enlarged block grant use and program cuts. [45]

By 1984, there was considerable polarization. But disaffection from politics was reduced according to the December, 983 <u>Washington Post-ABC News Poll.</u> People saw that Reagan had made a difference; and those with family incomes over 20,000 favored the Republicans 3 to 2, while those with incomes under $20,000 favored the Democrats 2 to 1.

The poll asked: "Do you feel things in this country are generally going in the right direction, or do you feel things [46] have gotten pretty seriously off on the wrong track." The <u>Washington Post</u> reported: "Three of every five in the first group said they were better off financially than when Reagan became President; only one-third of the latter group thought so. Five of every eight of the lower-income people said the cutbacks in social programs had created serious hardships for many people. Less than half of the upper-income people agreed." [47]

Other opinion surveys reveal the same sort of socioeconomic polarization. A return to racial separation is an aspect of that. The University of Michigan surveys, for example, showed that between 1980 and 1982, when an 8% overall upswing occurred in popular trust in government, attitudes of blacks dropped from +2 to -5. [48] During the five years ending in 1983, after tax income of the richest 20% of the population increased from a 37.0 to a 7.6% share while that of the lowest 20% fell from 7.1% to 6.6%. Michael Barone summarized the significance as follows: "Reaganites believe these changes will stimulate economic growth and make everyone better off in the long run. But for 1984 they had resulted in an economic polarization of the electorate greater than any we have seen in 20 years." [49]

Foreign policy also emerged as a polarizing issue by 1984, in contrast to 1980. The <u>Washington Post-ABC News Poll</u> showed a significant gap of 16 points between the income groups on Reagan's handling of foreign affairs, compared to a 26 point difference on the economy.

Yet, the <u>image of leadership,</u> the decisive variable in 1980, appeared to remain a key confidence factor in 1984 with respect to the President. Public interest in politics and elections had rebounded by the end of 1983. The Committee for the Study of the American electorate reported that in 1982 state contests, voter turnout in the 20 largest states increased in all but Pennsylvania. In half of these, the increase exceeded 10%. In December, 1983, both Reagan's pollster Richard B. Wirthlin and Mondale's Peter D. Hart, were projecting a 1984 voter turnout of 57% or 58%. That would be a recovery of nearly half the decline between 1960 and 1980.[50]

Conditions of Disaffection

From 1964 through 1980, a heavy accent was on negatives. In Ben Wattenberg's terms, an infrastructure grew which focused on crisis, failure, and guilt. President Reagan has sought deliberately to displace pessimism with optimism. Among the challenges, four categories of forces which demostrate a high preoccupation with failure are noted here. These four often feed disaffection: the media; academicians; internal governmental accountability; and negative/single interest politics.

Media Accent on Failure By examples, cases, and survey data, Ben Wattenberg documented the following conclusions in 1974:

> ...A case can be made that a good part of our domestic malaise can be laid precisely at the feet of a media system that underreports progress....What people know of firsthand, they think well of. What people know of secondhand, information gathered through the transmission belt of our system of communications, they think ill of!

> ...The only reason that Americans think things are lousy is because they are given a bum steer by a media system that lives by one cardinal rule; 'Good news is no news.'

> That is probably too all-inclusive a theory and probably far too harsh on the press. But the fact remains that the press has not learned how to present good news, and this is corrosive.[51]

Contrary in part to Wattenberg's views, Miller, Goldenberg, and Erbring, cited earlier, found political reporting in 94 newspapers "primarily neutral or positive." They did find, however, that readers of highly critical newspapers were more distrustful of government. They also concluded that "Media criticism serves as a 'mediator' of political realities which eventually, although indirectly, affects political malaise."[52]

Academic Perspectives   Ph.D.'s are educated to try to be objectively critical in research.   But they are also commonly taught to be problem-oriented.   Academic researchers look for problems to be studied and solved, not existing successes.   In political science, and most particularly in American public administration, the field emerged as an essential part of the governmental reform movement.   Research looked into corruption, inefficiency, diseconomy, and later, ineffectiveness, but it was not and is not now predominantly negative.   Reform was "the Good Government Movement," and reformers reported regularly on virtues of professional city management, governmental reorganization, and responsiveness of government.   An inclination to look for "what's wrong" persists, however.   Ben Wattenberg included three academic groups in his ranks of naysayers of the Failure and Guilt Complex: economists, sociologists, and "the internationally minded."   Charles Goodsell found extensive grounds for faulting academicians in public administration for excessive criticism of bureaucracy.[53]

A useful academic agenda in government and public administration might well be an assessment of the questions: To what extent can "critical" be translated as "negative" in research and teaching?   What are the impacts of academic research, teaching, and service on confidence in government?

Internal Governmental Accountability   Without demonstrated accountability, conditions for trust are absent from government. In the United States government, what Bernard Rosen calls "an awesome armada" of accountability methods are present.[54]   Audits by the General Accounting Office (GAO), Inspectors General, and other central offices tend to accentuate the negative and ignore the positive, contributing to an image of failure.   On the other hand, such audits and other accountability procedures promote responsibility and provide ways for citizens, media, officials, and public employees to correct deficiencies.

A negative focus on federal government auditing has been important in four major respects during the recent decades of disaffection.   First, single-interest political action groups and other advocacy organizations have sought to use internal accountability systems as instruments of advocacy.   For example, when the U.S. Civil Service Commission used inspections aimed at positive management improvement in the early 1970s, Ralph Nader and his associates severely criticized it as "the spoiled system" and charged coverups in agencies.[55]   Second, Members of Congress and committees in the 1960s sometimes attempted to use the GAO to pursue matters for political advantage, limiting the capacity for professional audit reviews.   That problem has been brought under general control by changing GAO authority and processes.   Third, since the mid-1970s, White House sloganeering about "wastefraudabuse" in agencies has conveyed an impression of both massive deficiencies in government and enormous dollar savings resulting from accountability procedures Fourth, reviews by GAO, Congressional committees, and executive agencies have been misused in undisciplined advocacy journalism.

Although accountability processes often have a negative impact and some corrections are needed, that has not been their intended or actual character generally. In fact, since the late 1960s, the GAO has been a leader in positive management improvement in the government.[56] Accountability processes including audits, remain the most fundamental foundation for citizen confidence in government.

Negative Politics Single interest and negative politics is a fourth category of factors which contributed to the disaffection of the 1960s and 1970s. Such politics both reflected and contributed to the confidence problems. Generally, competing interest groups have accepted compromises that further common goals; but this changed during the 1960s and 70s.

First, the efficacy of "customary politics" and elections was widely questioned. As noted, perceptions of personal efficacy fell, according to opinion polls, from 62% to 44% between 1964 and 1980. That perception may not have reflected reality--in an analysis of public opinion and policy data for the United States from 1935 to 1979, Benjamin I. Page and Robert Y. Shapiro found "considerable congruence between changes in preferences and in policies, especially for large, stable opinion changes on salient issues."[57] They concluded that "the evidence that opinion tends to move before policy more than vice versa indicates that opinion changes are important causes of policy change. When Americans' policy preferences shift, it is likely that congruent changes in policy will follow."[58] Nevertheless there was a prevalent perception of inefficacy in politics, and single interest fragmentation became dominant in the 1960s. Second, many advocates of particular interests became uncompromising in the 1960s. Often they were interested in only one issue. Third, new methods and arenas were used. Negative politics--attacks on opponents--became common. Interest groups employed subversive tactics within political and governmental organizations, as in Watergate in 1972 or the purloined Carter debate papers in 1980, violating fundamental norms of the political system.

The four sets of factors just reviewed--media, academic orientations, internal accountability systems, and negative politics--may be better understood by some comparison with conditions for confidence. That is the next and final topic in Part II.

Conditions for Personal and Civic Confidence

Two factors associated with confidence are briefly noted here: (1) success or excellence in personal and business affairs outside of government, and (2) upswings in public opinion during recent years of generally low confidence.

Personal, Organization, Social Confidence   In city management, the positive dimension of the executive's role is accepted as basic.   In its 1983 "flagship greenbook" on The Effective Local Government Manager, the International City Management Association's (ICMA) text teaches as follows: "Leadership requires accomplishment of common goals, and leaders structure such successes as they develop relationships with followers.   Local government managers are expected to schedule winning seasons every year, and successful managers usually accomplish this....But managers must understand that nothing breeds success like success in government, or in leadership generally for that matter....Over the long run, leadership requires coordinated group action to accomplish what will be perceived as a successful outcome."[59]   ICMA stresses highly expert and professional experience-based management.   It is deliberately positive.

A positive orientation also dominates private business practice.   The best-selling 1982 book by Thomas J. Peters and Robert H. Waterman, Jr. In Search of Excellence, chronicles numerous examples of "Lessons from America's Best-Run Companies."[60]   Their emphasis on the positive is as applicable to government as it is to the private sector.   The most hyped, big-profit version of what is known about confidence and accomplishment, The One Minute Manager, says simply what the preponderance of research reports: "People who feel good about themselves produce good results."[61]   In short, success breeds confidence which breeds success.

In contrast, negatives are routinely stressed in the federal government, positives are rarely noted, and detailed controls are glorified.[62]

Civic Confidence   Upswings in public confidence during recent years of civic malaise may be instructive.   One occurred in 1970-1972 and another in 1980-1983.   Moreover, as Ben Wattenberg stressed in 1974, many people felt personally confident even when there was widespread civic disaffection.

The two upswings occurred in periods of major policy changes.   The slight 1970-1972 opinion change occurred during the second two years of Nixon's first term.   Every effort was being made to accentuate the positive, including a strong push for a Vietnamese ceasefire and peace settlement.   The majority of

Americans perceived personal socio-economic gains. Only blacks showed a slide in confidence during this period.

In the 1980-1983 period, Reagan's consistent optimism affected public opinion. He accentuated the positives in his agenda of self-governance and limited government, avoided negatives, like taxes, and did not deal with details such as budgetary deficits.

Gains in civic confidence are most easily won through civic pride. Patriotism has been a key to success throughout American history. Even when appeals to patriotism occur in complicated contexts, this works. President Carter's 1979 malaise speech won some patriotic support, for example, until he thoroughly destroyed the effect two days later, calling for a full Cabinet resignation. Under Reagan, patriotism soared in 1983 with the invasion of Grenada and the Marine deaths in Lebanon. Confidence increased then wavered over nuclear and other war fears.

More sustained confidence seems associated with personal socio-economic well-being.[63] However, that confidence may remain strictly personal and not translate into civic confidence. The problem is how to transform private confidence into public confidence.

III. CONSTITUTIONAL NORMS AND POLITICAL INSTITUTIONS

Problems associated with confidence in political institutions and the underlying constitutional values and concepts may be dealt with by a critique of specific structures: the Presidency, Congress, the bureaucracy, the judiciary, and political parties and elections. That sort of analysis was done in 1980 by the Panel on the Electoral and Democratic Process of the President's Commission for a National Agenda for the Eighties. The group was set up by President Carter in 1979; it completed work in 1980; and its published report was issued in 1981, timed perfectly for oblivion. The panel concluded:

> This growing public alienation surely reflects an outlook among citizens that our political institutions have not responded adequately to the welter of troublesome problems confronting our nation. Timely action has sometimes been prevented because of the fragmentation that afflicts our American political institutions today. This framentation can be defined as the tendency for such organizations to break down into semi-autonomous units that act to further the interests of particular groups in society.[64]

Three clusters of interrelated confidence issues are examined here:

* Accountability, focusing on interrelationships between the federal bureaucracy, Congress, and the Presidency.
* Balance, dealing with reconciliation of values of change and stability, and of diversity and cohesion.
* Duty, centering on civic and public service values and responsible behavior.

Accountability and System Relationships

Three dimensions of accountability and governmental system interrelationships are discussed here: (1) assaults on the federal bureaucracy, particularly the 1970s neo-utilitarian critique and fashionable 1980s reforms proposed by public choice theorists; (2) concepts of politics in public administration; and (3) the trend since the 1960s to deinstitutionalize and politicize the federal bureaucracy.

Public Choice vs. Bureaucracy Public bureaucracies came under concerted attack in the 1960s and 1970s from citizens, politicians, and the media, with many blaming big government and high taxes for inefficiency and self-serving behavior in administrative institutions. The critics have found extensive support in academic criticism of bureaucracy. Distinctions need to be drawn, however, between sociological critiques of bureaucracy as an organizational model and assaults on the federal bureaucracy or other specific public career services. Some of the general criticisms may be self-perpetuating, contributing to popular dissatisfaction and other problems, like diminished public service morale. But many critiques of the organization of bureaucracies, such as those by Warren Bennis,[65] Harlan Cleveland,[66] and Daniel Katz and Robert Kahn,[67] have been aimed at improving that organization.

During the 1960s turmoil, many political scientists and economists became convinced that the national government had become overextended and/or unresponsive and that the federal bureaucracy was principally at fault. William A. Niskanen's Bureaucracy and Representative Government, published in 1971, was the most influential work to advance that view.[68] Niskanen, Assistant Director for Evaluation in the U.S. Office of Management and Budget under Nixon, used economic theory in a model of bureaucratic behavior to demonstrate that bureaucrats use their monopoly powers to secure budget authorizations that are above socially optimal levels. That viewpoint dominated segments of academic thought for the next dozen years, with substantial impact on public administration, political science, and economics.

The public choice theory that "a bureaucracy problem" is at fault for overextended and unresponsive government is based on concepts of supply and demand—neglecting how Congress, the Presidency, and various political interests engage in public policy processes. Niskanen's 1971 analysis implicitly combines the roles of legislative committees and the bureaucracy, focusing on bureaucratic power vis-a-vis the legislature. He concluded that alternative service delivery mechanisms were necessary. The two alternatives proposed by Niskanen were privatization, turning public functions over to the private sector, and competition, authorizing parallel suppliers of public services.

Alternative service delivery became a major interest in public administration in the 1970s. One suggestion was represented by the public choice attack on bureaucracy. Another theory involved pragmatic efforts to find alternatives that would provide public services at acceptable costs, without a fixed anti-bureaucratic bias.[69] A third proposal, made by some New Public Administration theorists, sought reforms that would result in more open systems, linking citizens and bureaucrats, and enhancing both citizen participation and bureaucratic realism.

By the 1980s, the public choice perspective was prominent in academic circles, and became integral to the philosophy of the Reagan Administration. But it also became subject to careful, penetrating assessment. A scholarly critique by Gary J. Miller of Michigan State University and Terry M. Moe of Stanford University was published in 1983 in the American Political Science Review.[70] Miller and Moe retained basic components of Niskanen's original budget maximization model in their research, but took into account the integral role of the legislature in decision processes. Their conclusions were as follows:

> When these legislative considerations are integrated into the analysis, bureaucratic behavior is placed in [a] larger, more meaningful context. Viewed from this standpoint, the dimensions of the "bureaucracy problem" begin to look very different from those stressed by Niskanen and other critics. In particular, the model implies that their negative assessments of bureaucracy are overdrawn, that their proposals for privatization and competition are often ill-advised, and that the legislature, not the bureaucracy, is primarily to blame for problems of big government.[71]

Miller and Moe maintained that, if some parts of government are overgrown while others are underfunded, the "interesting question is not whether we have a 'bureaucracy problem,' but where and to what extent the problem surfaces."[72] Their research led them to conclude that "The key to an answer rests with the underlying patterns of legislative organization and with empirical research to discover what those patterns are."[73]   They suggested several ways of enhancing legislative control of bureaucracy, such as changed criteria for committee assignments and jurisdiction.

Congress presently functions as a form of subcommittee government; the ways in which that affects relationships with the bureaucracy and the Presidency, and the confidence problems of government, warrants more attention.   Throughout most of the nineteenth century, Congress functioned along party government lines.   From the first part of this century until the "reforms" of the 1960s, committee government dominated, with leadership by a few powerful members.   The "democratization" of the 1960s resulted in a downward drift of power to the subcommittees.[74]

Following Presidential impoundments and Watergate, the 1974 Budget and Impoundment Control Act represented the beginnings of a departure from the 1960s fragmentation and an effort to strengthen leadership in the highly dispersed power system of the 1960s.   Creation of the Congressional Budget Office and similar steps to enhance staff support were aimed at correcting system difficiencies, but the bureaucratization of Congress has not succeeded in providing significantly strengthened leadership.

While Niskanen's critique of the "bureaucracy problem" was unrealistic in its neglect of Congress, it ignored even more important interactions between the Executive Office of the President, OMB, and the agencies.   A 1983 analysis of interactions between agency bureaucrats and executive branch politicians by Mark S. Kamlet and David C. Mowery demonstrates some of the serious deficiencies in the public choice assault on bureaucracy.[75]   They concluded:

> The Niskanen model of government growth is an inaccurate representation of federal budgetary processes, because it does not allow for the strong executive branch influence on budgeting; Niskanen's model resembles a staging of Hamlet without the prince of Denmark.   The dominance of the White House and the Executive Office of the President in resource allocation decisions suggests that the interaction of the White House politician and the executive bureaucrat is of greater importance than that of the federal legislator and the bureaucrat.[76]

Another 1983 study of nine models designed to explain the growth of government found that only one of the explanations-- Adolph Wagner's 1877 Law of Rising Public Expenditures--even barely survived econometric analysis of U.S. government developments during the period, 1948-1979.[77]

Contingency and complexity may be less satisfying explanations than the universals of neo-utilitarianism or other simple explanations of government. Complex reality is frustrating, compared to public choice and bureau voting theory. But a new realism is needed in political science and public administration, after the many overly simple prescriptions of the 1960s, 1970s, and 1980s.

Politicians and Administrators The old politics and administration dichotomy was resurrected during the turbulent 1960s and 1970s and reappeared as a problem in the 1980s. The "new public administration" of the 1960s was commonly perceived to assert that policy and its implementation are so intermingled that political policy roles and non-partisan administrative roles cannot be readily distinguished. Some 1960s radicals went much further, arguing (from the libertarian Left) that administrators are obligated to function as policy advocates, even as guerrillas who would undermine authoritative policy and rule systems to achieve "social justice." Certain politicians (often from the libertarian Right) countered that if everything is policy, then everything should be partisanly political. Pressures were mounted from the Left and Right for politicization and deinstitutionalization of public administration. In a 1979 analysis of "Jimmy Carter as Public Administrator,"[78] James L. Sundquist made a more representative professional call for realism on the politics and administration relationship. The revived importance of the issue was stressed by Dwight Waldo in 1979: "It is the area in which politics/policy and administration/management mingle that the crucial problems of the large modern polity are to be found."[79]

The peculiar separation of powers system largely accounts for the complexity of the politics/administration issue in the federal, state, and strong mayor-council forms of American government. That system contrasts with the council-manager form of government and with principal parliamentary forms. In the latter systems, power is concentrated in the legislative body, which sets general policy and has the authority to fire the manager, or it can vote no confidence in the executive and install a new administration. In turn, policy implementation is an executive function. By contrast, the federal and state governments perpetuate a Tudor model of fused functions shared by three separated branches. The result is a complex web of policy and implementation responsibilities shared by bureaucrats and politicians. Within that framework, the interdependence of bureaucrats, who bring expertise and professionalism to their roles, and politicians, who bring representation and political responsibility to theirs, is accepted as a workable paradigm for

American national government (although that view is rejected by some key Reagan Administration officials).[80]

An impressive analysis has been done by Joel D. Aberbach, Robert D. Putnam, and Bert A. Rockman of the differences and similarities between bureaucratic policymaking in seven countries: Britain, France, Germany, Italy, the Netherlands, Sweden, and the United States.[81] They characterized the United States government as follows: "American administrators have long had responsibility for promoting their policies and mobilizing their constituencies with an overtness and an intensity that is foreign to the European tradition. This practice, together with the weakness of American parties, has meant ironically that the U.S. bureaucracy has been recognized as a channel of representation rivaling Congress and, moreover, one that aggregates interests in a manner that is hardly less comprehensive or progressive."[82]

Analysis of bureaucrats and of the federal bureaucracy, as in the research of Aberbach, Putnam and Rockman, illustrates the hazards of mingling abstract conclusions about bureaucracy with defenses of assaults on specific governmental bureaucracies. Charles T. Goodsell achieved exceptional success in his brief for the defense, The Case for Bureaucracy, A Public Administration Polemic. As polemic, however, that effort lumps sociological and other critiques of traditional bureaucracy with ideological assaults such as public choice theory. It diminishes positive contributions like open systems theory, matrix organizations, and organization development, which grew out of critiques of traditional bureaucracy. Distinctions must be made between, on the one hand, bureaucracy and theoretical analyses of it and, on the other hand, the bureaucracy of a particular government and related critiques.

Deinstitutionalization and Politicization   A result of the assaults on the federal and other public service bureaucracies has been a trend toward deinstitutionalization and politicization of government bureaucracy--in plain terms, a significant return to transitoriness, amateurism, and spoils. In local governments, the same pressures resulted in attacks on professional local community management (the council-manager form of government) in the 1960s and 1970s. They also stimulated many positive efforts to involve citizens in the administration of local government, which enhanced popular confidence and career service knowledge and sensitivity. These developments are dealt with more specifically in the next two sections of this paper; they are raised here by way of introduction because of their bearing on acccountability and, ultimately, confidence in government.

Balance: Change and Stability; Diversity and Cohesion

The confidence problem of the 1960s and 1970s was not related only to politics and government. While Ben Wattenberg could easily find improved socioeconomic positions for people following the 1960s, growing disaffection stretched to most major American institutions from the mid-1960s to the 1980s, as shown in Exhibit 1.

Change, Diversity, and Fragmentation of Affections   In academic and applied business and public administration studies, change was the theme of the 1960s and early 1970s. Warren Bennis' and Philip Slayter's The Temporary Society[83] and Alvin Toffler's Future Shock[84] were in vogue, as were "sensitivity training" and personal and organizational change. It was a period of outrageous contrasts: Bennis' creative thought and Yippie Jerry Rubin's destructive anti-thought; landing a man on the moon and the growth of the drug culture. By the 1970s, concerns turned increasingly to balancing the forces of change and stability, as reflected in John W. Gardner's The Recovery of Confidence,[85] the American Management Association's Managing in Times of Radical Change,[86] and Harlan Cleveland's The Future Executive.[87]   Rather than a time of social disaffection, the 1960s and 1970s were a period of fragmentation of affections. Community fell apart, but communities of special interests proliferated.

This fragmentation characterized much of society by the 1970s. The single-interest group problem, for example, had an impact on many American organizations and institutions. For example, the International City Management Association (ICMA), the oldest professional public service organization and the only one to achieve institutional status, has experienced growing special interest politics within the association--county administrators, managers of small communities, managers of large cities, directors, assistants, blacks, Hispanics, and women all express frustrations and seek both special identities and inclusion. ICMA has dealt successfully with these developments, maintaining "essential internal community" by balancing forces for stability and change.[88]   The American Society for Public Administration (ASPA), another example, has both suffered and benefited from centrifugal forces which spawned 16 sections between 1973 and 1984, in addition to various committees and groups. Civic, social, religious, educational, business, and employee organizations experienced similar fragmenting forces in the decades of specialized realignment of affections. Many did not succeed in maintaining essential community.

Change and Federal Government Imbalance   The politics and administration problems in the federal government during the 1980s and the growing tendency toward deinstitutionalization and

-74-

EXHIBIT I

Percent of Poll Expressing a **Great** Deal of Confidence in Nine American Institutions, 1966-1979

Question: As far as people in charge of running [each institution on the list below] are concerned, would you say you have a great deal of confidence, only some confidence, or hardly any confidence at all in them?

	1966	'71	'73	'74	'75	'76	'77	'78	'79
Average of Nine Major Institutions	43%	27%	33%	28%	24%	20%	24%	25%	23%
TV News	25	--	41	31	35	28	28	35	37
Medical	73	61	57	50	43	42	43	42	30
Military	62	27	40	33	24	23	27	29	29
Press	29	18	30	25	26	20	18	23	28
Organized Religion	41	27	36	32	32	24	29	34	20
Major Companies	55	27	29	21	19	16	20	22	18
Congress	42	19	29	18	13	9	17	10	18
Executive Branch	41	23	19	28	13	11	23	14	17
Organized Labor	22	14	20	18	14	10	14	15	10

Source: President's Commission for a National Agenda for the Eighties, The Electoral and Democratic Process in the Eighties (Washington: U.S. Government Printing Office, 1981), citing surveys by Louis Harris and Associates as reported in Public Opinion (October/November, 1979).

politicization reflect the increased difficulties in reconciling rapid social change with community requirements of cohesion and stability. The history of the Executive's policy development since the 1960s illustrates this difficulty and its consequences. In the Golden Era of traditional American public administration, from the New Deal through the Eisenhower Administration, the Bureau of the Budget coordinated presidential policy involvement, with consistent reliance on the professional expertise of career public servants. That system began to change in the 1960s, moving toward a pattern of personal presidential loyalty; politicization became dominant in the policymaking of the Executive Office of the President (EOP) in the 1970s. Under Ronald Reagan, EOP policy processes became almost wholly partisan; the EOP deinstitutionalization extended to much of the Executive Branch.[89]

President Kennedy dismantled some of the institutionalized Cabinet and security affairs apparatus of the Eisenhower years. He employed ad hoc task forces for policy development prior to and following his election. However, he did not disturb the organization of the Bureau of the Budget (BOB). It was President Johnson who initiated changes there in the Golden Era model. In his memoirs, Johnson expressed his views on the institutionalized BOB policy machinery:

> I had watched this process for years, and I was convinced that it did not encourage enough fresh or creative ideas. The bureaucracy of the government is too preoccupied with day-to-day operations, and there is strong bureaucratic inertia dedicated to preserving the status quo....The cumbersome organization of government is simply not equipped to solve complex problems that cut across departmental jurisdictions.[90]

Johnson relied on White House appointees Joe Califano and Larry Levinson to coordinate his Great Society domestic policy, and the EOP and other resources were used without respect for traditional institutional patterns. Under Nixon, the BOB became OMB and the Domestic Council was created, with a prescription for a balance of institutionalized professional expertise and political leadership. Under John Ehrlichman, however, the operation was wholly politicized. Nixon's EOP became a peculiar mix of extreme centralization within a disastrously fragmented White House. President Ford restored Cabinet and agency influence, but by then the EOP policy machinery was routinely politicized. Under President Carter, the trend continued, but his Administration was characterized by incoherence and disorder. Under President Reagan, the Office of Policy Development has helped to facilitate adherence to the Reagan agenda, but it is wholly partisan.

This pattern extends across the government now. Key OMB offices are filled with political appointees, and incumbents of previously professionally-staffed positions commonly have dual appointments as political special assistants to the President. Inspectors General, created in 1978 through provisions aimed at developing them as institutionalized offices, were all fired in the initial days of the Reagan Administration to allow appointments consistent with a transitory, personalized, presidential loyalty model. Assistant secretaries and many bureau heads have been similarly politicized since the 1970s. The Civil Service Reform Act of 1978 has resulted in deinstitutionalization of the central personnel structure. The U.S. Office of Personnel Management had 36 political appointees in January, 1984, compared to the three in the former U.S. Civil Service Commission prior to 1977. This does not include nine other political appointees in the President's Commission on Executive Interchange and the White House Fellows program. Career personnel are routinely excluded from policy deliberations at OPM now.[91] That pattern extends to operating departments and agencies, and down through Assistant Secretary and many bureau offices.

A problem underlying this development was stated by Lyndon Johnson: lack of confidence among political leaders in the responsiveness and creativity of career bureaucrats. That attitude parallels, if it does not reflect, a larger problem of the social sciences and of political science in particular. The Golden Era of public administration was based on three conditions: (1) faith that science can positively transform society; (2) consensus that the government's role is to do right, not to discern it; and (3) general agreement on public management principles to execute the limited functions of government.[92] Those conditions no longer prevail. Faith in social science now applies more to technocratic expertise (like polling) and less to normative foundations; effectiveness issues are complex; and there is frequent disagreement on paradigms of political science and public administration. Lack of confidence in institutionalized, professional, and public service expertise had become pervasive by the 1980s.

For the nation, that perspective--the elevation of the subjective, personal, partisan, and transitory over values of objectivity, detachment, stability, and coherence--raises questions that warrant priority attention in research and commentary. A major question is: What stabilizing factors are required to promote cohesion in this era of diversity and rapid change?

The change between 1960 and the 1970s from an institutionalized to a highly partisan, personalized Presidency upset the previous balance created by the rise of large-scale administration. Developments since the 1970s are more serious.

The earlier shift in the EOP is now permeating the Executive Branch, deinstitutionalizing and politicizing much of the government around a personal loyalty.

Duty and Service: What are the Rules of the Game?

Constitutional democracy rests on the establishment of sufficient general agreement on fundamentals of society and government to withstand differences over less basic matters.   It assumes limits on advocacy and dissent in a climate of informed consent.   The decades of disaffection have raised many questions about these basic assumptions.   Three such concerns are discussed in this conclusion: The adequacy of agreement on constitutional norms;   changing conditions of community;   and interdependence of civic duty and public service values.

Does Agreement Exist on Rules of the Game?   The extended period of public disaffection from the national government indicates a need to examine the extent of understanding and agreement on constitutional fundamentals.   The United States government was founded on the premise that governmental politicians and bureaucrats can only be trusted with constitutionally defined and limited authority.   It is a system based on popular sovereignty and limited government,   with judicial review upholding the "rule of law" precisely because of a lack of confidence by the founders in "a rule of men."   But inquiry is needed into how those rules of the game, or others, are understood or followed.

The extent to which constitutional norms are observed today in Britain, without a written constitution, may serve to highlight the nature of the problem[93] in the United States.   Research by Donald D. Searing[93] is instructive about British politicians' attitudes toward constitutional fundamentals.   Based on interviews with Members of Parliament and candidates, Searing found an absence of assumed consensus on constitutional rules of the game.   Furthermore,   attitudes were   "deeply   and systematically divided" along lines of "political values and partisan advantage more than[94] traditional interpretations or recent democratic theory admit."[94]   The two distinct configurations of British rules of the game are classical ones: (1) a deliberative interpretation, built around parliamentarism, flexible tactics, and acceptance of limits (adaptation), and (2) a representational or responsiveness interpretation, revolving around "the role of the electorate, individual[95] responsibility, and vigorous and critical opposition."[95]   What was startling was that the commitment of British   politicians   was   not   to   coherence   of   constitutional principles;   they   were   malleable,   "permeated   by   party-political considerations."   That is, their attitudes about rules of the game were   determined   by   what   served   their   partisan   political advantage.

The American written constitution establishes a substantially different situation than exists in Britain, where some renewed support exists for written norms and judicial review because of a lack of trust in partisan interpretations of the unwritten constitution. But the behavior of politicians in the United States raises serious questions about their willingness to sacrifice constitutional principles and related rules of the game in favor of transitory partisan interests. Beyond the obvious crimes in Watergate and Abscam, the question of principled behavior is raised by President Carter's persistent assaults on the federal bureaucracy based, at least in part, on Patrick Caddell's polls indicating that it was politically advantageous to make these criticisms. Similarly, President Reagan dramatically staged the advocacy of a balanced budget amendment while insisting on grossly underfunded budgets, resulting in a series of deficits that tripled any previous levels.

More troubling because it is both less visible and possibly longer-lasting is the rapid deinstitutionalization and partisan politicization of the Executive Branch in only two decades, 1964-84. Is that also primarily a result of Presidents who seek transient partisan advantage, or is it a reflection of the failures of previous norms?

Major disagreements on fundamentals are also present among public administration practitioners and academicians. The constitutional principle of separation of powers in a system of mingled functions is often understood differently by academicians and politicians, who advocate either a rigid policy/implementation dichotomy or a lack of distinction between political and bureaucratic roles. In addition, certain public administration proponents have in the past supported the concept of an activist bureaucracy, which significantly conflicts with traditional principles of popular sovereignty and representative government through authoritative law.

In American political science, controversies since the 1960s have likewise centered on fundamentals. The conventional American paradigm of government as a common-benefit, conflict-resolving organization in a highly diversified pluralist society has come under sharp criticism. Dissenters assess the system as one of fundamentally conflicting interests, generally socioeconomic in nature.[96] The fact that the polarizing politics of the 1980s generated increased popular interest in politics (after the alienation of the 1960s and 1970s) attests to the serious character of this difference about fundamentals. It is not merely an academic debate; it is a question of which rules are being followed in the political game: politics of community, or of socioeconomic and racial division. How aware are political actors of the past rules of the game, and are they conscious of the implications of their actions?

<u>Essential Community</u> As noted, the old American paradigm focused on essential community. Politics and government were seen as vehicles to bring diverse people together, facilitating "the good life," balancing community and individual differences. The great issue from the constitutional era to the present has been how to achieve that in a nation as large and diverse as the United States.

Federalism has been one key to that, promoted early in this century by the development of extensive home rule for local governments. However, expansion of federal government activities, particularly intergovernmental transfer payments and regulations of the 1960s and 1970s, dramatically altered that relationship, building on more modest changes from the New Deal through the 1950s.

Currently there is renewed interest among many public administration practitioners and academicians in ways to strike a workable balance between the levels of government. Many of these individuals relate that challenge to more basic relationships of citizenship and administration, akin to interests at the time when the first schools of public administration were formed in the 1920s at Syracuse University and the University of Southern California and, in 1934, at The American University.

One conclusion, according to certain current thought, is that many personal dimensions of community and diversity are reconcilable only at local governmental levels, while others are essentially state or national concerns. It calls for dividing responsibilities between levels of government. The Reagan Administration initially advocated such an effort and in 1981 the "big seven" public interest groups, which represent local and state governments and their officials, generally supported it. When it became evident that the federal government's focus was more on funding cuts during a major recession than on practical reformulation, the effort foundered. But the roots of the ideas are far deeper than transient politics, and they merit longer term efforts to enhance conditions of essential community.

The 1960's and 1970's disaffection from government, retrenchment politics, and other political, social, and economic changes resulted in an extensive reexamination by local government managers of conditions for essential community in the future. In 1978, City Manager Robert Kipp, then President of the International City Management Association (ICMA), launched a "Future Horizons Project" which involved most local managers and many civic leaders in the United States and Canada, along with a few academicians. They faced the challenge of popular demands of "more for less" and accurately predicted major reductions in central governmental funding of local communities. They urged "Buy Back Federalism" as a strategy to retrieve local government authority that had been taken away by the rapid growth of national regulations since the 1960s. The orientation, however, was essentially positive and oriented to local responsibilities and actions. The managers worked on ways to network more effectively with scientific, academic, professional, and business communities. They explored and developed a wide range of ICMA initiatives ranging from applications of advanced technology to services adaptations in anticipation of demographic changes.

Idealism was ICMA's principal focus, however. Drawing on extensive inputs from professional managers, the committee summarized that perspective:

> The committee was struck by the degree to which the implementation of the strategies for contending with the future requires a profound idealism.

> Idealism is no stranger among professional managers. It has been the greatest distinction of this profession, which adopted the earliest code of ethics in the public service and has maintained a record of ethical behavior second to none; but the demands of the future, the potential costs and risks, will not be met without even higher ideals.[97]

Four ideals were stressed by these professional public managers: excellence of professional management; representative democracy; equity; and ethical conduct.

Civic Duty and Public Service   Recovery of longterm confidence, according to an impressive body of professional opinion in public administration, depends in part on precisely this kind of devotion to ideals among government leaders. It is an idealism which elevates effective citizenship as the most fundamental purpose of public service. The two classic ideals of Western civilization--civic duty and public service--are understood to be symbiotic.

Citizens, their politicians, and their public servants share responsibilities according to this ideal. Their alienation from one another in recent years has stemmed in part from dysfunctional separations among them. The development of ways to diminish those distances, particularly with respect to national government, is a challenge.

In their efforts to nourish citizenship as the foundation of constitutional democracy, most professional public administrators distinguished between governance and government long before that became a Reagan Administration slogan. It was a fundamental trust of the ICMA Futures study, for example.

Those professional public leaders generally understand that enriched citizenship involves opportunities in the private and independent sectors, including religious, charitable, educational, business, civic, and cultural activities. They also understand, however, that effective citizenship requires informed and sensitive exercise of authoritative public power. Contrary to the libertarian critiques of the Left and the Right, America's complex society cannot function without governmental excellence.

Enhanced quality in national political leadership is a desperately needed condition of such excellence, as this review of the decades of disaffection shows. A new devotion among politicians to combined values of civic duty and public service is essential to that. Many public administration leaders have turned with renewed vigor toward that sort of idealism as a result of the decades of disaffection. If this idealism should become a broad perspective, it could be an important contribution to the renewal of conditions for confidence in American government.

NOTES

1. Data from the University of Michigan's Institute for Social Research, as reported in Arthur H. Miller, "Political Issues and Trust in Government: 1964-1970," American Political Science Review, Vol. 58, No. 3 (September 1974): 951-972; Jack Citrin, "Comment: The Political Relevance of Trust in Government," ibid. 973-988; Arthur H. Miller, "Rejoinder to 'Comment' by Jack Citrin: Political Discontent or Ritualism?" ibid. 989-1001; Arthur H. Miller, "Is Confidence Rebounding?" Public Opinion, Vol. 6, No. 3 (June/July 1983): 16-20.

2. Ben J. Wattenberg, The Real America, A Surprising Examination of the State of the Union (Garden City, New York: Doubleday, 1974), 315.

3. Ibid., 6.

4. Ibid., 9.

5. Ibid., 7.

6. Miller, "Political Issues and Trust," 951.

7. Ibid.

8. Richard Scammon and Ben Wattenberg, The Real Majority (New York: Coward, McCann, and Geohagan, Inc., 1971).

9. Citrin, "Comment," 973.

10. Ibid.

11. Public Papers of the Presidents, Jimmy Carter, 1979, Vol. II (Washington, D.C.: U.S. Government Printing Office, 1980), 1235-1241, 1237-1238.

12. Caddell's memo, as quoted here, is reported in Theodore H. White, America in Search of Itself (New York: Harper & Row, 1982), 258.

13. Laurence L. Barrett, Gambling With History, Ronald Reagan in the White House (Garden City, New York: Doubleday, 1983).

14. Theodore H. White, America in Search of Itself, 382.

15. For a more detailed analysis of strategic Reagan behavior, see: Chester A. Newland, "The Reagan Presidency: Limited Government and Political Administration," Public

Administration Review, Vol. 43, No. 1 (January/February, 1983), 1-21; also, Newland, "Developing the Reagan Program: Executive Office Policy Management," Conference Proceedings, Governance: The Reagan Era and Beyond (Washington, D.C.: The Urban Institute, 1984).

16. A valence issue of one period may become a polarizing position issue at another time, of course. An example is inflation. While general tendencies were dominant on that issue before 1981, Reagan's policies resulted in bipolarization, with those having incomes over $20,000 most inclined to favor, and those below that level to reject, the Reagan policies. See David S. Broder, "America Appears Deeply Divided, Anxious to Vote," The Washington Post, January 1, 1984, A-1, A-6.

17. Arthur Miller, Edie Goldenber, and Lutz Erbring, "Type-Set Politics: Impacts of the Newspapers on Public Confidence," American Political Science Review, Vol. 73, No. 1 (March 1979): 67-84.

18. Ibid., 67.

19. Ibid.

20. Martin P. Wattenberg, "From Parties to Candidates: Examining the Role of the Media," Public Opinion Quarterly, Vol. 46, No. 2 (Summer 1982): 216-227.

21. Fay Lomax Cook, Tom R. Tyler, Edward G. Goetz, Margaret T. Gordon, David Protess, Donna R. Leff, and Harvey L. Molotch, "Media and Agenda Setting: Effects on the Public, Interest Group Leaders, Policy Makers, and Policy," Public Opinion Quarterly, Vol. 47, No. 1 (Spring 1983): 16-35, 33.

22. A textbook example is by Angus Campbell, "Types of Election Outcomes," in Presidential Politics, ed. James I. Lingle and Byron E. Shafer (New York: St. Martin's Press, 1983), 360-371.

23. Broder, "America Appears Deeply Divided."

24. Donald R. Kinder, "Presidents, Prosperity, and Public Opinion," Public Opinion Quarterly, Vol. 45, No. 1 (Spring 1981): 1-21.

25. Paul R. Abramson and John H. Aldrich, "The Decline of Electoral Participation in America," American Political Science Review, Vol. 76, No. 3 (September 1982): 502-521, 502.

26. Voter statistics are from Public Opinion, Vol. 5, No. 6 (December/January 1983): 24.

27. Gabriel A. Almond and Sidney Verba, The Civic Culture, Political Attitudes and Democracy in Five Nations (Boston, Massachusetts: Little, Brown and Co., 1963).

28. Sidney Verba and Norman Nie, Participation in America: Political Democracy and Social Equality (New York: Harper and Row, 1972).

29. For a valuable literature assessment and report of a random sample citizen survey in Wichita, Kansas, see Elaine B. Sharp, "Citizen-Initiated Contacting of Government Officials and Socioeconomic Status: Determining the Relationship and Accounting for It," American Political Science Review, Vol. 76, No. 1 (March 1982): 109-115.

30. U.S. Department of Commerce, Bureau of the Census, Social Indicators III (Washington, D.C.: U.S. Government Printing Office, January 1981).

31. America Enters the Eighties: Some Social Indicators (Philadelphia: American Academy of Political and Social Science, 1981).

32. Lady Bird Johnson, A White House Diary (New York: Holt, Rinehart Winston, 1970), 192.

33. The formal letter is printed in Mrs. Johnson's diary, (ibid.). The original 1964 handwritten letter and related materials are in the LBJ Library.

34. National Academy of Public Administration, Revitalizing Federal Management: Managers and Their Overburdened Systems (Washington: NAPA, 1983); and C.A. Newland, "Federal Government Management Trends," The Bureaucrat, Vol. 12, No. 4 (Winter 1983-84): 3-13.

35. Recalled by Lady Bird Johnson, A White House Diary, 680.

36. Ibid., 681.

37. National Academy of Public Administration, Watergate: Its Implications for Responsible Government (Washington: NAPA, 1974), vi.

38. Lee Sigelman and Kathleen Knight, "Why Does Presidential Popularity Decline? A Test of the Expectation/ Disillusion Theory," Public Opinion Quarterly, Vol. 47, No. 3 (Fall 1983): 310-324.

39. Alan K. Campbell, "The Institution and Its Problems," Public Administration Review, Vol. 42, No. 4 (July/August 1982): 305-308, 307.

40. White, America in Search of Itself, 1.

41. Gregory B. Markus, "Political Attitudes During an Election Year: A Report on the 1980 NES Panel Study," American Political Science Review, Vol. 76, No. 2 (September 1982): 538-560.

42. Ibid., 549.

43. Ibid., 558.

44. William K. Domke, Richard C. Eichenberg, and Catherine M. Kelleher, "The Illusion of Choice: Defense and Welfare in Advanced Industrial Democracies, 1948-1978," American Political Science Review, Vol. 77, No. 1 (March 1983): 19-35.

45. The effects of Reagan's domestic program on state and local governments is best documented in Richard P. Nathan, Fred C. Doolittle, and Associates, The Consequences of Cuts (Princeton, New Jersey: Princeton Urban and Regional Research Center, 1983).

46. Broder, "America Appears Deeply Divided," A-6.

47. Ibid.

48. Miller, "Is Confidence Rebounding," 17.

49. Michael Barone, "The Election Will Tell Us the Kind of Nation We Have Become," The Washington Post, January 1, 1984, H-8.

50. Broder, "America Appears Deeply Divided," A-6.

51. Ben Wattenberg, "From Parties to Candidates," 315-16.

52. Miller, et al., "Type-Set Politics," 67.

53. Charles T. Goodsell, The Case for Bureaucracy, A Public Administration Polemic (Chatham, New Jersey: Chatham House, 1983), 146-149.

54. Bernard Rosen, Holding Government Bureaucracies Accountable (New York: Praeger Publishers, 1982).

55. Robert G. Vaughn, The Spoiled System, A Call for Civil Service Reform New York: Charterhouse, 1975).

56. Broader aspects of evaluation and audits, including mid-1980s GAO developments, are summarized in C.A. Newland, The Bureaucrat.

57. "Effects of Public Opinion on Policy," American Political Science Review, Vol. 77, No. 1 (March 1983): 175-190, 175.

58. Ibid., 189.

59. Wayne F. Anderson, Chester A. Newland, and Richard J. Stillman, II, The Effective Local Government Manager (Washington, D.C.: ICMA, 1983), 114.

60. Thomas J. Peters and Robert H. Waterman, Jr., In Search of Excellence (New York: Harper and Row, 1982).

61. Kenneth Blanchard and Spencer Johnson, The One Minute Manager (New York: William Morrow and Co., 1982).

62. National Academy of Public Administration, Revitalizing Federal Management.

63. As noted earlier, Donald Kinder reported in 1981 that attitudes correlate more with perceptions of the nation's economic condition than with people's own perceptions. If correct, that apparent discrepancy may be accounted for by two factors: (1) people's conditions may determine their perceptions of the national economy, and (2) people may respond to queries to demonstrate "social" rather than "selfish" concern.

64. Panel report, The Electoral and Democratic Process in the Eighties (Washington, D.C.: GPO, 1980), 3. For the general commission conclusions, see Report of the President's Commission for a National Agenda for the Eighties, A National Agenda for the Eighties (Washington, D.C.: U.S. Government Printing Office, 1980).

65. Warren G. Bennis, Changing Organizations (New York: McGraw-Hill, 1966).

66. Harlan Cleveland, The Future Executive (New York: Harper and Row, 1972).

67. Daniel Katz and Robert L. Kahn, The Social Psychology of Organizations (New York: John Wiley & Sons, 1st ed, 1966; 2nd ed., 1978).

68. William A. Niskanen Jr., Bureaucracy and Representative Government (Chicago, Illinois: Aldine Publishing Co., 1971).

69. A good example of the lack of connection to anti-bureaucratic idelogy and an orientation to pragmatic government improvement is a case study of the use of recreation vouchers in South Barwon, Australia. See John L. Crompton, "Recreation Vouchers: A Case Study in Administrative Innovation and Citizen Participation," Public Administration Review, Vol. 43, No. 6 (November/December 1983): 537-546. For a comprehensive analysis of applied practices in governments in the United States, see Harry P. Hatry, Review of Private Approaches for Delivery of Public Services (Washington, D.C.: The Urban Institute, 1983). For a partisan, public choice perspective, see E. S. Savas, Privatizing the Public Sector (Chatham, New Jersey: Chatham House, 1982).

70. "Bureaucrats, Legislators, and the Size of Government," American Political Science Review, Vol. 77, No. 2 (June 1983): 297-322.

71. Ibid., 298.

72. Ibid., 321.

73. Ibid.

74. For a perceptive textbook analysis of Congress, see Lawrence C. Dodd and Richard L. Schott, Congress and the Administrative State (New York: John Wiley and Sons, 1979). For a theoretical analysis of Congressional influence on bureaucratic decisions concerning geographical allocation of expenditures, see R. Douglas Arnold, Congress and the Bureaucracy (New Haven, Connecticut: Yale University Press, 1983). Arnold's analysis includes a brief critique of public choice theories.

75. "Budgeting Side Payments and Government Growth: 1953-1968," American Journal of Political Science, Vol. 27, No. 4 (November 1983): 636-664.

76. Ibid., 659.

77. "The Growth of Government in the United States: An Empirical Assessment of Competing Explanations," American Journal of Political Science, Vol. 27, No. 4 (November 1983): 665-694.

78. James L. Sundquist, "Jimmy Carter as Public Administrator: An Appraisal at Mid-Term," Public Administration Review, Vol. 39, No. 1 (January/February 1979): 3-11.

79. Dwight Waldo, "Public Management Research: Perspectives of History, Political Science, and Public

Administration," Public Management Research Conference sponsored by OPM/GAO/OMB/GSA, at The Brookings Institution, Washington, November 19-20, 1979.

80.   Donald J. Devine, "Public Administration and the Reagan Era," paper presented at the national ASPA conference, Detroit, April 13, 1981. Also, Divine, "Escape from Politics," The Bureaucrat, Vol. 11, No. 4 (Winter 1982-83).

81.   Joel D. Aberbach, Robert D. Putnam, and Bert A. Rockman, Bureaucrats and Politicians in Western Democracies (Cambridge: Harvard University Press, 1981).

82.   Ibid., 23.

83.   Warren G. Bennis and Philip E. Slater, The Temporary Society (New York: Harper and Row, 1968).

84.   Alvin Toffler, Future Shock (New York: Random House, 1970).

85.   John W. Gardner, The Recovery of Confidence (New York: W.W. Norton, 1970).

86.   John J. Fendrock, Managing in Times of Radical Change, (New York: American Management Association, 1971).

87.   Harlan Cleveland, The Future Executive (New York: Harper and Row, 1972).

88.   Laurence Rutter, The Essential Community, Local Government in the Year 2000 (Washington: ICMA, 1980).

89.   For a detailed analysis of these developments, see C.A. Newland, "Developing the Reagan Program."

90.   Lyndon Baines Johnson, The Vantage Point (New York: Holt, Rinehart and Winston, 1971), 328.

91.   C.A. Newland, "Crucial Issues for Public Personnel Professionals," Public Personnel Management, Special Issue (Spring 1984).

92.   Daniel Bell, The Social Sciences Since the Second World War (New Brunswick, New Jersey: Transaction Books, 1982); Samuel H. Beer, "In Search of a New Public Philosophy," in The New American Political System, ed. Anthony King (Washington, D.C.: American Enterprise Institute, 1979).

93.   Donald D. Searing, "Rules of the Game in Britain: Can the Politicians Be Trusted?" American Poltical Science Review,

Vol. 76, No. 2 (June 1982): 239-258.

94. Ibid., 240.

95. Ibid., 243.

96. This disagreement was assessed by Charles E. Lindblom in his 1981 presidential address to the American Political Science Association: "Another State of Mind," American Political Science Association, Vol. 76, No. 1 (March 1982): 9-21.

97. Laurence Rutter, supra, 136.

Part I: The Public Sector: Responsibility and Accountability

B. Promoting the General Welfare

Chair: Dorothy B. James, The American University

Presentation by: Nelson Polsby, University of California at Berkeley

Comments by: Hon. Martha Keys, Association of Former Members of Congress

Respondents: Hon. Stuart E. Eizenstat, Powell, Goldstein, Frazer and Murphy
Hon. John A. Svahn, The White House

Rapporteur: Michael Hansen, The American University

PROMOTE THE GENERAL WELFARE

Michael G. Hansen

An analysis of general welfare provision in the 1980s is problematic. Besides issues of definition, locus, and focus, a number of factors have converged in recent years to alter profoundly the parameters of debate. Using Nelson Polsby's paper as a starting point, this chapter reviews the evolution of these factors, highlights various aspects of the current debate, and concludes with several key implications for public administrators and public management education. The current debate over the means and ends of general welfare promotion has tremendous significance for public administration. But the field and its professionals appear ill-prepared to move beyond their traditional preoccupations and make a creative contribution during the present period of redefinition and flux.

The Polsby Argument

Polsby describes welfare in general as a situation where society somehow looks after the physical condition of a given population. There are minimum standards of income, nutrition, health, housing, and education. When the private sector contributes directly to the maintenance of such minimum standards, it is either as self-help or philanthropy. Public sector intervention is traditionally called "welfare." Promotion of the general welfare is, however, more fundamental and profound than this. Polsby notes that the successful expansion of the economy is in large part responsible for our contemporary level of general welfare. Capital investment created economic growth, which created jobs, which created widespread prosperity and large markets for goods and services. The crux of Polsby's argument is that our general welfare is the result of roles played in both the private and public sectors. It is government's role, though, that tends to be deprecated and little understood.

Echoing the arguments in such books as Lindblom's Politics and Markets[1] and the more recent America's Hidden Success,[2] by Schwarz, Polsby highlights elements of the federal government's role in general welfare promotion. There are, for instance, political conditions which sustain capital formation and permit entrepreneurs to maneuver and innovate. Government itself is a significant source of capital and of resource aggregation, particularly through land grants and an educated citizenry. In addition, taxes are an important element in investment, as are public expenditures on material and human capital.

My argument is that the role of government in the provision of welfare is great. Government has not merely collected a tithe and distributed it to the less fortunate, but has also played a creative and useful role in the formation of economic prosperity.[3]

Polsby concludes that the government's role in providing for the general welfare has gained considerable legitimacy and has achieved an impressive measure of success.

Public Responsibility

The appropriate role of government in promoting the general welfare is once again a factor in the national agenda. Contemporary debate focuses on three areas, traces of which can be found in the Polsby paper. The first area is the degree to which our economic system alone can and should provide sufficient opportunity and support for general welfare. The second is the relationship between the public and private sectors in welfare promotion. The third area focuses on the effectiveness and appropriateness of specific public sector programs and policies, such as minimum wage laws, equal employment opportunity regulations, tax policy, and income support through social insurance and public assistance.

The degree to which the climate of debate over general welfare policy has been dramatically altered is illustrated in Reagan Administration initiatives. As described by Bawden and Palmer (1984), these initiatives constitute a "coherent ideological attack on the principles that have governed social policy in this country for the last half century."[4] The authors describe a number of prevailing assumptions that the President has called into question:

1. The extent to which the public--any "public," local, state or federal--is responsible for the social and economic well-being of its individual members. The historic trend has been toward an increasing assumption of responsibility at all levels of government.

2. The appropriate goals of social policy. Public debate on this issue in recent years has been preoccupied with questions of equality, whether of conditions or opportunity, but this word is conspiciously absent in this administration's rhetoric.

3. The most efficient means--level of government and type of program--for discharging public responsibility, however defined. The presumption should favor state and local governments as the most efficient vehicles for

delivering whatever largesse the public purse has to offer; ... in general, the federal government should look more to the private sector for the answers to social problems.[5]

Historically, direct government participation in issue resolution and problem solving has consisted of formal policies and structured programs. Despite the decidedly rational, social engineering aspects of welfare promotion, however, government's role grew by accretion rather than conscious design. In fact, until just fifty years ago, there was little direct federal spending in the social arena at all.

Beginning with the New Deal, the federal government became involved in what has turned out to be a major national social commitment to income support. Dolbeare describes the initatives as divided into two types: contributory programs, sometimes called "social insurance;" and non-contributory programs, also known as "public assistance" or "welfare."[6] Bawden and Palmer refer to the former as "upper tier" insurance programs, funded primarily through payroll taxes; and the latter as "lower tier" or means tested programs for those without such insurance or with inadequate protection by their present insurance.[7] Contributory programs include: Social Security (Old Age, Survivors, and Disability Insurance), unemployment insurance, and Medicare. Means tested or non-contributory programs target such groups as the elderly, blind, disabled, and women with dependent children. Programs include: Supplementary Security Income; the Food Stamp Program; Medicaid; Housing Assistance; and Aid to Families with Dependent Children. The basic eligibility criterion to receive benefits from these latter programs is demonstrated need.

The development of the income support commitment, particularly (but not only) through non-contributory entitlement programs, has been controversial:

Public assistance turned out to be politically one of the most unpopular programs ever adopted by Congress. It is disliked by national, state, and local legislators who must vote the skyrocketing appropriations for it; it is resented by the taxpayers who must bear the ever-increasing burdens of it; it is denounced by the officials and caseworkers who must administer it; and it is accepted with bitterness by those who were intended to benefit from it.

Certainly our public assistance programs have not succeeded in reducing dependency.[8]

In addition to "lower tier" programs, the federal government has been involved in other aspects of income maintenance which have also often been controversial: expanding government responsibility for managing the economy; maintaining price stability and maximum employment; and even providing jobs as the employer of last resort when necessary.[9] Although consolidation of social programs and expenditures began more than a decade ago, it has been President Reagan who has attempted to change their scope, goals, and the means used to achieve them. Palmer and Sawhill observe that the President "has successfully shifted the nation's social policy agenda from problem solving to budget cutting, and as long as the federal deficit remains a problem, there is little room for the agenda to shift back."[10]

The Commitment in Flux

The national social commitment to promote the general welfare has entered a period of shifting means and ends. Traditional support for the welfare system and its programs was bolstered by Depression-era politics of the 1930s and the expanding economy of the early Great Society years. At present, the coalition forged during the era lasting from the New Deal to the Great Society confronts the politics of retrenchment, privatization, unparalleled budget deficits, a transfer of budget priorities from the social to the defense sector, and a general perception of renewed national well-being. There does not currently exist a value or goal consensus concerning national social policy.

Paradoxes abound. For example, while public opinion surveys reflect a general feeling that we are, on the whole, better off than we were four years ago, government data indicate that more people are actually below the poverty line now than four years earlier. Furthermore, opinion surveys repeatedly demonstrate that a majority of the population favors shrinking government programs, budgets, and the deficits; yet individuals continue to support programs that benefit them in particular rather than the general welfare. A final illustration: While tax cuts, growth of the GNP, and lowered inflation suggest a marked increase in real disposable family income over the past four years, disparities between the incomes of poor families and those of the more affluent have also grown during this period. Do such paradoxes suggest a shift in the national commitment to protect individuals and relieve poverty? Not according to many of the panel members; rather, the current period is seen as one of redefinition and reconceptualization of government's role. According to Martha Keys in her panel presentation, the real issue is: Where do we need to go to maintain our national social commitments and how do we get there?

Although unable to agree on answers to ends and means questions, panel members did identify various perceptual, structural, economic, and political factors that have an impact on the policy debate:

1. There is conceptual confusion when general welfare promotion is considered. Social welfare is variously considered as a philosophy, in terms of the welfare state (e.g., in Great Britain), or as a number of policies and programs and their objectives. Clearly, the general welfare is distinguished from what is inherent to and provided by the welfare system. General welfare is also differentiated from other societal goals, such as justice and equality. Finally, there are varying perceptions of the efficacy of general versus special interest welfare promotion. Understanding is enhanced by separating the concepts of welfare, the welfare state, and welfare programs.

2. There is a general perception that welfare means "relief" or "public assistance." The pejorative connotation of "welfare" masks the reality that the majority of welfare programs are geared toward and in support of the middle class.

3. Rarely are the multifaceted impacts of government influence on welfare promotion clearly understood. Ideological, political, and perceptual differences, coupled with considerations of self-interest, subject government initiatives to a variety of interpretations. For instance, in America's Hidden Success, Jack Schwarz reinterprets the effects of various government social programs over the past 20 years. He laments the "myth of failure" that surrounds government initiatives in low income nutrition, health, and housing. Statistical evaluations of programs demonstrate marginal, if any, improvements in these areas over time. But Schwarz argues that the results of these programs have been greatly misunderstood.

    [New policies persist] in the belief that the nation's economic difficulties, such as the spread of unemployment, arose over the 1960-80 years from essentially unhealthy economic conditions spawned by an overgrown and mismanaged government. In this, [new policies] continue to underplay the crucial point that our difficulties arose far more from demographic and social factors (e.g., increased population due to the baby boom) than from the government's alleged growth or ineptitude or from a falling economy.[11]

Divergent conceptual, perceptual, and political interpretations exacerbate the search for common policy ground and mutually acceptable means and ends.

4. There is a perception, accentuated in recent years, that government cannot effectively run social welfare programs—that they are rife with waste, fraud, and abuse. Given the federal nature of our constitutional system, administrative rationality cannot possibly exist to the degree that is expected by the general public and that is basic to accountability and control systems. This reinforces the belief that government should not be involved with such programs and that promotion of the general welfare would be guided more effectively by the private sector.

5. Contemporary social policy of any type cannot be considered without examining tax expenditures and the incentive structure of our fiscal policies.

6. There appears to be bipartisan support to halt cutbacks in means test welfare programs. The current political debate concerns income transfer programs. Although a national social commitment still exists in our society, any more fundamental reforms of the welfare system risk destabilizing the support coalition. The political challenge for the future is to shape the welfare system and its political constituencies so that they include lower tier clientele groups. Such an arrangement, as opposed to the current fragmentation, could constitute the necessary aggregation of political interest and power to sustain the national coalition through its current period of uncertainty and flux.

The panel agreed that a key question for determining future social welfare policy concerns the locus of responsibility: What is the state's responsibility for the general welfare and what should individuals be required to do for themselves?

Implications for Public Administrators and

Public Management Education

At the beginning of this chapter it was argued that the appropriate role of government in general welfare promotion could be viewed from three perspectives. The first was the degree to which the economic system alone could and should provide sufficient opportunity and support for the general welfare. The second—a "mixed" view—advocated that the public and private sectors share responsibility. The third perspective focused on specific public sector policies and programs for which the government had full responsibility. Clearly, the government influences to differing degrees the programs, policies, and initiatives in all three areas. Historically, the field of general welfare has been most concerned with the third perspective: specific public sector policy and implementation.

Kaufman argues that public administration has been basically concerned with procedural and structural values: representativeness; neutral competence; and presidential leadership.[12] In a similar vein, a more contemporary analysis suggests four central commitments and beliefs widely shared by practitioners and students of public administration:

1. Belief in the need for a strong executive.
2. Belief in the need for a unified and comprehensive budget and a coherent budget process.
3. Belief in a civil service based upon expertise but responsive to legitimate political direction.
4. Belief in the accountability of political officials and the civil service to Congress and the public through oversight processes.

The beliefs express the continuing struggle to achieve public objectives by reinventing a measure of order out of the disorderly fragmentation and dispersion of power in the American constitutional system.[13]

The central tendencies of public administration appear to diverge sharply from the policy concerns involved in general welfare promotion. If social welfare is an offshoot of private sector activities (the first perspective), then little initiative will be expected of or desired from public institutions and administrators. This is the Reagan Administration's position at the present time. Social welfare policies and programs administered by public agencies (the third perspective) are those historically controversial activities that are currently subject to cutbacks, privatization, and decentralization. The public sector is not the solution to problems, according to the President; the government is the problem. Thus, experimentation, risk-taking and creativity will be precluded--the emphasis is on control systems and accountability.

It is the area of mixed public-private initiatives (the second perspective) where public administrators appear to have the opportunity for creative contributions to the social policy debate. Unfortunately, core values in the field offer little in the way of guidance. American public administration has traditionally focused on the management and direction of government institutions. There are relatively few precepts and principles to guide the future development of public-private relationships. The same holds true for contemporary intergovernmental relations. The massive funding of federal programs administered by state and local governments in recent years has generated confusion and uncertainty about the effectiveness of many programs and has diffused responsibility for the expenditure of public funds. The focus and methods of[14] the past are not adequate to meet present and future needs.

The pursuit of technical rationality by public administrators limits what the field can contribute when issues like social welfare policy transcend organizational and public sector boundaries. Public management research only reinforces this limitation: Agencies continue to emphasize instrumental rationality in their funded projects. Scientific management, which stresses the politics/administration dichotomy[15] is promoted at the expense of basic field development projects.

Public management is significant as a link between rational-instrumental concerns and those of politics and policy.[16] The evolution of social welfare policy could benefit from such linkage, since current and future administrative policy will rest in both private and public hands. Moreover, the implications of this linkage are significant for public administration education. While tying together technical and normative concerns is desirable, the process suffers when there is too much specialization and insufficient integration. Ideally, practitioners would juggle democratic political theory with technical demands[17] environmental constraints, and an ethical perspective.[17] A public administration curriculum emphasizing synthesis, not specialization, can contribute most to the linkage of technique to policy, and thereby to the achievement of public policy objectives.

1. Charles E. Lindblom, Politics and Markets (New York: Basic Books, Inc., 1977).

2. Jack E. Schwarz, America's Hidden Success: A Reassessment of Twenty Years of Public Policy (New York: W.W. Norton and Company, 1983).

3. Nelson Polsby, "The Role of Government in Providing for the Public Welfare," Paper presented at Public Affairs-50, The American University, March 2, 1984.

4. D. Lee Bawden and John L. Palmer, "Social Policy: Challenging the Welfare State," in The Reagan Record: An Assessment of America's Changing Domestic Priorities, ed. John L. Palmer and Isabel V. Sawhill, 177.

5. Ibid., 177-78.

6. Kenneth M. Dolbeare, American Public Policy (New York: McGraw Hill Book Company, 1982), 216.

7. Bawden and Palmer, "Social Policy," 180.

8. Thomas R. Dye, Understanding Public Policy (Englewood Cliffs, New Jersey: Prentice-Hall, Inc., 1978), 124-25.

9. Dolbeare, American Public Policy, 236.

10. John L. Palmer and Isabel V. Sawhill (eds). The Reagan Record: An Assessment of America's Changing Domestic Priorities (Cambridge, Massachusetts: Ballinger Publishing Company, 1984), 16.

11. Schwarz, America's Hidden Success, 152.

12. Herbert Kaufman, "Emerging Conflicts in the Doctrines of Public Administration," American Political Science Review 50 (December, 1956), 1057-73.

13. James D. Carroll, "Public Administration in Mixed Society," in Improving the Accountability and Performance of Government, ed. Bruce L. R. Smith and James D. Carroll (Washington, D.C.: The Brookings Institution, 1982), 111-12.

14. Ibid., 122.

15. G. David Garson and E. Samuel Overman, Public Management Research in the United States (New York: Prager Publishers, 1983), 76, 159.

16. E. Samuel Overman, "Public Management: What's New and Different?" Public Administration Review 44 (May/June 1984): 275-78. See also James L. Perry and Kenneth L. Kraemer (eds.), Public Management: Public and Private Perspectives (Palo Alto, California: Mayfield Publishing Company, 1983), 278.

17. Louis L. Gawthrop, Public Sector Management, Systems, and Ethics (Bloomington, Indiana University Press, 1984), 7, 137.

THE ROLE OF GOVERNMENT IN PROVIDING

FOR THE GENERAL WELFARE[1]

Nelson Polsby

This paper will discuss the role of government in providing for the general welfare. As I mulled over this fascinating topic, the whole idea of "welfare" became increasingly complicated. The dictionary was not much help. On page 1480 of my "concise" Oxford Dictionary the word is defined as: "Satisfactory state, health and prosperity, well-being." When combined with the word "state" it means, "One having national health insurance and other social services."[2]

That, at least, is the story as told by the Oxford dictionary, no doubt under the influence of the form of government most familiar to its editor.

I looked in three specialized political dictionaries and discovered that there was no entry for the word "welfare" at all, though they all defined "welfare state," albeit somewhat divergently. William Safire's dictionary described the latter almost entirely in terms that could serve as ammunition for those who want to attack the idea of welfare.[3] The Walter Laqueur dictionary once again showed British roots, mentioning the Attlee government of 1945-51 and defining the welfare state as:

Legislation and state-sponsored social insurance designed to raise minimum standards of living. It usually includes the provision of health services, housing, insurance against sickness and old age and relief for employment.[4]

I think this gets us into the ball park. Welfare generally refers to a situation where organized society, or government, looks after the physical condition of a given population. It follows that there are implicit social agreements upon minimum standards of income, nutrition, health, housing, and education. In principle these can be maintained through private or public provision, or through some combination of the two. But when it is done privately we think of it as "self-help" or "philanthropy," and when it is done publicly it is called "welfare."

I should like to argue at the outset that welfare-like functions are nearly always activities shared by the public and private sectors. People provide for their physical health and comfort both by using their private resources and by pooling collective resources. On the whole, the great debates concerning public versus private responsibility for maintaining a socially acceptable standard of living have flown in the face of a simple fact: at least in the United States, welfare is and has been both public and private for a very long time. Moreover the two domains are quite inseparable in all but the most primitive living circumstances. This inseparability is illustrated in the following account, drawn from a standard history of American medicine:

In 1928, Alexander Fleming, in London, found that a mold had gained access to a culture plate on which he was growing colonies of a common staphylococcus. He noted that the colonies near the mold, which previously had been developing normally, were now showing signs of dissolution. Since this was an unusual phenomenon, the mold was isolated and was identified as Penicillium notatum. Fleming later showed that this mold produces a substance that strongly inhibits the growth of the organisms which cause certain common infectious diseases. He named the substance penicillin. Ten years later, Howard W. Florey from Australia and Ernst B. Chain from Germany, along with their English associates at Oxford University, began an intensive study of earlier scientific work, searching for ideas that might be carried further by the new techniques and newer knowledge. During this search they ran across Fleming's almost forgotten paper (1929) about penicillin. They made some penicillin and tried to develop methods to improve the yield of this substance and to purify it without impairing its activity. They gradually accumulated a small store of pure penicillin for a trial on mice infected with a virulent strain of hemolytic streptococci (1940). All of the control (untreated) mice were dead within 16 hours, but the penicillin-protected mice survived.

The American part of the story came at this juncture. With the advent of World War II, there was great difficulty in obtaining supplies and apparatus in England. At the same time, there was need for improved medication to care for the war-wounded. Efforts were made to produce penicillin in larger quantities, but progress was slow. Making ingenious use of available apparatus, the Oxford group succeeded in producing enough penicillin for a clinical trial in 1941, when an Oxford policeman dying of septicemia was administered the drug. There was marked improvement in his condition until the supply of penicillin was exhausted. English pharmaceutical firms were unable to invest the time and equipment needed to perfect mass production of the new drug. Therefore, in 1941, Drs. Florey and Heatley came to the United States and were in touch with Ross Harrison, then chairman of the National Research

Council. Harrison, in turn, introduced them to Charles Thom of the Bureau of Plant Industry, who years before had identified Fleming's mold as <u>Penicillium notatum</u>. Ultimately they were sent to the Northern Regional Research Laboratory of the Department of Agriculture in Peoria, Illinois. There, on July 14, the problem of producing more penicillin was outlined to the Director of the laboratory, Orville E. May, and to the Director of the Fermentation Division, Robert E. Coghill. It was Dr. Coghill who suggested that the deep-tank fermentation methods then used to produce gluconic acid might be applied to penicillin production. Several methods of increasing production were implemented at the laboratories in Peoria. For example, the addition of corn-steep liquor to the culture medium increased the output of penicillin 20 times. Substitution of lactose for glucose further improved output. A search for more productive species of <u>Pencillium</u> was undertaken, and from a rotting cantaloupe found in a Peoria market, a species of <u>Penicillium chrysogenum</u> was obtained that improved the yields of penicillin still further.

In addition to the work in Peoria, United States pharmaceutical manufacturers began to apply to the penicillin problem the experience gained in other industries which use yeasts and molds, such as brewing and the manufacture of citric acid and other chemicals. By this time (1942), the United States had entered the war, which added a further stimulus to the effort. Finally, large quantities of penicillin began to be produced. The government took control of the entire penicillin output, assuring its availability for war needs and the most urgent civilian needs. In 1942, there was barely enough penicillin to treat 100 patients; by late 1943, the United States was producing enough for both its armed forces and those of our allies. In 1945, there was sufficient penicillin to meet civilian needs, and in 1958 more then 440 tons of crystalline penicillin were produced--enough to give penicillin in an amount of two million units to every individual in our population of 175 million people.[5]

This is a wonderful story. What combination of private and public endeavor trained Fleming and Florey and Chair, transported them to England, and gave them facilities for their work? The National Research Council itself is a public body organized in the United States for the purpose of using public and private resources to help solve national problems. That rotting cantaloupe moved from the private to the public sector in a truly timely fashion.

The joint effort of public and private resources in the development of penicillin suggests that there will be no easy answer when we ask the difficult political question: what are the limits to the welfare responsibilities of the state as opposed to the responsibilities that individuals ought to shoulder for themselves? Many ingenious and sophisticated theories of human motivation and human behavior are invoked in the course of battles over the problem. However, I am going to sidestep these arguments in order to attempt a far less entertaining pursuit, namely, a simple appraisal of the condition of welfare in the United States over the last 50 years or so, and an evaluation of the government's responsibility for this condition.

I

On January 20, 1937, the School of Public Affairs at The American University was only a few years old, and the President of the United States was taking stock of the welfare of the American people. Because we have come a very great distance from the position he described on that day, it is well worth quoting his words at length:

> I see a great nation, upon a great continent, blessed with a great wealth of natural resources. Its hundred and thirty million people are at peace among themselves; they are making their country a good neighbor among the nations. I see a United States which can demonstrate that, under democratic methods of government, national wealth can be translated into a spreading volume of human comforts hitherto unknown, and the lowest standard of living can be raised far above the level of mere subsistence.

> But here is the challenge to our democracy: In this nation I see tens of millions of its citizens--a substantial part of its whole population--who at this very moment are denied the greater part of what the very lowest standards of today call the necessities of life.

> I see millions of families trying to live on incomes so meager that the pall of family disaster hangs over them day by day.

> I see millions whose daily lives in city and on farm continue under conditions labeled indecent by a so-called polite society half a century ago.

> I see millions denied education, recreation, and the opportunity to better their lot and the lot of their children.

I see millions lacking the means to buy the products of farm and factory and by their poverty denying work and productiveness to many other millions.

I see one-third of a nation ill-housed, ill-clad, ill-nourished.[6]

One third of a nation. Actually, President Roosevelt arguably understated the problem. And where are we today?

To begin with, we are now a nation of two hundred thirty million--one hundred million more than the nation led by Franklin Roosevelt. We are far richer than we were then. Economist James Tobin estimated that in 1935, 51% of the population had incomes of less than $3000 measured in 1965 dollars. By 1965 that number had shrunk to 17%.[7]

We have an official poverty line, measured in current dollars adjusted for inflation, below which people are considered to be very badly off indeed. This is a shifting line, which can be drawn to refer to individuals, households, or families of varying compositions. It can designate some absolute standard, such as nutrition stated in daily calories, or a relative standard, which compares the standard of living for different groups of people.[8] But for our purposes, the so-called "official poverty line" is a good initial approximation of our position from a comparative and historical perspective. In 1960, 18.1% of the population was below the poverty line; during the 1970s that number shrank to between 4% and 8%, and in 1981 it was 11.2%.[9] That is roughly 25 million people who still live below the poverty line--not an inconsiderable number, and one well worth worrying about. But recently it would have been only "one tenth of our nation" instead of "one third" below the poverty line; John Kennedy, on the other hand would have had to say, "one fifth of our nation."

What has been true of incomes has been even more true of housing. In 1940, 40% of dwelling units lacked bathtubs, but by 1980 only 2.6% lacked "some or all plumbing."[10]

Although our performance on health care and prevention falls below that of many other rich countries, we are healthier than in previous times. In 1940 the infant mortality rate was 47 per 1000 live births; in 1979 the rate was 13.1 per thousand.[11] Life expectancy has increased from 62.9 years at birth in 1940 to 73.7 years in 1979.[12]

Other measurements of the standard of living of Americans show similar patterns. Our society has become much wealthier over the last five decades. A larger proportion of Americans is living decently today than was true 20, 30, or 50 years ago, even though the number of people who have needed some kind of welfare has mushroomed during the same period.

II

The next question is this: What has caused these changes? Especially, what accounts for the improvements in the general conditions of life? A substantial argument can be made for the proposition that the successful expansion of our economy achieved this success. Capital investment created economic growth, which created jobs; jobs created widespread prosperity and large markets for goods and services. Therefore, political conditions that fostered capital investment have been at the root of the improved welfare condition of the nation.

This explanation is good as far as it goes, but it does not go far enough. Explanations of this sort rarely give adequate credit to the actual political conditions that sustain capital formation. The customary description--primarily by right wing analysts--emphasizes conditions that allow entrepreneurs the freedom to flourish, providing them with room to innovate and to maneuver. Deprive them of that freedom, it is argued, and business incentives disappear, investment lags, and economic growth slows.

If we had to point to one accomplishment by government that has had the most important economic consequences, it would have to be the maintenance of civil peace. Without peace--and the expectation of peace--there can be no hope of investment. People invest in the future when they can contemplate a future, and the maintenance of civil peace makes investment a rational and profitable prospect.

Two further facts should be mentioned. Capital formation has not merely been encouraged by law and order and by hands-off governmental policies. Government itself has been a significant source of capital and resource-aggregation in the historical development of the American economy.

Government action has contributed two kinds of capital in particular: first, land in the form of immense gifts to states, homesteaders, and transportation companies;[18] second, an educated citizenry. With respect to the latter, free universal education has long been a part of the American experience, and educated, literate people constitute a far more sophisticated, maneuverable, civil, and productive workforce than do uneducated people.

As for capital contributions to the development of transportation, the numbers during the 19th century are quite staggering: tens of millions of dollars for canals, roads, and railroads. For example, the National Road was a project of the Jefferson administration and the Eisenhower administration funded the federal highway program.

Thus, a revised causal model might explain that political decisions favoring civil peace and economic accumulation foster capital formation and investment, leading to economic growth, which creates jobs, which in turn raises incomes. The model continues: This generates taxes, which in turn are invested in the next generation, as well as redistributed to those members of the population who are unable to engage in paid work--that is, the young, the old, the sick, the severely handicapped, and many single parents.

This redistribution is crucial in providing for the general welfare. John Schwarz has done some valuable calculations which show the following:

> When one takes all income except that transferred to individuals through governmental programs, census evidence for 1965 indicates that about 21.3% of the public would have been living in poverty; in 1972, again considering all sources of income except that received from governmental programs, census figures show that about 19.2% of the public would have been living in poverty, about one tenth less than in 1965.[14]

This was a time of enormous growth in the economy, a seven-year period during which real disposable income rose, on the average, by 3 percent a year. But some people fell far below the average: the impoverished elderly, families headed by women, and especially women under the age of 25. Schwarz's figures suggest that "whereas economic growth reduced the poverty of one in ten Americans, governmental intervention reduced that of more than one in two Americans over the same period."[15] Here Schwarz refers to mainline government welfare programs: Aid to Families with Dependent Children, Medicaid, and food stamps. He shows further that specialized programs have improved housing for Americans, and medical aid programs have increased the access of the poor to doctors and improved their health.

An understanding of government's contributions to the general welfare does not stop here. Taxes are invested as well as spent, and public expenditures contribute to capital formation as well. Those tax revenues that pay for education--including a significant number of local taxes in addition to the federal taxes designated for military training--also go into capital formation of a most important kind: human capital. In the public sector, we have been spending about as much on education as we do on defense. (That does not include the defense appropriation for education and training, or what is spent on education privately.)[16]

Perhaps the most striking story of public-private cooperation in economic investment during the last 50 years is the saga of American agriculture. It will take a more knowledgeable historian than I am to disentangle the mass of public and private endeavors which produced the massive mechanization of agriculture, freed an immense farm population for productive labor in the cities, brought electricity to rural places and refrigeration to the railroads, invented hybrid seed, disseminated modern techniques of farming as well as fertilizers and pesticides. While no government official invented the combine or ran the railroads, the western railroads did run on land given to them by the federal government. State universities--a number of which began with the proceeds of federal land grants--developed innovations that improved crop yields. And county agents--government employees--channeled them to private farmers, who implemented the new techniques.[17]

Let us follow another cycle far enough to see the web of public and private relationships. The major medical breakthroughs of the last century--those with the greatest impact on the life expectancies of most people--have been: (1) basic improvements in public health, sewage, sanitation, water supply, sterilization of surgical materials and so on, and (2) the cures for infectious diseases. Both are artifacts of increased prosperity--people could afford dwellings with sanitary toilets and hot and cold running water, while municipalities could safeguard their water supplies and install modern sewer systems. But these amenities also were developed because legislators wrote laws and regulations channeling private expenditures into these innovations and making the requisite public expenditures for them.

III

Thus, my argument is that government's role in providing welfare is very great. It has not merely collected a tithe and distributed it to the less fortunate, but it has also played a creative and useful role in the formation of economic prosperity. It has invested in entrepreneurship, protected markets by imposing tariffs and providing patents, and subsidized capital growth. It has invested heavily in promoting the next generation's skills, employability, ingenuity, and enlightenment. There remains the question of retraining the adult population, which, I believe, will occupy an increasing share of the education agenda.

We now reach the government's role as a direct provider of welfare. Here, once again, the story is far more complicated than it appears at first blush. There are significant welfare implications in a great deal of the government's actions over and above simple transfers of cash.

To begin with the direct transfer payments, the following figures reflect the orders of magnitude. In 1982, a year of heavy unemployment, the government distributed $23.1 billion to unemployed workers. The aged, who constituted a significant portion of the poverty population, received $137 billion in Social Security benefits, and the disabled received $18 billion. Medicare benefits amounted to $50 billion in 1982. On the whole, despite inflated costs that might not correspond to improved benefits, the experience of most rich countries suggests that the spread of medical and health benefits to larger parts of the population does pay off in better health.

But what about governmental activity facilitating self-help? There are three major social groups whose capacities and opportunities for self-sufficiency have changed radically in the last 50 years: the elderly, women, and blacks. I have already mentioned the elderly. The proportion of people over the age of 64 who are able to live by themselves in separate households was 67% in 1952 and 86% in 1975, a gain of 19% over a 23-year period.[18] This implies a significant net change in the welfare position of the aged, irrespective of whether they receive government payments. Many do continue to receive these payments; in some cases, such as with social security, whether they need it or not.

The direct role of government in women's welfare has not been large. This may principally be due to the fact that there were women on all economic levels of the social structure 50 years ago. Since then, they have entered into the workplace by the millions; American families have changed their shape, structure, sizes, and expectations largely (though not entirely) unaided by government. Indirectly, of course, government has been of crucial importance: It fought World War II, which created demands for women in the workforce to replace absent men in the workforce and to help operate the wartime economy. Nevertheless, it seems that since the war most governmental actions with respect to the newly independent roles of women have lagged behind rather than led economic development. The more interesting aspects of this evolution are the changes in women's aspirations and controlled--often delayed--childbearing.

Finally, we must consider the complicated story of black Americans. At the beginning of our 50-year period, most blacks were living in the South, in rural conditions. The majority were poor, uneducated, suffering legal as well as customary discrimination and were barred from meaningful citizenship. Today black Americans are still not equal to whites according to many measures of well-being. But the changes are also striking: The black population has urbanized (overwhelmingly: 81% by 1970), moved north (about half of the black population now live in the North), and while this population is not living as well as the white population according to most economic indicators, it is living better than it did. For example, measured in constant 1967 dollars, the median income of black families slightly more than doubled between 1947 and 1970. The proportion of black people living below the poverty line has gone from 53% in 1959 to 34% in 1981 (these figures do not include the effects of transfer payments). The life expectancy at birth of a black baby in 1920 was 83% of that of the whole population; by 1979, it was 93%.[19]

In 1970, there were 1,472 black elected officials in the United States, a figure which grew to 5,606 by 1983.[20] Studies suggest that black public officials do make a difference in the delivery of welfare related benefits on the black community.[21]

These statistics and arguments indicate that a social welfare strategy for a society is not necessarily an economic equalization strategy. Equalization usually entails taking from the top while giving to the bottom, and paying less attention to the overall size of the pie. This has not generally been the strategy followed in the United States where, as mentioned earlier, the government has boosted economic growth as well as attempted to aid the unfortunate.[22] The result has been a sharply unequal distribution of wealth and income, maintained more or less over a 50-year time span, although some studies show a slow shift toward equalization.[23]

Money, however, is not everything, and not all real-life games are zero-sum. A decline in infant mortality benefits those segments of the population whose babies used to die, while it does not in the slightest harm that segment of the population whose babies lived and continue to live. The fact that there are more black voters does not detract from the voting rights of those whites who used to vote and continue to do so. Even in the economic realm, it is worth remembering that if Rockefeller diets, the hungry are not necessarily fed. Indeed, it helps to have money in order to redistribute it. Thus, a meaningful redistribution stategy clearly has to consider the production side of the equation as well as the redistribution side.

This is a very controversial issue. Some people value equality so highly they are willing to contemplate leveling downward, sacrificing some growth for a better distribution of economic goods. These people measure progress differently from the view proposed here, and deplore the typically American strategies I have described. For them, welfare and equality are inseparable. I believe that they are separable, and can be measured and assessed separately. We pay a considerable intellectual price for merging the two conditions. Because our economic inequalities are so great and so persistent, our preoccupation with them may overwhelm our capacity to understand the rest of our politico-economic system, especially that which provides for the formulation and implementation of various welfare strategies.

By virtue of its overall prosperity, our society supplies many public goods, among them public order, virtually free television, free libraries, and free public education. Although many of these public goods are more frequently used by upscale members of the population, their elimination or diminution would have a greater impact on downscale segments. The rich can always buy on private markets those goods that the public sector fails to provide. The poor cannot. Thus, even though middle class citizens may use a public good such as a state university more than poor people do, a sufficient number of poor students have access to higher education to justify state universities as a public good on welfare grounds. If there were no such places, a fair number of rich students would still find their way to Princeton or Stanford, but the bright and diligent children of poor people would nearly all have to forego quality education.[24]

Some people find this argument repulsive, and believe they know how to target welfare more efficiently. Voices on the Left talk of equalization strategies, of finding means for depriving the well-to-do, and of leveling down. Voices on the Right discuss reducing waste and focusing on the truly needy. They are both probably wrong. I have seen them try. The net effect is to harm the needy as well as to increase their numbers and reduce the size of the constituencies supporting institutions that supply welfare benefits in the largest sense of the term.

Let me conclude by observing that welfare turns out to be a good topic for a birthday celebration. On milestones such as this one, do we not wish one another long life, good health, and prosperity? When we construct and maintain welfare systems, are we not trying to do the same thing? And despite the economic waste and conceptual confusion for which Americans are famous, when we look at the results over a 50-year period, it seems that the government's role in providing for the general welfare has gained considerable legitimacy. It operates through many channels and devices, and--though there is far more to do in areas such as infant mortality--the government has achieved an impressive measure of success.

NOTES

1. Many thanks to Michael Goldstein and John Gilmour for helping me produce this paper. My colleagues Harold Wilensky in Berkeley and Stanley Lebergott at Wesleyan gave enormous aid and comfort, but are absolved from responsibility for anything said here. They and I know that if either of them had done this paper it would have been sounder and better informed.

2. H.W. Fowler and F.G. Fowler, The Concise Oxford Dictionary of Current English (Oxford: Clarendon, 1964), 1480.

3. William Safire, Safire's Political Dictionary (New York: Random House, 1978), 784-785.

4. Walter Laquer (ed.), A Dictionary of Politics (New York: The Free Press, 1973), 537.

5. James Bordley III and A. McGehee Harvey, Two Centuries of American Medicine (Philadelphia: Saunders, 1976), 452-453.

6. President Franklin D. Roosevelt's Second Inaugural Address, 1937.

7. See James T. Patterson, America's Struggle Against Poverty, 1900-1980 (Cambridge, Massachusetts: Harvard University Press, 1981), 79; James Tobin, "It Can Be Done," New Republic, 156 (June 3, 1967), 14-18.

8. Harold Wilensky, "The Political Economy of Income Distribution," Major Social Issues, ed. Milton Yinger and Stephen Cutler (New York: Free Press, 1978), 87-108.

9. U.S. Bureau of the Census, Statistical Abstract of the United States, 1982-1983, 103rd ed. (Washington D.C.: U.S. Government Printing Office, 1982), 442.

10. Patterson, supra, 42; and Statistical Abstract, supra 752.

11. Statistical Abstract, ibid., 75.

12. Statistical Abstract, ibid., 71.

13. Carter Goodrich estimates the value of the governmental contribution to transportation companies (canals and railroads) in the 1850s-70s at about 30% of capitalization. Government Promotion of American Canals and Railroads 1800-1890 (New York: Columbia University Press, 1960), 265ff. See also Robert

W. Fogel, Railroads and American Economic Growth: Essays in Econometric History (Baltimore: Johns Hopkins Press, 1964).

14. John Schwarz, America's Hidden Success (New York: Norton, 1983), 34.

15. Schwarz, ibid., 38.

16. National Center for Education Statistics, Digest of Education Statistics 1982 (Washington, D.C.: U.S. Government Printing Office, 1982), 21.

17. Willard W. Cochrane, The Development of American Agriculture (Minneapolis: University of Minensota Press, 1979).

18. Daniel Scott Smith, "Historical Change in the Household Structure of the Elderly in Economically Developed Societies," in Aging: Stability and Change in the Family, ed. Robert W. Fogel, et. al. (New York: Academic Press, 1981), 100.

19. Figures on migration of blacks are from U.S. Bureau of the Census, Historical Statistics of the United States, Colonial Times to 1970, 22-23. Income figures come from Historical Statistics, ibid., 297. Voting registration figures are from U.S. Bureau of the Census, Current Population Reports, Series 20, No. 383, 4ff. The source of information on blacks below the poverty line is Statistical Abstract, supra, 442. Information on life expectancy is from Statistical Abstract, supra, 71.

20. Statistical Abstract, supra, 488; and Gerald Boyd, "Black Electoral Gains Grew Last Year," New York Times, January 9, 1984, 11. These data are collected by the Joint Center for Political Studies.

21. Peter K. Eisinger, "Black Employment in Municipal Jobs: The Impact of Black Political Power," American Political Science Review 76 (June 1982): 380-396; Judith Gruber, "Political Strength and Policy Responsiveness: The Results of Electing Blacks to City Councils." Paper presented at the meeting of the Western Political Science Association, March 26-29, 1980, San Francisco.

22. Arthur Okun, Equality vs. Efficiency: The Big Tradeoff (Washington: Brookings Institution, 1975).

23. Wilensky, supra; and Wilensky, The Welfare State and Equality (Berkeley: University of California Press, 1975).

24. W. Lee Hansen and Burton A. Weisbrod, "The Distribution of Costs and Direct Benefits of Public Higher Education: The Case of California," The Journal of Human

Resources 4 (Summer, 1964) 176-191. This article provoked many responses. For example: Elchanan Cohn, Adam Gifford, Ira Sharkansky, "Benefits and Costs of Higher Education and Income Distribution: Three Comments," The Journal of Human Resources 5 (Spring, 1970): 222-236; Joseph A. Pechman, "The Distributional Effects of Public Higher Education in California," The Journal of Human Resources, 5 (Summer, 1970): 361-370; Robert W. Hartman, "A Comment on the Pechman-Hansen-Weisbrod Controversy," The Journal of Human Resources 5 (Fall, 1970): 519-523; W. Lee Hansen and Burton A. Weisbrod, "On the Distribution of Costs and Benefits of Public Higher Education: Reply" The Journal of Human Resources 6 (Summer, 1971): 363-374; Joseph A. Pechman, "The Distribution of Costs and Benefits of Public Higher Education: Further Comments," ibid.: 375-376; John Conlisk, "A Further Look at the Hansen-Weisbrod-Pechman Debate," The Journal of Human Resources 12 (Spring, 1977): 147-163; Joseph A. Pechman, "Note on the Intergovernmental Transfer of Public Higher Education Benefits," Journal of Political Economy 80 (May/June, 1972): 256-259.

THE FEDERAL ROLE

IN A

NATIONAL SOCIAL WELFARE POLICY

Martha Keys

I do not have the wealth of academic background of Mr. Polsby, but rather a different kind of experience and expertise: that born of working to win and then assuming public responsibility in the U.S. Congress. As a result, I am very pragmatic, and I view the discussion of an "ideal role of social welfare" as one that offers little prospective utility.

We all recognize that it is a constitutional responsibility for government to promote the general welfare and, indeed, it has done so. As Herbert Croly said in 1909:

> "The social problem must, as long as societies continue to endure, be solved afresh by almost every generation: and the one chance of progress depends both upon an invincible loyalty to a constructive social ideal and upon a correct understanding by the new generation of the actual experience of its predecessors."[1]

It seems to me that it is where we are, where we need to go, and how we are going to get there that are the terribly important questions.

First, we must have the broadest possible understanding of the federal role before we can begin to strengthen our ideals or correct the course of social welfare policy. Second, the federal role includes a factor that is often overlooked in social policy: the tax structure and the $345 billion federal tax expenditures that are an integral part of social policy in this country. If one looks at the entire amount of government involvement in social policy, it is quickly apparent that the direct beneficiaries of social policy actions by the federal government are, for the most part, the middle class.

We should also look at several reasons for federal involvement in social policy--a need to remedy the problems of a free market economy, which was the reason for most federal government actions; and the necessity for redistribution of income between working and non-working people and between various income levels. These forces and motivations continue to grow even stronger in today's complex, technological, internationally competitive workplace and economy.

I do not believe that our commitments, which are really an expression of our national social conscience, have changed at all. Those promises to protect individuals and to relieve poverty are as strong as ever in our national community. There may be dissatisfaction with the complicated and overlapping ways in which we try to address those problems, but the commitments are solid. Again, the real problem is where do we need to go and how do we get there. The attempt to deal with those questions brings us to an enormous array of forces--demographic change; transformations in the social structure and the roles of women, men, and family; economic forces; and political forces.

I would like to present three observations from my recent experiences in government. First, the welfare reform, which the Carter Administration and Congress attempted in a very strong way in 1977, was an excellent effort and reform should have been accomplished. It would have consolidated three specific programs to alleviate poverty--Aid to Families with Dependent Children, Supplemental Security Income, and Foodstamps--into one single cash program with simpler eligibility rules and a less complicated administrative mechanism. It would also have added a program to provide reasonable jobs for able-bodied individuals. I was a member of the House Select Welfare Reform Committee working on the proposals, which then had to go through four different committees. The experience was an education in the forces arrayed against constructive changes that aim to keep our national social commitments effective and current.

My second point was indirectly expressed by Mr. Polsby, when he stated that the direct federal role concerning women has not been large. The government has had some positive effect in this area; but it has probably had a greater impact by virtue of its omissions and tremendous blindness to the differences of women's work patterns and lives. Consequently, the status quo of the male establishment has been reinforced, along with the continued socialization of women. While the Constitution was written without thought of equality under the law for racial minorities or women, most of the legal restrictions to equality have been removed for minorities. But legal restrictions remain for women at state and national levels.

Government has perpetuated institutional discrimination in employment, establishing far lower pay levels for sex-stereotyped jobs (for example, clerical and service positions) than for other jobs, such as truck drivers and parking attendants. The latter types of employment obviously do not demand more preparation, are not more important and do not merit a higher wage. In short, government has indeed had a strong effect on women.

In the health area, the decisions about research dollars have been made with a blindness to the differences between men and women that has only begun to change in the last ten years. Our health systems are ill-equipped to deal with the chronic illness problems that plague women who live longer than men--this is one of the prime public policy problems that we face in the years ahead.

Thus, the political gender gap derives, very simply, from a gender gap in jobs, in pay, in retirement income, and in other areas. Government has institutionally supported this gap by its indifference to the necessity for understanding the different life patterns of men and women.

Social Security is my last example of the difficulty of change. I have spent a good deal of my public life interested and involved in that subject, in the Congress, on the House Ways and Means Committee, in the executive branch at Health, Education, and Welfare, and recently on the National Commission on Social Security. Social Security has been one of the finest achievements in public policy for our whole society. It has revolutionized the way of life for older people, widows, orphans, and disabled people in our society. It is certainly the retirement system that has been most important to women. But that great system is lagging far behind the kind of progress that would make it responsive to the current roles of work and women. One change that must be made soon is the treatment of a married couple as an economic unit so that retirement credits earned by the couple are shared equally during the years of marriage. Although the system does not discriminate between single women and men, it does treat married men and married woman much differently.

One cannot examine social policy without looking at tax expenditures and understanding the role they play. We now, in fact, provide more incentives and public support to those who have the discretionary income to put into IRAs by allowing them to deduct that contribution from gross income. We actually support them through a tax expenditure. I would suggest that it makes considerably more sense, in view of the incentives offered by IRAs, KEOUGHs, and other retirement plans, to equalize the burden of contribution to Social Security by deducting the tax contribution from the gross income of every working person.

It is my hope that these brief examples of effective reform or reorganization of our national social commitments will be useful to future discussion. We must not forget the policy impact of ignoring the developments in society, and of neglecting to revise the structure of programs that serve our people, especially women. Nor can we continue to avoid confronting the hidden incentives and inequities of tax expenditures, which are important and deliberate aspects of social planning. These concepts are basic to creative changes in our national social welfare policy.

NOTES

1. Herbert Croly, <u>Promise of American Life</u> (New York: Macmillan, 1909).

Part II: Science, Technology and Government:

Harnessing the Technological Revolution for the Public

Good

Introduction: Robert P. Boynton, The American University

SCIENCE, TECHNOLOGY AND GOVERNMENT:

HARNESSING THE TECHNOLOGICAL REVOLUTION

FOR THE PUBLIC GOOD

Robert P. Boynton

This section of the College of Public and International Affairs' fiftieth anniversary volume explores problems resulting from the intersection of three dominant communities: science, technology, and government. Their interrelationships and their institutions provide considerable grist for public policymaking and much of the content of policy implementation in the United States.

The constituent units of the College of Public and International Affairs have long manifested interest in and supported educational and research activities geared toward the understanding of management and policy issues. The Center for Technology and Administration has been the particular focus for much of this effort. Founded in 1958 within the newly established School of Government and Public Administration, it has served as an institution for studying the effects of new technologies upon the administrative process. In 1964, the Center was made a separate administrative unit.

Throughout its history, the Center for Technology and Administration has offered a variety of multidisciplinary specializations designed to meet the technological needs of public servants. The mainstays of its graduate program have been the management-related fields of computer systems applications and management information systems. Closely related specializations have included science/technology policy and administration, scientific and technical information systems, operations research, environmental systems management and records management. At present, most of the Center's academic efforts are concentrated in the application of technologically-based information systems to the solution of public management and policy problems, both in the domestic public sector and in the international sphere.

The panels sponsored by The Center for Technology and Administration during the fiftieth anniversary celebration looked at two closely related issue areas: (1) the role of government in regulating scientific and technological activities and the consequences of these activities for the structure and operation of the private economic sector, and (2) the impact of international competition on the American scientific and technological communities and their relationships with government.

Few issues are more intertwined with America's future than those which surround the government's responses to private enterprise and its products. The American government's dominant role has often been adversarial, characterized by regulation interspersed with non-systematic support and encouragement for selected sectors and industries. International economic competition is now eroding the country's once dominant economic position. Competition comes from nations that have chosen alternative, cooperative relationships between government and their vital industries and enterprises. Does this indicate that our system of economic development is wrong or inappropriate for the current and emerging internationalized marketplace?

The panel discussions explore the complexities of these issues and suggest certain changes that are necessary in the way public servants--elected and career--approach them if America is to remain economically strong and internationally competitive.

Part II: <u>Science, Technology and Government: Harnessing the</u>

<u>Technological Revolution for the Public Good</u>

A. <u>Science, Technology, and International Competition</u>

<u>Chair</u>:   Louis G. Tornatzky, National Science
Foundation

<u>Presentations By</u>:   John Holmfeld, Committee on Science and
Technology, U.S. House of
Representatives
Bruce Merrifield, Assistant Secretary,
U.S. Department of Commerce
Walter Plosila, Deputy Secretary for
Technology and Policy Development,
Commonwealth of Pennsylvania
Ronnie Straw, Communication Workers of
America

<u>Respondent</u>:   Robert Stern, Institute of
Public Administration

<u>Rapporteur</u>:   Nanette Levinson, The American
University

SCIENCE, TECHNOLOGY, AND INTERNATIONAL COMPETITION:

AN OVERVIEW

Nanette S. Levinson

Lewis Carroll once wrote that "When you don't know where you are going, there are many ways of getting there." The presentations and comments of the Science, Technology, and International Competition Panel reveal that even if there is agreement about the goal of improving the U.S. position in the international economic arena, there are still myriad ways suggested for bringing about that improvement. This paper reports on the ways suggested by panelists and discussants as well as on their perceptions of the U.S. position in science and technology. It also provides a conceptual framework which aids in understanding not only specific recommendations made in support of U.S. science, technology, and innovation but also the actions of science and technology-related organizations.

The U.S. Position In Science and Technology

The U.S. position in science and technology is changing, but the panelists and discussants disagreed about the exact position of the United States vis-a-vis other nations. A speaker from the British Embassy, as well as others, expressed great admiration for U.S. science and technology, noting that government and industry leaders from England and other countries visit the U.S. to learn about our success, especially in biotechnology and microelectronics.

A recent Washington Post article by Joel Kotkin corroborates these comments and argues that European and Asian leaders are "looking toward America's dynamic, if somewhat chaotic, entrepreneurial economy as their role model for the future." Kotkin quotes Jiro Tokuyama, Dean of the Nomura School of Advanced Management in Tokyo: "I don't think our large organizations can move quickly enough to make the changes. We must find our model among the entrepreneurs like in your Silicon Valley."[1]

These qotes highlight some of the problems inherent in any discussion of U.S. science, technology, and international competition. They focus on our high technology industries, but do not deal with the role of high technology in our traditional smokestack industries or with these industries themselves, in which we are not "on top of the heap." (And discussants remind us that even were we "on top of the heap," we should not be complacent about maintaining our position.) Thus, there are major differences in types of industry and our world leadership position.

There are also those who say that irrespective of the industry grouping, the true measure of our position in economic competition is our adaptability. Professor Robert Z. Lawrence of the Brookings Institution claims that "This economy has been adaptable to changing economic conditions and more adaptable than many other industrial economies, particularly those in Europe. And, according to this measure, the U.S. is in excellent shape."[2]

WHAT NEEDS TO BE DONE: AN INTRODUCTION

Panelists, discussants, and leaders in government and industry express concern about strengthening the U.S. science and technology base in support of international competition. But once these concerns are articulated, there is often a parting of the ways regarding what needs to be done. 'Experts' in the field identify numerous actions (and almost as many actors to implement these actions) that would enhance our competitive position. These recommendations reflect the personal perspective, organizational affiliation, and special focus of those making them. These recommendations can also be distinguished on the basis of whether they involve implementation at the federal or state levels. The controversies regarding actions as well as actors seem to be greater at the federal level than at the state level. Perhaps this reflects the current Administration's emphasis on the role of the state as well as the greater flexibility for action at the state and local levels. Moreover, current public confidence in state and local governments appear to be stronger than that in the federal level.

There are several reasons for this stronger public confidence in state roles. Traditionally states have been concerned with their own economic development; they have wanted to attract new industries. Therefore, they already have in place departments of economic development or commerce charged with these functions. Additionally, they have assumed a responsibility to provide public education and to aid public employment; they already have departments of education and employment, often with longstanding informal linkages. Thus, the public has grown accustomed to state performance of these functions and to state offices charged with these responsibilities. The jump from attracting new businesses to promoting greater cooperation among existing or newly-formed state agencies, concentrating on attracting and enhancing a state's industries, is not a large one.

It is a much larger jump from state to federal levels. Not every member of the public feels comfortable with broadened federal powers or new federal structures to enhance industrial competition. There is also a gap in actions that involve coordination and support across federal (both defense and non-defense), state, and local levels.

THE FEDERAL LEVEL

At the federal level there are, of course, numerous recommendations. Some have been around for a number of years, such as those to improve tax, patent, and regulatory policies, and government funding for basic research.

More recent suggestions involve significant changes in the science and technology infrastructure: changing the Executive level structure responsible for dealing with science and technology in a global context (e.g., establishing a Department of International Trade and Industry or a Council of Industrial Competitiveness, as an independent government agency, or a Bank For Industrial Competitiveness); changing the antitrust laws; including more applied research in federal government funding; structuring industry and university relationships so as to provide another alternative to promote needed linkages between basic and applied research; and changing the nature of U.S. trade policy.

These recommendations revolve around a popular term-- "industrial policy"--which graces countless article and book titles and stirs countless debates. The notion of industrial policy presupposes the types of major structural changes outlined above; it requires a holistic, government-wide approach to the problems of international competition.

Although panelists, discussants, and experts on international competition do not agree on all the elements of an industrial policy, most concur that the counterpoint to industrial policy is the free market system. In fact, the recent Committee on Economic Development's Report on Industrial Competitiveness comes out strongly against a "top down industrial policy" and instead calls for increased reliance on the market system as the best means of enhancing U.S. competitiveness.[3] But this greater dependence on the market system does not preclude recommendations on changes in federal approaches. For instance, the Heritage Foundation and its scholars argue that greater reliance on the free market process, coupled with changes in laws and regulations "that add unnecessarily to the costs of doing business in the United States," will improve the U.S. position in international competition.[4]

The recent preliminary recommendations from the President's Commission on Industrial Competitiveness (Business-Higher Education Forum, 1984) seem to agree with this moderate approach and focus on the "interrelated issues of educational

-126-

excellence and industrial productivity."[5] In addition to suggesting improvements in the education and research sphere, he Commission calls for developing public-private sector partnerships in the technical assistance area and changing antitrust, patent, and trade regulations to strengthen research and develpment efforts. It does not, however, suggest any major structural changes or targeting policies.

Just as there are a number of proposals for improving our international competitive position, there are numerous approaches to industrial policy. Indeed, some argue that the United States actually has an industrial policy--an unspoken one--by default. Others argue that industrial policy has four key elements:

* restructuring (changing management and labor practices in return for government benefits);

* worker retraining (providing training benefits/incentives for workers to move to positions in rapidly growing parts of our economy);

* infrastructure reconstruction (rebuilding and building roads and bridges, etc.);

* targeting (coordinating government aid and identifying specific priority growth areas).[6]

Of all the proposed elements of industrial policy, the notion of targeting has come in for some vitriolic comment. Most of the criticism stems from the question of who would make the decision as to which industries would be targeted for special funding and growth. Proponents suggest various panels of industry, government, and labor representatives; opponents reply that any mechanism for setting priorities provides an invitation for lobbying and special interests to run rampant.

This particular element of industrial policy highlights the absence of widespread public confidence in federal decision-making regarding winners and losers. The prospect of the federal government targeting specific industries and restructuring the management of science and technology raises the hackles of some members of the public, who believe that these actions are not appropriate for the federal government.

Whether one is a proponent or opponent of targeting, it is important to note that a type of targeting already exists in the federal Research and Development (R&D) budget. One of the changes introduced by the President's Science Adviser, George Keyworth, when he assumed the Directorship of the Office of Science and Technology Policy, was to set specific, explicit priorities for federal R&D funding. Additionally, the defense section of the R&D budget has its own set of funding priorities. While this type of targeting is more limited than the practices recently suggested, decisions stemming from these targeting philosophies are already being made.

The major difference between this limited, budget-related targeting and recent recommendations calling for targeting is the latter's call for an increased, coordinated, yet multi-faceted, government role supporting U.S. international competition. Additional arguments against targeting and, in fact, against the whole notion of industrial policy pit this increased, coordinated government industrial planning mechanism against the free market concept. These arguments are summarized by George Gilder, who writes that the notion of industrial policy is inefficient compared with the free market.[7]

There is also a time element dimension to the anti-targeting arguments. The proponents of this approach maintain that today's industrial policy formulations are based on industrial policy formulations that worked in another setting at another time. The other setting is Japan and the other point in time is post-World War II, when targeting was, it is argued, an appropriate and effective strategy for Japan's economic and industrial policy. Today rapidly changing technologies in both Japan and the United States make the practice of targeting industries much more challenging than in the immediate post-World War II period.

What is particularly interesting about recent discussions of industrial policy, including targeting recommendations, is the extent to which even supporters of free market theory are beginning to express their confidence in some government role. A recent statement from Lee A. Iaccocca provides evidence of support for a stronger government role: "I believe in the free market but I see what the Japanese are doing to me."[8]

There is a noteworthy contrast between the above viewpoints and those from a growing and major industrial grouping, the biotechnology area. An Office of Technology Assessment (OTA) study, "Commercial Biotechnology: An International Analysis," identifies factors "potentially important to international competitiveness in biotechnology."[9] The three most important factors: providing financing and tax incentives for firms (especially for new firms); increasing government funding for generic applied as well as basic research; and increasing the availability of qualified personnel and initiating training programs in applied areas.

The study considers another three factors to be of moderate importance in supporting international competitiveness in biotechnology: decreasing health, safety, and environmental

-128-

regulations; modifying U.S. intellectual property law; and promoting university/industry relationships.

Four factors with the least importance in terms of international competitiveness are: improving U.S. antitrust laws to enhance technology transfer; modifying U.S. export control of laws; investigating the feasibility of government targeting policies; and awareness of public perceptions of the risks and benefits of biotechnology.

This ranking of factors is certainly useful. It tells us which policy elements are important within a given industry grouping and demonstrates that the proponents of industrial policy do not advocate the same factors proposed by biotechnology leaders. Biotechnology business leaders do not appear to have confidence in targeting or restructuring approaches.

As Elliot Richardson's address warns, we need to learn how to use government to achieve our objectives without causing unnecessary consequences. We do not yet know enough about the consequences of the changes advocated in the Office of Technology Assessment study, let alone the consequences of major structural changes, especially at the Federal level.

The State Level

Currently there seems to be state action that is consistent with the needs of the biotechnology industry as portrayed in the OTA survey. Many states are placing a high priority on improving and providing education responsive to industry's needs.

The National Governors Association Task Force reports on a flurry of state activities in support of economic development.[10] No two states have identical plans or approaches, but almost all of them are focusing not only on financing and tax policies, but also on systems-based actions to improve linkages among state government, industries, and educational systems. In a variety of ways, states seem to be enhancing weak linkages in order to strengthen science and economic policy at the state level. And this enhancement, depending upon the state, is found in traditional industrial areas as well as in new high technology.

Some state level initiatives include: organizing or continuing foundations or commisssions on science and technology (mechanisms for generating proposals and/or funding in support of economic development); policies for supporting and training needed personnel; creating or enhancing linkages among industries, universities, and state government agencies; encouraging management and technical support for small business (e.g. incubator programs at local universities or research parks); and providing economic support and incentives for the development of new businesses and the growth of existing businesses.

States do seem to be paying less attention to the connection between their efforts and federal government efforts. The National Governors Association Task Force's only comment on federal linkages is: "Federal policies and programs formulated by Congress and executive agencies must recognize and be consistent with forms of state leadership that are emerging."[11]

Several elements identified in the Task Force Report appear to be important in providing a successful foundation for state efforts:

> * longterm commitments (analogous to the need for stable federal policies in support of U.S. international competition);
>
> * public involvement and understanding of needs for promoting innovations;
>
> * comprehensive approaches "linking research and development, education and training, entrepreneurial development and small business innovation support into an overall, cohesive strategy. Successful innovation, itself, depends precisely upon developing these kinds of linkages."[12]

Concluding Concepts and Assessments

This final element--comprehensive approaches--appears to be more problematic at the federal level. On the one hand, infrastructure recommendations reveal the importance placed by some proponents of industrial policy on a holistic coordinated approach. On the other hand, the OTA study indicates that the biotechnology industry places lesser importance on this approach.

Taking a broad view of state as well as federal recommendations related to industrial competitiveness--those that have been around for a while as well as those which have either resurfaced or been newly introduced--even discussion of the recommendations themselves is clearly bringing change. Longstanding adversarial antagonism between business and government, labor and management appears to be lessening. This development is reinforced by the technological scene as well as the changing international competition scene. There is greater informal and formal communication among organizations and individuals interested in international competition.

A recent update of the Business-Higher Education Forum on industrial policy issues highlights a number of recent studies, reports, and opinion pieces.[13] There is a fascinating symbolism in the plethora of writings discussing international competition and the concomitant absence of major industrial policy legislation. The interest shown by some members of Congress and the executive branch in science and technology, especially over the last two years, has activated/energized intense communication and action among various industrial, labor, and professional organizations, not to mention among various government agencies themselves. This activity is reflected in media coverage and public debate. There appears now to be an inverse relationship between Congressional action and industry action on most industrial policy issues relating to U.S. international competition. While legislative actions in this area have been few and limited, industry and government agency actions have been manifold and varied. Industry has been primarily either lobbying for possible legislation or taking the initiative in collaboration on projects of mutual benefit to U.S. organizations competing in the global arena. And both state and federal agencies have become more activist in promoting the health of these organizations.

An interorganizational approach would be useful in understanding science and technology in the international context and private voluntary actions related to these issues. Recent studies of interorganizational relations (particularly of those involving community agencies) reveal that these relationships may simultaneously exhibit conflict, cooperation, and consensus. These studies focus on relationships among similar types of organizations.[14] In the case of U.S. science and technology issues, the organizations are not all of the same type. These organizations range from private sector companies to public sector agencies and legislative, executive, and judicial bodies. Each of these organizations has its own needs and resources, as well as potential formal and informal linkages with other organizations. This setting can be characterized as having a distribution of general resource factors (including economic, manpower, and knowledge resources), professional/trade associations, and federal, state, and local government agencies and representatives.[15]

Depending upon the industry type and age, and of course needs, a specific organization becomes aware of possible collaborating organizations as well as of potential benefits from this joint effort. For instance, in the semiconductor industry, a number of major computer companies can collaborate in applied generic technology or even in support-gathering for a specific bill before Congress. The resource composition of their specific environmental setting becomes important in determining their propensity to collaborate.[16]

In addition to resources, several other elements which characterize a specific setting may influence inter-organizational relations, such as the presence of third parties including representatives of state, local, or federal government, professional associations or public interest groups, or regulations, policies or laws perceived as facilitating, hindering, or having no effect on interorganizational relations. For instance, individual and corporate perceptions of antitrust laws may affect an organization's willingness to collaborate with other organizations. These 'third party' elements can play[17] an important catalytic role in inter-organizational relationships.

What seems to be most effective in stimulating these relationships is a meshing of personal and organizational needs with perceived benefits, leading to strong individual and then organizational support for collaboration. A major perceived benefit, especially in the science and technology field, is stability. Exchange situations may bring about more stability because of the value of the relationships to the participating organizations.[18] This is especially true when turf issues are present--for example, the founding of the Chicago Board of Trade stemmed from Chicago-area business organizations' uncertainty about turf issues. In the case of the semiconductor industry's formation of its cooperative generic research group, the uncertainties and threats stemmed from U.S. international competition.

Thus, organizations experience simultaneous conflict, cooperation, and consensus. This becomes particularly clear at the professional association level where member organizations compete with one another in the free market. At the same time, they can be cooperating and sharing information and technology research. And, at the public relations level, they can be banding together through their professional organizations to express support for (or opposition to) a particular industrial policy-related bill before Congress.

It is important to remember that each organization has its own unique goal set, cultural climate, and key values. The development of relationships which recognize the uniqueness of collaborating organizations involves negotiating contracts specifying rules and regulations for these relationships.

While this framework is not necessarily accurate as a basis for predictions about organizational behavior in the face of international competition, it is helpful in understanding the current U.S. science and technology scene. The international uncertainty (e.g., from Japanese competitors) in a specific environmental setting, coupled with the specific needs and resources of given organizations, appears to color the propensity of organizations to collaborate in at least some areas of their operation. In this way they begin to combat the uncertainty in their environment. Thus, we can understand the formation and interactions of industry groups such as the American Electronics Association or even the non-government semiconductor research group.

These relationships do not occur in a vacuum. Federal, state, and local government can influence the inter-organizational relationships in a given territory through laws, regulations, and personnel. This can happen haphazardly--allowing only free market influences to dominate--or it can occur in a more coordinated, holistic fashion to counteract the impacts of a potpourri of laws and agencies with differing interests, goals, and values.

The role of the public and of consensus politics permeates these relationships among science and technology organizations. Public support that is communicated to elected state and federal officials influences political propensity for action. There have been at least two years of great visibilty for "high technology" issues, but public confidence in the federal government's ability to "manage" U.S. science and technology is not as strong. This lack of confidence reflects the lack of public agreement on the appropriate roles for the federal government in the industrial policy arena.

There is no clear consensus on the way to proceed in strengthening U.S. science and technology. This buildup covers options of tremendous complexity, ranging from enhancing the U.S. climate for innovation to providing trade protections for U.S. companies. The uncertainties stemming from these complexities, as well as from competitors in other nations, have set the stage for two types of behavior.

The first is the absence of major or unified action on the part of Congress or the executive agencies. While public confidence in science and technology itself is relatively high, it is not high in terms of the federal government's support of science and technology. Moreover, Congress has failed to pass any major industrial policy bills, reflecting a lack of agreement on the appropriate federal government roles. Additionally, the unique organizational climates of specific federal agencies dealing with science and technology issues, each with their own set of goals and groups of clientele, contribute to the lack of unified action at the federal level.

The second is major action by individual industries themselves. Without the benefit of major legislative action, business organizations with competing products are voluntarily collaborating in a variety of ways to reduce the uncertainties. These businesses are placing particular emphasis on generic

R&D--potentially key areas in international competition. Industry-university connections are also growing, both with and without the involvement of local, state, or federal government agencies.

Future consideration of U.S. science and technology in an international context should not only look to economic theory for solutions to problems. Recognizing the complexity and the range of salient issues, this work should add an inter-organizational dimension which integrates not only federal, state, and local action options, but also explains industry's voluntary action options.

NOTES

1. Joel Kotkin, "In This New Age of Entrepreneurs, We're Number One Again," Washington Post, 29 April 1984, B1.

2. Ibid.

3. Committee on Economic Development, Strategy for U.S. Industrial Competitiveness (Washington, D.C.: Committee on Economic Development, 1984).

4. Richard B. McKenzie, ed., Blueprint for Jobs and Industrial Growth (Washington, D.C.: The Heritage Foundation, 1983), 1.

5. Business-Higher Education Forum, America's Competitive Challenge: The Need for a National Response - One Year Later- A Status Report (Washington, D.C.: Business-Higher Education Forum, 1984).

6. Sidney Blumenthal, "Drafting A Democratic Industrial Plan, "New York Times Magazine, 28 August 1983, 31-60.

7. Ibid., 59.

8. Ibid., 31.

9. Office of Technology Assessment, U.S. Congress, Commercial Biotechnology: An International Analysis (Washington, D.C.: U.S. Government Printing Office, 1984).

10. National Governors Association Task Force on Technological Innovation, Technology And Growth: State Initiatives in Technological Innovation (Washington, D.C.: National Governors Association, 1983).

11. Ibid.

12. Ibid.

13. Business-Higher Education Forum, America's Competitive Challenge.

14. See Charles L. Mulford and Mary A. Mulford, "Community and Interorganizational Perspectives on Cooperation and Conflict," Rural Sociology 42 (Winter 1977): 569-585. See also Keith G. Provan, "The Federation as an Interorganizational Linkage Network," Academy of Management Review 8 (1983): 78-89.

15. See Nanette S. Levinson, "Initiating University-Industry Research Arrangements: Theories and Practices," American Educational Research Association (April 1983).

16. See Howard Aldrich, Organizations and Environments (Englewood Cliffs, New Jersey: Prentice-Hall, 1979).

17. Provan, "The Federation as an Interorganizational Linkage Network."

18. See H. Leblebici and G. Salancik, "Stability in Interorganizational Exchanges: Rulemaking Processes of the Chicago Board of Trade," Administrative Science Quarterly 27 (1982): 227-242.

Part II: Science, Technology, and Government:

Harnessing the Technological Revolution

for the Public Good

B.   Science, Technology, and Government:

Regulation of Private Enterprise

Chair: William D. Rowe, The American University

Presentations by: William Cavanaugh, President, American
Society for Testing and Materials
Charles Elkins, Director, Office of Policy
Evaluation, Environmental Protection
Agency
Neil Kerwin, The American University
Henry Piehler, Carnegie-Mellon University
Jim J. Tozzi, Director, Multi-National
Business Services, Inc.
Leon Weinberger, President, Leon
Weinberger Associates

Rapporteur: Marilyn Bracken, Vice-President, Environment
Testing and Certification Corporation

"Science, Technology and Government:

Regulation of Private Enterprise"

MARILYN C. BRACKEN

As science and technology developed in the United States and in the world, government intervention increased. Initially, government played the role of benefactor, providing funds for science and technology, particularly when it was critical for the common interest and the survival of this country. During World War II and the post-war years, there was a great influx of federal monies to support science and technology. Sputnik was a prime example of a massive interjection of federal funds into the solution of a technological problem. The economy was thriving and, as a result, little attention was given to the need to examine the adverse effects of science and technology.

During the sixties, however, the people of the United States began to experience a change in their environment. The air was being polluted, natural resources were being squandered, public lands were being defaced, and the health and safety of many of our workers were affected. The Congress stepped in and began to pass legislation. New agencies were created with the authority and responsibility to write and enforce regulations. Private enterprise was regulated at every stage, and the increases in costs of operation were being passed on to the consumer. In the late seventies, industry increasingly protested that the costs of regulation were seriously affecting their competitive posture in the world markets.

The cries of "excessive regulations and impacts on technological innovation" were heard repeatedly at industry association meetings and in the press. An adversarial relationship grew among the regulators and the regulated. Public interest groups became articulate spokespersons for those who were potentially at risk from the adverse effects of science and technology development. Industry formed strong trade associations who lobbied Congress, the regulatory agencies, and the Office of Management and Budget. The courts frequently became the mediators as regulations were litigated over procedural and due process issues on the one hand, and action levels and economic impacts on the other hand.

Implications of Regulations in Controlling Adverse Impacts of

Scientific and Technological Innovation

When examining the impact of regulations in controlling adverse effects of scientific and technological innovation, the panel agreed that most of the attention to date has focused on health and environmental regulations. Regulatory reform groups, particular in the most recent administration, have focused on their costs and benefits. Lesser attention has been given to economic regulations affecting trade issues, entry into markets, financial transactions, and the like. These, in fact, may have a greater impact on society and private enterprise; consequently, greater emphasis is needed on the substance and effects of economic regulations.

Assuming then, that government regulation is inevitable, the panel addressed the issue of improvements to the process. "Regulatory reform" became a political issue in the last Presidential campaign; as implemented by the present Administration, the term has meant deregulation or regulatory relief.

There are three problems with this approach, which must be overcome if it is to be effective in regulatory reform:

1. The perception that rulemaking would result in using the lowest common denominator, thereby skipping over complex issues and unique industry characteristics;

2. The belief that a consensus means that not everyone will be satisfied.

3. The idea that the private sector rather than the public sector will make all the decisions.

Some participants disagreed with the proposition that the consensus approach would moderate the adversarial nature of the regulatory process, pointing out that there is no precision in the consensus system. The courts have had difficulty in enforcing and interpreting consensus language because it is imprecise. In addition, agencies have encountered problems when voluntary standards have been converted into regulations.

Methods and material standards are much easier areas in which to gain consensus. Difficulties surface when the decision-maker goes from a technical determination to a risk management resolution, which requires definitions of acceptable margins of safety or acceptable levels of risk. More attention is needed in the risk management definition area.

Critics of the consensus process agreed that "who is invited to the table" is critical. Consensus can be easily obtained if the only participants are those with similar ideas. That is infeasible in the regulatory process where, while the technical issues may be resolved easily, risk management decisions are made with a politically-motivated bias.

The regulatory process historically has created many unnecessary burdens, with hidden costs or unidentified impacts, that generally result in excessive litigation.

The Impacts of Standards and Regulations on Technical

Innovation

Critics of the regulatory process frequently state that the costs incurred in meeting the requirements of regulations are so great that they preclude many new products from ever entering the market. Frequently cited examples are new drug and pesticide regulations which call for extensive health and safety test data. With the passage of the Toxic Substances Control Act in 1976, similar arguments were raised with respect to the testing requirements for the introduction of industrial chemicals to the market place. Agencies do not know how serious a problem such demands pose, as documentation and empirical evidence supporting the above mentioned arguments have not been widely available.

Regulatory reform measures initiated during the Reagan Administration have attempted to examine the cost benefit ratios associated with new testing regulations. Government agencies and international organizations have begun studies to determine if technical innovation is being stymied. Public interest groups have raised the concern that regulatory reform has been translated into "regulatory relief" and that, by reducing testing requirements for new products, the public may be subjected to greater health and environmental hazards.

While regulation can severely restrict innovation, it can also occasionally redirect it. Innovation must extend beyond the innovator's basement or laboratory. Innovations must reach the production mode, with likely entry into the market place. In this respect, performance standards tend to stimulate creativity and innovation as compared to technology-based standards. The latter, once established, rarely provide incentives to improve efficiency, even when new technology is available and installation costs are relatively minimal.

Creativity is also impeded by a regulatory bias against new products. Agencies may require new chemicals, new drugs, other new products, and new manufacturing sites to meet higher performance requirements. While new source performance standards are more stringent, they are also easier to meet as industry becomes more technologically innovative.

Although performance standards may have less impact on innovation than technology-based standards, they may not always work. Performance standards must include tests to determine their efficiency and effectiveness, but a test can only serve as a model of the actual use. There is also a demand for post-market surveillance to incorporate new ideas and improvements into the regulatory process.

Alternatives for Efficient Regulation

The Federal Energy Regulatory Commission uses a consultative approach in the licensing of hydroelectric power plants. The regulator, the regulated, and the environmental community representatives are brought together early in the licensing process to articulate concerns. The regulatory process proceeds on a case-by-case basis, with intensive dialogue among the various groups. The work group participants recognize that the incentive to license the plant forces consultation. Moreover, experience showed reduced recources are utilized by the agency; there is less litigation and the process itself is less adversarial.

It is crucial to examine the regulatory process and its entities. Regulations cannot be generalized; individual situations require different approaches and techniques.

In summary:

*   Regulations and standards are inevitable. But the adversarial role does not work efficiently.

*   Litigation and time delays created by the regulatory process hurt the United States in the competitive trade markets associated with science and technology (particularly in maintaining the U.S. lead in biotechnology).

*   Industry does want regulation--it provides a protective shield in litigation. If a company is in compliance, liabilities are reduced, insurance coverage is less complex and less expensive, etc.

*   Methods like the consensus approach have potential-- they provide a more fruitful exchange of ideas and

force compromise. But this approach works better in resolving technical standards development.

* Regulations involving risk management require more study; researchers must gain a better understanding of the nature of assumptions, uncertainties in the data, costs of establishing margins of safety, etc.

What is the role of the public administrator and what can university programs in public administration contribute? Analysis of the apparatus and administration of the regulatory process lends itself to university research. Specifically, a determination of the complexities of the process and the legitimate roles of intergovernmental overlap is critical. While case-by-case regulation is necessary, there does need to be an oversight role, as well as frequent scrutiny of the aggregate effects of regulations. A forum was recommended to provide an opportunity to discuss the broader policy issues such as the equity and value aspects of regulatory policy.

Students should be educated more in the interdisciplinary approach to problem solving. They should be provided with better communications skills if they are planning to become involved in the regulatory process. The student should be trained to progress from the analyst role to the role of arbitrator or mediator. Conflict management skills are useful, as is knowledge of strategies and tactics for solving problems or building consensus.

The university might focus attention on the nature of regulatory law in the future. What kinds of regulations will be needed? What types of organizational structure will be required? What will be the roles of the "third party?" What will be the nature of enforcement policies and the role of the courts? How will the continued growth of the multinationals affect the regulatory process? A number of these questions may be relevant to the study of public administration over the next 50 years.

Part III: Social Justice: Beyond Criminal Justice

A. Integrity in Justice Institutions

Chair: Rita J. Simon, The American University

Presentations by: Edward Codelia, Associate Director, The
                              Prison Fellowship
                          Patrick V. Murphy, President, The Police
                              Foundation
                          James Q. Wilson, Harvard University

Rapporteur: James J. Fyfe, The American University

INTEGRITY IN JUSTICE INSTITUTIONS

James J. Fyfe

Public corruption--profit-motivated misconduct by government officials--is, in the popular view, a particularly detestable variety of criminal behavior. It is a betrayal of the taxpayer by those he pays to act in his interests, and therefore involves crimes against the people to a greater degree than do most other offenses.

Corrupt police officials are viewed as especially reprehensible. In addition to violating the same general responsibilities of other public employees, they pervert the very specific mandate of the police. They are charged with working to prevent and detect crime, and to assure that the behavior of the rest of us stays within legal bounds. Instead, they commit--and permit--crimes for their own personal benefit.

Thus, it is not surprising that we vilify corrupt police and we lionize those who resist great temptation or expose corruption: We are believers in heroes and villains. One of the folkheroes of American law enforcement, for example, is Elliot Ness, the Prohibition era "Untouchable." There is little evidence that his enforcement activities stemmed the flow of bootleg liquor--or of blood--in Chicago, but he and his associates did manage to remain untainted despite the fortunes apparently offered them by Al Capone and Company.

A more recent police folkhero is Frank Serpico, who helped bring to public attention the fact that widespread corruption existed in the New York City Police Department.[1] Serpico's status as a police celebrity is less attributable to the substance of his revelations than to the fact that he made them--he became a hero because he had the courage to focus attention on corruption that was obvious to any insider (and to many concerned outsiders), rather than because he demonstrated investigative brilliance in finding the corruption.

What Serpico did find was not surprising: Corruption has been periodically exposed in urban police departments since they were founded. In every odd-numbered decade since the 1890s, for example, there has been a major corruption scandal in the New York City Police Department.[2] Prior to the 1890s, corruption in policing, and in the rest of government, was apparently so widespread that it was accepted as part of New York City's natural order.[3] Police corruption has not been unique to New York City: The police departments of Chicago, Denver, Philadelphia, Seattle, and countless smaller jurisdictions have also experienced repeated corruption scandals. During one four month period, the Police Foundation news clipping service found stories describing police corruption in 30 states.

Defining Corruption

Analyses of police corruption must begin with careful definitions; like "crime," police "corruption" has occurred in many places, but its substance and extent have varied. "Corruption" is not a legal term denoting a specific activity; rather, it is a convenient but imprecise term used to describe a great variety of offenses.

The Knapp Commission[4]--the investigative body created in response to Serpico's allegations--found that corruption among New York City officers included: acceptance of small gratuities (meals, cigarettes, small "Christmas gifts," etc.); solicitation of bribes from merchants whose businesses were open in violation of Sunday closing laws and from building contractors who operated in violation of myriad administrative regulations (e.g., failing to have permits to drive cement trucks across sidewalks, blocking more than half a sidewalk at any one time, permitting dust to fly); theft during the course of burglary and death investigations. Even this great variety of misconduct, however, does not cover all the corruption in New York at that time. The illegal activities of many members of the Special Investigating Unit (SIU) (e.g., stealing cash and drugs from narcotics arrestees; supplying informants with narcotics), the elite narcotics unit to which Edward Codelia was assigned, were contemporaneous with those described by Serpico and Knapp but did not come to public attention until after the Knapp Commission had finished its work.

Thus, because it takes so many different forms, discussions of "corruption" may be as meaningless as discussions of "crime." Before we can discuss either in a manner that has implications for public policy, we must make our terms more specific.

Organized and Opportunistic Corruption

Patrick V. Murphy of the Police Foundation suggests that is administratively useful to think of corruption in terms of two broad classes.[5] The first, organized corruption, is amenable to control by managerial intervention because it is continuing and usually involves longterm relationships between offenders and those whom we entrust to eliminate their activities. Officers involved in organized corruption are vulnerable to detection if only because they must periodically meet with those who pay them off.

The second type of corruption described by Murphy is opportunistic. It involves ad hoc profit-making by police who, during the course of their work, come upon and take advantage of serendipitous opportunities for illegal windfalls. Some of these officers, he states, are "meat-eaters" who aggressively seek out, or even create, such opportunities. Others are "grass-eaters," who are not so aggressive but who regularly exploit such chances when they arise.[6]

Thus, Murphy concludes, organized corruption is a symptom of organizational defects, while opportunistic corruption is more closely associated with individual deviance or weakness. Because opportunistic corruption is sporadic and unpredictable, it is far less amenable to administrative control than is organized corruption. Consequently, administrative effectiveness in fighting corruption is best judged by the strength of efforts to control organized corruption; and occasional demonstrations of opportunistic corruption should not be interpreted to mean that whole agencies are corrupt.[7]

Individual and Systemic Explanations of Corruption

Closely related to this attempt to describe corruption are attempts to explain its causes. Traditionally, administrators (in police and other agencies) have analyzed corruption in terms of "rotten apples"--a few deviant officers who spoil the otherwise fine barrel of the police agency. This theory of corruption is inviting for police administrators because, in blaming the rotten apple, it absolves a department, its administrators, and its political and social environments from responsibility for officers' corrupt activities. But, despite the occurrence of individual, opportunistic corruption, this explanation is usually inadequate, and does little to prevent future corruption.

In Serpico's New York and in Ness's Chicago, corruption among police was highly organized. In the former case, it was ignored or condoned by administrators whose own personal integrity has never been otherwise questioned: There is no evidence whatsoever that the top administrators who "overlooked" gambling related corruption did so for profit. In the latter case, as in many others, those at or near the top of the local law enforcement establishment actively participated in corruption and reaped huge profits from it. The highly organized nature of these activites and the large numbers of officers involved raise questions about the "rotten apple" theory that police corruption (or other misconduct) is a problem of individual deviants, or "rotten apples."

It is true that corrupt police officers are deviants insofar as their activities vary from the societal norms that most of us expect them to follow. But where corruption is highly organized, the acts of these officers may not be signs of individual deviance, but rather of conformity to the more immediate departmental--or squad--norms governing their behavior. It may be that the organization and the enforcement system of which it is a part, rather than the individual, are the real deviants; and the organization simply makes it easier to follow its corrupt norms than to fight them. If that is so, it is fruitless to focus anti-corruption efforts on individual police officers while ignoring the role of deviant departmental norms.

In New York City, for example, corruption was the norm among the gambling enforcement officers with whom Serpico worked, and they apparently all conformed to it and/or to the norm of ignoring the misconduct of one's colleagues.[8] Serpico violated both of those norms and, from that point of view, he--not his colleagues--was the deviant who broke the rules by which they lived. He certainly had received little encouragement to do this and, in retrospect, it was far more difficult for him to break those rules than to have concurred with them.

How does it happen that corruption becomes the norm in whole squads--or whole departments--of police officers? In most places, officer candidates are tested and subjected to extensive character and background investigations, and are therefore presumable honest when they enter policing.[9] One of the major actors in the Serpico scandals, for example, came from an impeccable background, had attended only parochial schools, and had graduated from St. John's University before becoming a police officer (at a time when such educational achievement was a rarity among police in New York or elsewhere). Was he corrupt when he entered the police force, or did certain characteristics of the department and his work lead him--along with the majority of his colleagues--down the primrose path he eventually followed? Were the criminal charges that were ultimately brought against a large number of his colleagues caused by their individual deviances, or by some other variables?

There are, no doubt, individual "rotten apples" in police work. The evidence, however, suggests that organized police corruption is largely attributable to the characteristics of some police departments and of some police work, rather than to the characteristics of individuals. Thus, the causes of organized police corruption are generally systemic, while the causes of opportunistic corruption by lone officers are individual, such as the "rotten apple" who exploits his position on a catch-as-catch-can basis, and the weak individual who unexpectedly encounters an "offer" that meets the price at which he is willing to compromise himself.[10]

There are several systemic considerations relevant to this discussion. Police departments are very sensitive to the political environments in which they work and, in general, internal police norms reflect the views and priorities of local politicians. The police know what the mayor wants, how much of it can be safely withheld from him, and what he does not care about. Police departments are nearly total institutions, characterized by great solidarity, mutual loyalties, a high degree of peer pressure, and a fairly conservative respect for tradition and precedent; both police work and police organizations exert a great degree of influence on the behavior and views of individual officers. As an old saw among management theorists has it, "the best predictor of a person's performance in a job is the performance of the person who had previously held the job;" individual characteristics (integrity, education, etc.) are usually secondary to the already existing organizational standards that affect the new jobholder. That is certainly true of policing, where officers are under constant pressure to conform to the norms of their departments. When those norms, and the norms of the police department's clientele, encourage misconduct, it is likely to occur.

Serpico's colleagues, for example, were assigned to enforce gambling laws in the South Bronx, an area in which "numbers"[11] and other illegal gambling are social institutions, and where numbers operators are trusted members of the community-- nobody would place a bet with a numbers operator absent the certainty that he would pay off. There was no way that police efforts would eliminate this gambling and there was little concern about illegal gambling among residents of the community (a good number of whom were regular bettors). Indeed, arrests of numbers operators in such areas have even precipitated mini-riots involving bettors who feared that they would not be able to document winnings when operators' records were seized by police as evidence. Further, the penalties suffered by those arrested for illegal gambling were minimal (usually a fine of less than $25.00).

A situation conducive to corruption exists in such places. It is important to gamblers that they continue to operate and to be accessible to their bettors. They can be successful only if they have reputations for stability, reliability, and professional integrity. But, in providing accessibility to bettors, they also become visible to the police. Their visibility makes them vulnerable, and in order to retain their working reputations and credibility, they must find means to immunize themselves against the police. The police feel little or no local pressure to enforce gambling laws, and are evaluated by a distant headquarters and city hall only in terms of the numbers of arrests they effect. It is consequently in the best interests of all concerned that there be established some longterm working arrangements between gamblers and police. They do so by setting up regular payoffs (e.g., monthly "pads"), and by colloborating in "convenience" arrests of low-ranking gamblers to fill arrest quotas. This makes everybody happy: The mayor and the police chief demonstrate the extent of their anti-gambling efforts by counting off a high number of arrests for those concerned with public morality (who are usually far removed from ghetto streets); gamblers continue to operate and, occasionally, ask the police to put their competition out of business; bettors continue to play; and police officers both make a profit and fill their arrest quotas without having to engage in the onerous activity of enforcing laws that nobody seems to want enforced. When scandals occur (as when an independent investigative agency catches a police officer with his hand in the till), the administration condemns the "rotten apple," replaces him with someone else, and all concerned continue business as usual.

Integrative and Disintegrative Corruption

According to panelist James Q. Wilson such corruption is integrative[12]: A popular, illegal service is provided; virtually unenforceable laws are quietly circumvented without the criticism that might accrue to any official or administration suggesting that the laws be abolished or formally ignored; and it is difficult to determine what tangible public interest is being hurt.[13] He distinguishes this kind of corruption from "disintegrative" corruption, in which officials profit individually while causing clear and measurable harm to the public interest. Serpico's colleagues made the same kind of distinction; they generally regarded money taken from gamblers as "clean," but viewed money "dirty" if it involved police collaboration with narcotics dealers or other offenders whose crimes caused discernible injury or loss to victims.[14]

These distinctions may seem like semantics or an apologia for corrupt officials, but they are important for the purposes of this discussion. Certainly, integrative corruption has social costs,[15] but these are often far less discernible and far less valued by its participants (and by observers) than are its benefits. The point is that integrative corruption and "clean" money are arguably more tolerable than disintegrative corruption and "dirty" money. Isn't taking bribes from a gambler less evil than accepting bribes from a heroin dealer or murderer? Because the symbolic costs of disintegrative corruption are so great, integrative corruption is far more likely to be open, organized, and condoned by high officials. Many people in the New York City Police Department knew that gambling enforcement was a sham. Most, however, were shocked to find that there also existed widespread corruption among narcotics officers. Whereas the former was general information, the latter was a closely held secret among the officers who were directly involved in it.[16]

Other Dimensions of Corruption

While these attempts to define and explain police corruption are useful, the experiences of Mr. Codelia and his SIU colleagues suggest that they may be incomplete, and that it may be informative to examine corruption along other dimensions as well.

It is by now evident that the top administration of the New York City Police Department knew about and tolerated the gambling related corruption exposed by Serpico, which involved "clean" money, and integrative corruption. But, conversely, can one assume that they took no action concerning the narcotics related corruption of Mr. Codelia and his colleagues--presumably "dirty" money and disintegrative corruption--because they did not know about it? Or, is it also possible that they were part of the closely held secret, that they did know about it but did not discern any violations of the unofficial prohibition on "dirty" money, and therefore decided to ignore it? Is it conceivable that the corruption of SIU was not so clearly disintegrative as it might at first appear? A convincing argument be made affirming these last two questions.

Like New York City gambling enforcement officers of that period, narcotics officers were faced with a virtually impossible task. Their mandate was to reduce the flow of drug traffic, a mission several subsequent "wars on drugs" suggest may be impossible even when enforcement resources are limited.[17] SIU did not have unlimited resources: The New York State Commission of Investigation[18] reported of Mr. Codelia's unit in 1972 that it was under-funded, under-equipped and, because it had virtually no "buy money," could make only low level drug purchases. Officers also had virtually no funds with which to pay informants and, like Serpico's colleagues, were evaluated by their superiors solely on the basis of the number of arrests effected. They too had a quota of four arrests per month, and were required to meet it even when their normal working hours were filled by lengthy investigations that kept them off their regular assignments.[19]

This operating mode generated interesting results. The State Commission reports that during 1970, the 70 officers in SIU[20] made 7,266 heroin buys, which resulted in 4,007 arrests (a monthly average of approximately 4.8 per officer, and a strong suggestion of the degree to which police officers respond to organizational norms). These officers were clearly quite busy, and were also involved in work that placed them at great personal risk.[21]

The question of the impact of their work upon narcotics traffic, however, is a different matter. The Commission reports that the total amount of "compounds containing heroin" seized during these 1970 buys and arrests was 4.97 pounds.[22] Further, only five to six percent of this amount was actually heroin, the remainder being the milk sugar quinine, and other impurities with which heroin is "cut" before it is sold on the street. In this environment, several of Mr. Codelia's colleagues told the Investigations Commission, even the most dedicated officers became disenchanted and cynical.

As subsequent events demonstrated, many officers also employed extralegal means of reducing the flow of drugs and of "hurting" drug dealers. Illegal wiretaps and illegal searches became common (often, according to Mr. Codelia, at the urging of prosecutors and high police officials); large amounts of cash were stolen from drug dealers during the course of arrests; informants were paid out of this cash or with drugs that were seized during arrests but stolen by officers.

Thus, with some exceptions[23], most of the unlawful acts of these narcotics officers were different from those of Serpico's partners. The latter were part of a very sophisticated system in which gamblers were sold immunity from arrest. They went to work every day with no intention of enforcing the gambling laws; their regularized payoffs had become the central focus of their police careers. That was not so among the narcotics officers. While Serpico's colleagues had surrendered to the gamblers, the SIU officers were engaged in a war without rules. They enforced the law, made arrests, and brought prosecutions, but also felt free to violate rights, to divert evidence, and to seize unto themselves the spoils of their war with narcotics offenders.

A critical difference between the narcotics officers' corrupt acts and those of the gambling enforcement officers may be obscured by the fact that "narcotics related" corruption are generally regarded as a more egregious activity than "gambling related" corruption. But that superficial categorization ignores a more fundamental distinction. The gambling enforcement officers had been neutralized by the gamblers and, for all intents and purposes, took no valid enforcement action against them. It is not at all clear that that was true of the narcotics officers. Instead, it is probably realistic to dichotomize between corruption that is central to officers' conceptions of their police work, and corruption that is incidental. By and large, the evidence indicates that--no matter how profitable--the corruption in SIU was incidental, while the corruption of Mr. Serpico's colleagues was central.

Further, the corruption in Serpico's gambling squad was negotiated and immunizing, in the sense that police and long established offenders developed well-defined working arrangements that immunized offenders from vigorous enforcement and provided means by which officers could meet the formal demands of their organizations (e.g., by effecting convenience arrests in fulfillment of quota requirements). In contrast the misconduct in SIU was sometimes negotiated and/or immunizing (e.g., providing informants with narcotics; intervening on informants' behalf in criminal cases), but these activities were rarely corrupt because they generally produced no profit for the officers involved. Instead, the corrupt activities of SIU officers were generally non-negotiable and non-immunizing: They were forcible thefts from persons who were also arrested and prosecuted by officers driven by different--and perhaps less venal--motives than those of the gambling enforcement officers. Perhaps, had their administrators and political superiors known of their activities, they, like the misconduct of Serpico's colleagues, would have been tolerated.

Conclusions

We have only recently begun to learn about the dynamics of official misconduct generally and of police corruption specifically. Recent events in New York and elsewhere--including those in which Mr. Codelia was implicated--proved that the mere recruitment of high caliber personnel and the personal honesty of administrators are not adequate measures for eliminating or, more realistically, minimizing corruption. Instead, as Mr. Murphy points out, what is needed inside police agencies are systems by which managers can be held accountable for corruption among the personnel who work for them.

Those in academe and other institutions outside police agencies need to examine this misconduct more closely, and from a variety of dimensions. Corruption is not a one dimensional problem and, until we discern the differences between various types of corruption, we will never recognize that they require different curative measures. In doing this, we would be well-advised to heed admonitions given by Dr. Wilson. He asserts that administrators have an obligation to explain carefully to the public the limits of their authority. The public often views easy availability of illegal goods and services--drugs, gambling, and prostitution--as indications that social control agencies have been corrupted. But this is not always the case; because of due process requirements and resource shortages, it is often difficult for even the best run and most honest agencies to act against offenders as quickly and as effectively as we would like. Even had SIU been corruption-free, for example, it is doubtful that it would have been more effective reducing drug trafficking.

Finally, as Wilson notes, it may be possible to reduce corruption to a minimum, but it is neither realistic nor possible to pursue one virtue--a pure government--without regard to the costs involved in other government activities. We may be able to eliminate corruption, but in doing so we may lose local political prerogatives, impose a universal standard on a pluralistic population, and find ourselves using Orwellian measures.

1. Robert Daley, Prince of the City (New York: Houghton-Mifflin, 1978) is based on the Serpico revelations and the consequences.

2. In 1894, the Lexow Commission, headed by a Republican upstate New York State senator, conducted hearings on police corruption in New York City. Nearly 700 witnesses testified: that police bought appointments and promotions from the Democrats' powerful Tammany Hall; that they protected gambling and prostitution; that they shook down legitimate businessmen who had committed minor violations of municpal regulations; and that, in return for a share of the proceeds, they permitted pickpockets, thieves, and con-men to operate without interference. In 1915, the Curran Committee reported very similar findings. In the early 1930s, the Seabury Committee, headed by a judge, reported that prohibition had only worsened this situation, and uncovered corruption on a scale large enough to force the resignation of the city's mayor, the flamboyant Jimmy Walker. In the early 1950s, Harry Gross, who allegedly paid police more than $1 million annually in order to protect his Brooklyn gambling operations, testified against scores of police officers in a scandal characterized by suicides, convictions of high ranking officers, and more than 100 dismissals from the department. In the 1970s, the scandals involving Frank Serpico and the Special Investigating Unit of the Narcotics Division came to light. See generally, Robert M. Fogelson, Big-City Police (Cambridge, MA: Harvard University Press, 1977).

3. Fogelson notes:

The police [in American cities] served themselves and the machines a lot better than the citizens. They drew an adequate salary; if they put in a full day, which was highly unusual, they worked no harder and no longer than other Americans; and they enjoyed greater security. They also supplemented their salaries with payoffs; most patrolmen preferred taking graft to raiding gamblers and most detectives preferred collecting rewards to arresting criminals. For most policemen, as indeed for most judges, teachers, and other municipal employees, public service was first and foremost a livelihood, and a relatively accessible one at that. Whether licensing vice, regulating crime, preserving order, or helping the citizenry, the police usually kept the interests and concerns of the machines uppermost in their minds. Not only did they realize that their positions were controlled by the ward bosses, but they also understood that their careers were inextricably bound up with the organization's fortunes. For most policemen, as indeed for most firemen, sanitationmen,

and other public employees, personal aspirations and organizational imperatives were virtually synonymous. From their perspective, which was shared by most lower and lower-middle-class immigrants, the police best served the public by first serving themselves and the machines.
Fogelson, ibid., 35.

4. The Commission to Investigate Allegations of Police Corruption and the City's Anti-Corruption Procedures was popularly called the Knapp Commission, after its chairman, Wall Street lawyer Whitman Knapp.

5. Patrick V. Murphy, Paper presented at Public Affairs-50, The American University, March 2, 1984.

6. A third participant in opportunistic corruption might also be identified: the ordinary--and ordinarily honest--man who fails to resist a one-time-only extraordinary temptation. One example is a New York City police officer who was walking out of a police station when he was stopped by a citizen and given a bag containing $110,000 in small bills. The citizen, an airport worker, explained that he had just found the bag in his parked auto at the end of his working day. The officer complimented the finder on his good citizenship, assured him that he would "handle the case," and the citizen continued on his way home from work. When he arrived there, he told his family about his remarkable find. They told him that an airport bank had been robbed of $110,000, a dramatic high-speed pursuit through the airport's parking lot had followed, and that, despite a near apprehension there, neither the robbers nor the money had been found. He called police to determine whether his $110,000 was the bank's $110,000 (of course, it was, apparently dumped in his auto by the fleeing robbers), and was told that police had no record of his find. The officer involved was subsequently identified, arrested, tried, and dismissed from the police department.

7. Opportunistic and organized corruption are probably better described as the two extremes of a continuum, rather than as a clear dichotomy. At one end, there might appear incidents like the one described in note 6 and, at the other, there would be highly routinized regular payoffs between offenders and large numbers of officers. In between, there are several less readily classifiable gradations. Were the groups of narcotics officers in SIU--who regularly "ripped off" cash from the drug dealers they arrested--guilty of opportunistic or of organized corruption? Their activities appear to have been a mixture of both.

8. Peter Maas, Serpico (New York: Viking Press, 1973), 153-154), describes the following conversation between Frank Serpico, who had been newly assigned to gambling enforcement ("plainclothes") and Robert Stanard, a plainclothes veteran who had known Serpico when both had previously been assigned to the Seventieth Precinct (the "Seven-oh"):

Stanard swung away from the curb, and almost idly asked, "Hey, how much time you got on the job?"

"Six, seven years, around that."

"And so now you're in plainclothes. You know what plainclothes is all about?"

Serpico decided to keep his answer as vague as possible. "Yeah. Some things I hear, and some things I guess for myself." He took out his meerschaum and lit it.

"Christ, roll down the window a little," Stanard said. "How can you smoke that thing?"

"It relaxes me."

"Anyway, the guys were saying that...look, let me tell you something. You have an opportunity to make some easy, clean money."

"What do you mean?"

"I mean, you can make eight hundred a month, just like that."

"Just like that?"

"Yeah, that's what I said. I'm saying you can. I--" Stanard seemed to have second thoughts about what he was going to say. He drove perhaps the length of a block before he spoke again, his voice lower, less assertive. "We got a call about you from someone--I don't know who, and they didn't even have your name right, 'Sertico' I think they called you--and it was that you couldn't be trusted."

Serpico allowed himself a caustic laugh. "What were they bitching about? That I didn't like to take money?"

"Yeah, something like that. But it doesn't matter. I told the guys that you were OK. What we do is check a guy out with the other cops he hangs around with, but you're kind of weird. You don't hang out with cops, so there's nobody we can really talk to. So I told the guys you were OK in the Seven-oh, and when plainclothes came up for you, you asked me about it and I told you to grab it. I told the guys, 'Yeah, he's weird and has a beard and he's around the village a lot and stuff, but he's all right.' I mean, I told them you wouldn't hurt another cop."

Serpico stared ahead, puffing on his pipe. Out of the corner of his eye, he saw Stanard glance at him. "Would you hurt another cop?"

"I don't know what you mean, 'hurt another cop.'"

"You know. Would you do anything to hurt another cop?"

"Well, that depends on what he's doing."

"Hey," Stanard said, "nobody does anything bad here. The only thing we do is we make a little clean money off gambling. They're going to operate anyway, and they give us money so we don't bother them."

9. See, e.g., John H. McNamara, "Uncertainties in Police Work: The Relevance of Police Recruits' Background and Training," in The Police: Six Sociological Essays, ed. David Bordua (New York, John Wiley, 1966); Arthur Niederhoffer, Behind the Shield (Garden City, NY: Anchor Books, 1969); Police Corruption, ed. Lawrence W. Sherman (Garden City, NY: Anchor Books, 1974); William Westley, Violence and the Police (Cambridge, MA: MIT Press, 1970)

10. This is, of course, a somewhat simplistic explanation because, for example, the causes of even the most highly organized corruption are both systemic and individual. In an ideal world, officers confronted with even the most highly organized, sophisticated, and normatively supported corruption would neither particpate in it nor ignore it: they would work to eradicate it.

11. Numbers are a form of lottery betting, in which bettors choose their own numbers, and winners are selected on the basis of parimutuel horse racing results and cash handles. Numbers bets are typically small (in New York City, $5 would be considered a very large bet), but great numbers of players bet daily so that profits are quite handsome.

12. James Q. Wilson, "The Nature of Corruption," Paper presented at Public Affairs-50, The American University, March 2, 1984.

13. The subject of one of David Susskind's more bizarre television interviews, for example, was a man who argued that it served the public interest to permit illegal gambling in New York City. A lobbyist, he had been retained by a group of illegal numbers operators to fight against the proposed legalization and licensing of such betting. He argued that licensed numbers gambling would not generate as much tax revenue as anticipated, because most veteran players would continue to bet with illegal operators in order to avoid paying taxes on any winnings and in order to continue to bet on credit, a practice that probably would not be permitted in licensed betting establishments. More

importantly, he asserted that illegal numbers betting in New York City provided 400,000 part-time and 100,000 full-time jobs. These individuals, he argued, would not be permitted to hold jobs in licensed (or state-run) betting establishments because many of them had accumulated records of arrest for illegal gambling. Thus, if licensed numbers gambling were successful, many of those currently employed would go onto the welfare rolls, while those who took jobs in legal gambling establishments would generally not be inner-city residents, and would therefore not circulate back into the inner-city economy the salaries they would be paid through the bets of inner-city players. It is impossible to check the accuracy of his figures but, even if his claims are exaggerated, no knowledgeable observer would dispute his contention that illegal gambling in New York does result in the flow of enormous amounts of cash.

14. Maas, supra.

15. Patrick V. Murphy has previously observed that:

Police corruption does particular damage in the following ways: (1) it undermines the confidence of the public; (2) it destroys respect for the law; (3) it undermines departmental discipline; and (4) it harms police morale.

Patrick V. Murphy, "Corruptive Influences", in Local Government Police Management, ed. Bernard L. Garmire (Washington, D.C.: International City Management Association, 1981), 66. While Murphy's observation is accurate, it deals with outcomes that are often nebulous from the point of view of the field officer.

16. Many officers anxious to leave uniformed duty during that era declined assignments to gambling enforcement units and sought out narcotics duty specifically in order to avoid exposure to corruption.

17. See, e.g., Arnold Trebach, The Heroin Solution (New Haven, CT: Yale University Press, 1982).

18. New York State Commission of Investigation, Narcotics Law Enforcement in New York City (New York, 1972).

19. Id., 60-62.

20. Id., 115. The difference between the numbers of "buys" and "arrests" is generally attributable to four factors. First, officers sometimes buy from the same individual several times before arresting him. Second, some buys are attempts to build credibility among low level distributors in order to obtain access to higher level operators. Third, officers sometimes

elay arrests for drug sales until after analyses of the
erchandise has been accomplished; by then, it is occasionally
ipossible to find suspects again. Fourth, officers, like
idicts, are sometimes "burned" by dealers who sell them milk
igar or quinine under the guise of heroin. When this occurs,
rosecutions for drug sale are not possible because no drugs
ave changed hands.

21. During 1971, 671 officers were assigned to the New York
ity Police Narcotics Division. Of these, one was shot and
illed, six were shot and wounded, four were stabbed, eight
ere seriously injured in assaults with other weapons (autos,
ubs, chains, etc.), four were seriously injured in weaponless
hysical assaults, two were bitten by watchdogs at premises they
ere raiding, and three were burned by lye that had been
irown at them. In addition, they shot and wounded seven
uspects, and shot and killed four. James J. Fyfe, Shots Fired:
n Examination of New York City Police Firearms Discharges
?h.D. dissertation) (Ann Arbor, MI: University Microfilms
iternational, 1978), 329-344.

22. Police laboratory testing of narcotics seized in buys and
rrests typically does not specify the amount of actual heroin (or
:her controlled substance) included in suspect compounds.
istead, because the gravity of charges is determined in part by
ie total weight of the compound including cutting materials and
:her impurities, laboratory analysts typically report, for
cample, that "the substance analyzed weighed 15 grams, and
intained heroin."

23. Three officers were convicted of the sale of five
ilograms of heroin withheld by them from evidence in a case in
hich they had seized 105 kilograms (processing the other 100
roperly); two other officers were convicted of attempting to sell
1 incriminating tape recording to a drug trafficker; another was
:quitted of similar charges in a separate incident; and others
ere tried and acquitted on charges that they had sold freedom
one of two persons seized in a drug raid. Daley, supra.

THE NATURE OF CORRUPTION

James Q. Wilson

I would like to speak somewhat abstractly about the subjec of corruption: to ask why it exists and under wha circumstances its frequency will change. I will define corruptio as following a course of action contrary to what duty require that is undertaken in exchange for some material consideration This does not include the commonplace "corruption" that occur for reasons of friendship, ideology, or passion; this discussio is restricted to corruption based on material considerations.

Doing as one's duty requires--that is to say, the opposite o corruption--is a fragile and vulnerable value in any society. A example illustrates the violation of a duty so profound that, fo most of us, it is simply an abstraction.

Professor Stanley Milgram[1] opened a storefront office in Ne Haven, Connecticut and, through newspaper advertisements invited the public to sign up for what was described as "learning experiment." When people arrived in response to th ad, they were confronted by a white-coated person who had th aura of a Yale scientist, although it is not clear that he eve made this explicit. The "subject" was shown a machine; he o she would see, through a window, a person in another room attached to a machine. The subject was told that the tw machines were linked by a wire and that the other person wa engaging in a learning experiment trying to master some lessons The job of the volunteer was to sit behind the first console an administer an electric shock to the individual in the other roo every time the latter gave a wrong answer on the vocabular test. The two rooms were connected by a loudspeaker, and th shock was to be administered on a machine which had a kno labeled "safe," "moderate," "dangerous," "very dangerous," "extremely dangerous."

The person in the other room--a confederate of th experimenter--was a trained actor who would writhe, twist, an moan from the shock which was, of course, fake. He woul make the same mistake repeatedly; each time the "scientist" i the white coat would instruct the volunteer to turn the knob little more until finally that person, in over one-third of th cases, had the knob pointing to "highly dangerous" while th individual in the other room could be heard to shriek "M heart!" and could be seen writhing while tied down in his chair.

These were ordinary, middle-class citizens, of both sexe and all races. If people can violate a norm solely because stranger in a white coat tells them to do so while assuring them that it is all right, how much more likely is it that a police sergeant would find it easy to persuade an officer to take a bribe from a car wash?

The norms of integrity, which are so fragile, vary in their force across time and between countries. We do not have a well-developed theory about the reasons for corruption, but if we consider why it appears in some places more commonly than in others, and at certain times more frequently than at others, we might begin to create such a theory.

No country, no region, no group of people anywhere is immune to corruption. It is sometimes said that the London Metropolitan Police--the Bobbies of Scotland Yard--are paragons of police virtue. I once asked Sir Robert Mark, then Commissioner of the London Police, whether it was true that Scotland Yard detectives were above corruption and brutality. He answered (paraphrasing the Duke of Wellington): "Sir, I don't know whether my detectives scare our criminals, but by God they scare me." It was later confirmed that pornography, prostitution, and drug trafficking were tolerated with both police knowledge and police payoffs in many parts of London and possibly other cities, albeit not to the same degree as in the United States.

In short, no country is immune, but some countries do appear to have less corruption, especially organized corruption. Similarly, certain regions in the United States seem to have more of it than others. The Northeast, including New York, Chicago, and Philadelphia, seems constantly embroiled in major corruption scandals at the state and local level. There are fewer such stories in Los Angeles, Oakland, and San Diego, although they occur there as well.

What is going on? What could possibly explain these differences? There are at least three possible explanations, which are not mutually exclusive.

First, corruption seems to be more likely to occur where political power is fragmented. Any governmental institution providing services must reconcile many competing, conflicting claims for authority, not all of which agree as to how that authority should be exercised. A police department in a city where ward committeemen, aldermen, city councilmen, and state legislators have lateral access to precinct captains, beat sergeants, and the commissioner's office lends itself to corruption far more than a department where the chief is responsible to only one center of power, although that condition by no means guarantees the absence of corruption. The more decentralized political authority is in any regime, the cheaper it is to buy a piece of it. The higher the concentration of authority the more expensive it is to buy it. And other things being equal, which of course they never are, the more expensive it is to purchase corruption, the less corruption will be purchased.

A second factor is that in many areas--and in every nation at certain points of time--some people are less willing to accept those universal norms of duty that are the essence of resistance to corruption. Such individuals have what social scientists call a "particularistic" value system. The United States is especially likely to reflect such a system because we are a nation of immigrants, people who, in many cases, came from countries where government was distrusted. While these immigrants were just as principled as native Americans, they took a different view of government. And why not? In many cases, they had lived under oppressive governments, had been exploited, and had travelled to the United States partly to escape that. In their eyes, government did not side with the citizens, it stood against them. Governmental integrity seemed an implausible abstraction. Survival in their countries of origin required the ability to outwit and evade the government through friends and contacts and depended, above all, on personal loyalties, not abstract values.

Third, corruption is more likely where the government controls a highly valued resource, to which the people have access only on the government's terms. This phenomenon is exemplified in Prohibition; indeed, it is still apparent today because alcohol, though not banned, is so highly taxed that many people believe there must be a cheaper way to get it. Building permits, housing inspection services, health permits--all represent resources which people value. The higher the number of such resources controlled by the government, the greater the incentive to pay somebody to overlook rule violations.

The greatest center of bureaucratic corruption in the world today seems to be the Soviet Union--it is there that one finds the government in command of virtually all valued resources. Between the lines in the speeches about problems of production and problems of hooliganism, Yuri Andropov and other senior officials have also alluded to the pervasive corruption that affects all levels of Soviet society. If anything is to be accomplished--production quotas, the purchase of valued Western commodities, escape from prison or the Gulag Archipelago--somebody has to be paid off. The Russian word for it is "blat," a form of corruption in which one buys a little freedom from governmental control.

The United States does not monopolize resources in the same way as the Soviet Union, but we do subject many areas to public control. Perhaps the example par excellence of the way in which corruption is stimulated is the government restriction on access to certain drugs. The existence of a valued commodity, which is tightly controlled by the government, provides a powerful incentive for corruption. Is this an argument, as many people say, for making access to drugs legal? I think that our society has implicitly answered this question in a way which I personally find acceptable, though I am keenly aware of its cost. If we allowed open, unrestrained access to heroin, its price would be reduced; people would not have to steal to obtain it, nor would police officers have to overlook drug trafficking. But the cost for all this would be a manyfold increase in the number of heroin users.

The U.S. government has stated its preference for maintaining the illegality of heroin in order to reduce the number of users, the argument being that minimizing the recruitment of new users is worth the cost of some increase in crime. This leads to my last point: Like much else, the elimination of corruption from society is not unequivocally good. We cannot pursue any virtue, even the virtue of honesty, to the exclusion of all other considerations. Virtues are inevitably in conflict, as are rights and liberties. Consequently, when we try to purge society of corruption we pay a price. This is dramatically illustrated in the case of the narcotics trade; but it is equally real, if less sensational, in other areas.

We could in principle design a system of inspection, internal affairs, audits, grand jury investigations, and the like, which would reduce virtually to zero the chances of a police department engaging in corruption. But it would entail the creation of a very large and intrusive apparatus, centralizing jurisdiction over the police. That apparatus in turn would become vulnerable to certain inefficiencies, perhaps even to the risk of corruption itself. Moreover, as we insulate a police department from corrupting influences, we also, to a degree, insulate it from other civilian influences. The Los Angeles Police Department and the Oakland Police Department, for example, have both in the past been corrupt agencies which were reformed by farsighted, determined and brave mayors, city managers, and police chiefs. Although they have not been free from corruption problems, they have served as models for other police departments. But the price--perhaps a necessary one--was such rigid insulation of those police departments from outside influences as to confer total power on the chief.

Now these departments have other problems: The Los Angeles Police Department is regularly accused of excessive use of force, for example. The current struggle is to reassert outside political authority over the Department to deal with that situation, but in a way that will not lead to the same kind of influence that produced the corruption of the 1930s and 1940s. How do you do this? That is a task of statesmanship. Social science has nothing to contribute to it.

NOTES

1. See Stanley Milgram, "Some Conditions of Obedience to Authority," International Journal of Psychiatry 6 (October 1968): 259-276.

Part III: <u>Social Justice: Beyond Criminal Justice</u>

B. <u>Punishment in a Just Society</u>

<u>Chair</u>:   Jeffrey Reiman, The American University

<u>Presentation by</u>:   Hugo A. Bedau, Tufts University

<u>Respondent</u>:   William Hemple, Probation Office, U.S.
                         District Court for the District of
                         Columbia

<u>Rapporteur</u>:   Ronald Weiner, The American University

Punishment in a Just Society

Ronald I. Weiner

Hugo A. Bedau believes that it is not possible to eliminate punishment in society until we have abondoned all control over convicted offenders and all liability to such control for violation of our laws. In spite of the fact that there are those who advocate abandoning the use of imprisonment as a mode of punishment, he does not believe that anyone favors completely relieving the offender from responsibility and from some form of control and punishment. Instead, he thinks that we have moved away form harsh and destructive modes of punishment, save for the death penalty, to what he refers to as "productive modes of punishment." These are, in his judgment, quasi-punitive humanistic regimes designed to produce some good in the offender and to teach others compliance with the law. For example, restitution or rehabilitation programs are not true alternatives to punishment because they are still coercive and because the threat of imprisonment is still used to back up the less severe modes of intervention against the law violator.

Professor Bedau suggests that the only non-punitive form of dealing with the law violator is "denunciation" or "verbal castigation," an idea first suggested by Hyman Gross in his book A Theory of Criminal Justice.[1] This approach emphasizes publishing the names of all offenders in the daily newspaper and requiring lawbreakers to endure lengthy castigations in a courtroom by judges of the bench. A similar tactic was used locally when a judge required a drunk driver reponsible for the death of a person to witness the autopsy of another person killed in an accident caused by a drunk driver. Professor Bedau believes that this type of social policy comes as close as is possible to being non-punitive while still retaining seemingly coercive and punitive features. He also maintains, however, that a social policy of this sort is not in society's best interest when we are dealing with hardened recidivists and those convicted of the most egregious offense.

The elimination of punishment would be impossible in his view; and even if we could, we would probably inflict mora damage to society by such complete abandonment. Such a policy would be far worse for the well-being of our society than policies that inflict severe forms of punishment on wrongdoers.

Jeffrey Reiman pointed out that Professor Bedau predicates punishment on the assumption that there are just laws. Professor Reiman questioned this assumption, commenting that laws may appear to be just, but we must examine them and their consequences in the context of the social systems they seek to protect. He emphasized that we can never be "too competent in our intuitions about the justice of our own society; and this means we cannot quiet our doubts about the justice of punishment with anything less than an adequate and reasoned defense of the justice of the society it protects, matched with honest efforts to rectify injustices when they are found."

William Hemple examined the role of punishment from the standpoint of the practitioner who works in the field of probation and parole, and who believes that most of these officials view their work as non-punitive insofar as they try to gain an offender's compliance with lawful behavior. He believes that they are quite successful in their attempts to help violators comply with the law using what Professor Bedau refers to as quasi-punitive modes of intervention.

Professor Hemple comments that the greatest difficulty for probation officers lies in their responsibility for making recommendations to judges about appropriate sentences for offenders, e.g., which ones should go to prison and receive the harsh regime of a total institution, and which ones should remain free in the community under the less severe modes of quasi-punishment. He shows that the punishment deserved by defendants is often unclear, given their offenses and the related circumstances of their crimes.

NOTES

1. Hyman Gross, A Theory of Criminal Justice (New York: Oxford University Press, 1979).

PUNISHMENT IN A JUST SOCIETY: COULD IT BE ELIMINATED?

Hugo Adam Bedau

Punishment plays an important role in our society, and despite its enormous cost in economic and emotional terms, we are, as a society, inseparably wedded to its practice--notwithstanding, of course, doubts and even severe criticisms here and there about particular cases or certain styles of punishment. At least since the time of Plato, philosophers have wondered whether there is any legitimate role for punishment in a just society. They have wondered whether the widespread practice of punishment in their own day might not be merely one more manifestation of the incontestable fact that the society in which they lived was anything but just or fair. Such doubts have been, on the whole, as inconclusive as they have been widespread. For every philosopher who has raised fundamental doubts about the practice of punishment, there have been two others who have exerted their best efforts to reassure us that punishment is required both in principle and in practice.

In the remarks that follow, I want to focus directly on this large topic, and to do so from a point of view too infrequently exploited. I shall not discuss directly (except at the very end) the time-honored philosophical question of whether punishment is justified. Nor shall I depart from abstractions to concentrate attention on whether this or that form of punishment as practiced in our society is justified. My concern is not to explain why we should punish the guilty, nor even to explain the prior question, why we should threaten punishment on the innocent--though, as we shall see, I do have something to say on these topics. My approach will be to ask instead whether punishment can be eliminated from human life as we know it. I want us to contemplate a world without punishment in an attempt to decide what kinds of general considerations tell for and against our longstanding and too often unreflective practice of punishment. Let me add immediately that when I ask, "Can punishment be eliminated?" I am not confining myself to a narrow interpretation of these words. I mean to explore whether we should eliminate it, if we can. Of course, if we are unable to dispense with it, then there seems little point in trying to explain why we should not. But, first, let us see whether it can be eliminated.

Before we can face this issue in its full generality, we need to be in tolerable agreement about what punishment is. This is not the occasion in which to launch into a full-scale investigation of what punishment is: yet the elimination of punishment, whether desirable or merely possible, does turn to some extent on what we take punishment to be. At one extreme are those who think of punishment as any form of deliberate use of violence against another person or group. This is a far broader notion of punishment than discussed here, and asking whether punishment in this broad sense can be eliminated is tantamount to wondering whether peace can reign in human affairs. Police use of lethal force in apprehending felons, the nation's use of military force against other peoples, a householder's use of force against an uninvited intruder—none of these are instances of punishment as far as I am concerned; in any case, nothing I shall say about punishment is relevant to these kinds of deliberate violence against other persons.

At the other extreme are those philosophers who have come to think of punishment as a complex expressive and communicative act, whereby one person or group uses force against another person or group only after the former has judged the latter to be in violation of some important law, rule, or norm. The purpose is to allow the former to express their moral indignation against the latter, causing the latter to see themselves as being regarded as moral reprobates by others. This view of punishment may be the best one. But it depends for its validity on a central role for retributive purposes and expressive communicative acts that are controversial (and I have criticized them elsewhere); so for present purposes I shall regard this as too narrow a view.

What I shall say about the elimination of punishment may not extend to punishment as conceived in this narrow and sophisticated way; but this idea of punishment itself may well—and I think it does—fall far short of characterizing what actually goes on in the criminal courts, the prisons, and other related institutions in our society. Accordingly, I shall try to walk a path between these two extremes, and assume that the punishment under discussion here is not so broad as to include what police do on the street in the heat of trying to prevent a crime nor so narrow as to be confined to what a morally sophisticated parent might do with a loved child who has deliberately caused harm to the family dog.

I should say from the beginning that I do not have in mind—or take seriously—the idea of eliminating punishment by reference to certain empirical considerations and contingencies. Suppose, for instance, no one was ever arrested for a crime; then, we arguably would have eliminated punishment through the side door as it were, because we lack persons on whom to visit punishment. Or, to take another example of the same sort, suppose that although many people were indicted and arrested for crimes, none were ever convicted: Here again we would have eliminated any possibility of punishing anyone. The same result follows from any of the following suppositions: No one is ever sentenced to be punished, or no one is willing to carry out a punishment on anyone, or no one is willing to pay for criminal courts and punitive institutions. I put to one side all such considerations as essentially uninteresting for our purposes, both because they are so unlikely given the reality of our social world and because they shed little or no light on the moral aspects of the practice of punishment, which are uppermost in my mind even if they are not always under immediate discussion.

Historically, punishment has been under assault from three main directions, and it is best to look first at these sweeping arguments. One direction of assault is from the pacifist anarchist, who argues that no end--not even that of preventing the violation of just laws--ever justifies the use of coercive force or the threat thereof by a society's government. A second direction is from the cost-benefit behaviorist, who maintains that punishment is less efficient in securing compliance than reward, and that given the alternatives of more and less efficient ways to secure compliance, a reasonable person always will choose the more efficient. The third direction from which punishment can be undermined is that of the metaphysical determinist, who posits that no one is truly eligible to be punished because all of those whose violation of the criminal laws seems to warrant punishment could not help their actions and so do not deserve to be treated as if they could have changed their behavior. Should we credit any or all of these categorical objections to the practice of punishment?

The metaphysical determinist can advance his claims in either of two major forms. In the broadest version, he claims that everyone--lawbreaker or not, adult or child, normal and rational agents, as well as the deviant and the impulsive--act as they do and could not act otherwise because their choices, decisions, and preferences could not be other than they are. In this view, the very idea of human agency is out of place in the picture of human life. This view, as others have often pointed out, would not in fact undercut any rationale for punishment. Rather, it would leave everything--including both criminal conduct and punitive behavior--exactly as it is. That is, if universal metaphysical determinism of this sort were true, then we could not use it to pry off and eliminate punishment of the guilty and the threat of punishment for the innocent if they transgress. The reason is that these activities are somehow inseperable from the interwoven warp and weft of human affairs under the iron rule of causal determinism. These activities are themselves the product of the same uncontrollable causes as the law-breaking behavior itself. Where everything we do is caused by forces beyond our control, no part of the effects--in this case, the practice of punishment--can be treated separately, as though we were free to alter or eliminate it.

In its narrower and somewhat more interesting form, metaphysical determinism claims that only those who violate the criminal law are not responsible for their actions, owing to causes over which they have no control and for which they are not accountable. Such a claim is tantamount to the view that every lawbreaker has the excuse that he or she could not help what was done. Whatever else we might say about such a view, surely it is highly implausible. Indeed, it verges on the miraculous that there should be a perfect fit between those who break the criminal law and those whose conduct is always a manifestation of involuntary causation. I know of no determinist who has ever advanced such a doctrine, and it is extremely difficult to think of grounds (empirical or a priori) that might be advanced to defend it. As an inductive hypothesis, it has little or no chance of gaining favor with those who actually study the behavior of lawbreakers.

I have no doubt that there are valid excuses as well as justifications for breaking the law and even for harming other persons. Both law and morality are in complete agreement on this general point. But the hypothesis that everyone has or might have a plea that would nullify his or her eligibility for punishment truly boggles the mind. We do not believe any such thing, and are hardly likely to be persuaded to accept it by nothing more plausible than a version of metaphysical determinism specifically tailored to yield such a result.

In reply to the behaviorist, there are two fundamentally different objections. First, as Jeremy Bentham pointed out nearly two centuries ago, the cost of a system of reward, not to mention its administration, would be staggering. The idea seems to be that society should pay each person in some kind of coin--money, retirement credits, food stamps, whatever--every time they do not commit a crime, so that the prospects of such reward would serve as an incentive to compliance with the law. But there are virtually endless occasions on which any given person does not violate the criminal law, so that it takes no great ingenuity to reduce the whole idea of general rewards to absurdity. Such a reward system would, for example, require us to confer more benefits on people who sleep ten hours a day than on those who sleep only eight hours--for the longer sleepers are by that very fact generally less dangerous than those who are still awake and thereby potentially able to break the law.

The second objection is that the chief evidence in favor of the efficacy of reward over punishment in shaping conduct is derived from laboratory experiments involving animals. But it is doubtful whether animals understand punishment as we do. Whereas we know that persons (except perhaps for sociopaths) can clearly distinguish between, on the one hand, violating a command of someone who is in a position to bestow rewards or impose punishment, and on the other hand, acting unfairly or harming another person, there is no good reason to suppose that animals do. Virtue is its own reward, according to folk wisdom; so is compliance with the law.

In reply to the pacifist anarchist, I would argue that the authority of some over others, and of the state and its government over its citizens, is in principle defensible. I say "in principle" because one can, of course, think of cases where governments have seized power illegally, or once in power have become in effect criminal regimes, exploiting the citizenry and creating that "long train of abuses" which, as John Locke and Thomas Jefferson argued, amply warrants revolution. The use of force and the threatened use of force—or, to speak more precisely, the creation of laws imposing liability to be punished if they are unjustifiably violated—are also defensible in principle. What the anarchist must do is to convince us that, on moral grounds and moral grounds alone, (a) no one has or can ever acquire authority over another to prohibit conduct however harmful, unfair, or ruinous that conduct may be, and—even if this were false—(b) no one has authority to enforce such prohibitions and requirements, should they be violated, with punitive methods.

However, attractive the pacifist anarchist outlook may be in some settings and however noble a goal it may be, it seems impossible to find sufficient reasons to believe it. To most of us, it seems utterly inequitable that some should have to endure the violation of their rights by persons who are willing to commit crimes and yet who are free from any liability to be punished. And it is especially aggravating to contemplate such impunity if there is reason to believe that some of these crimes might have been prevented by effective law enforcement plus the liability to punishment for criminal acts.

I conclude from this necessarily brief examination that these three sweeping lines of argument against the practice of punishment are not persuasive. However skeptical of the threat and use of force we may be, the pacifist anarchists do not convince us that it may never be justly employed. On the contrary, we believe, and rightly so, that it is a legitimate weapon to use in defense of just laws and institutions; it is not always merely a cover for exploitation or an expression of hostility and violence against others. Behavioristic utilitarianism also fails to persuade us to switch from a policy of punishing the guilty to rewarding the innocent; it is too expensive and absurdly complex to hope to administer it on a national scale, and this scheme's success—even if these obstacles could be surmounted—is doubtful. Finally, metaphysical determinism fails to be convincing in either of the forms in which its extreme claims can be asserted. Moreover, it has the disadvantage of clouding the issue of the legitimate role to be played by a valid excuse or justification for harmful conduct.

In the course of the discussion so far, we have alluded to at least two other lines of reflection that are potentially powerful enough to warrant the elimination of punishment. The first is the idea that there might not be any laws, rules of conduct, or norms of sufficient validity or importance to merit an effort to secure compliance via a system of punishment. It is important to take this objection seriously--it is a constant reminder that, were we to believe it and yet continue to practice punishment, punishment would be a weapon of immoral violence. I believe that laws against murder, assault, arson, and the like are certainly of sufficient importance to warrant an attempt to secure general compliance with them, even including liability to be punished as a disincentive. But I am willing to grant that, to the extent that the laws we enforce are not just or incapable of just enforcement, we jeopardize the moral authority with which we proceed to punish violators. Victimless crimes, political offenses, religious conformity are all examples of conduct that can be and has been made criminal; but there is little or no moral authority in my view to punish those who commit these "violations."

The other sweeping argument I would consider is this: Punishment could be eliminated if no one was eligible for it. In other words, no one would be eligible because the only way to incur liability would be by committing a crime. Without crime there cannot be, morally and logically speaking, any punishment. So crime is a necessary condition of punishment; by removing the one, you eliminate the other.

One must grant the validity of the above argument, even as we cancel its impact by each of two different reasons. First, there is little likelihood of this eventuality coming to pass. The Bible assures us that the poor we shall always have with us. The rest of human experience seems to promise us that lawbreakers we will also always have with us, so long as some people find it in their apparent interest to harm others, to cheat and steal, to bribe and lie. Though it may be logically possible to eliminate punishment by not committing any crimes, there seems to be no likelihood that this can be accomplished in this way.

The other objection to this line of reasoning is more important and somewhat less obvious. Even if we could be assured that there would be no more crimes, and therefore that no one would be punished (there would not be anything to punish!), this would not by itself be a reason for abolishing the liability to punishment in the first place. In fact, some might argue (though I am not among them) that the best way to go about ensuring that we never have to punish anyone is to threaten to punish everyone more convincingly than we now do. We have encapsulated here the visionary dream of every deterrence advocate: Make the eligibility conditions for punishment so sweeping, and the certainty and severity of the punishments so acute, that no one in his or her right mind will ever again commit a crime. Thus, the very condition sufficient to guarantee that no one is ever punished is also a condition that makes absolutely necessary the presence of a system of vigorous law enforcement, including the threat of swift and savage punishments. So, if we could eliminate punishment by eliminating crime, it might well be because we would leave intact the entire system of punishment, perpetually on the brink of application should any foolish miscreant invite its sanctions.

This suggests another line of reasoning that, were it to persuade, would provide a basis for eliminating punishment. If we believed that the threat of punishment served no useful purpose--that the doctrine of general deterrence is a complete myth--then it could be argued that punishment in the sense of making persons liable to criminal sanctions should they violate certain laws would be irrational and a waste of energy and effort.

However, we can expect to encounter two objections, which I will call respectively the Benthamite and the Kantian. The Benthamite will argue that indeed, if it were true that general deterrence is a failure across the board, then we should do away entirely with punishment. Of course, no Benthamite will grant that punishment is an utter failure as a deterrent. Such a generalization about the behavior of human beings when they are facing the threat of pain is virtually impossible for him to accept; it contradicts too much that is fundamental to his creed and conception of human nature.

The Kantian, on the other hand, may well have doubts not only about the morality of general deterrence but about its efficacy as well; but he would not in the least be perturbed by the discovery that punishments never deter. In his view, lawbreakers should be punished because they deserve it in light of their wrongdoing, not because of any dubious consequences for someone's future behavior.

There are at least two other general arguments, each of which provides a possible rationale for the elimination of punishment. One argument holds that wrongdoers should not be punished; rather, they should be forgiven. The other argument holds that, rather than being punished or forgiven; they should be tried and, if found guilty, subjected to non-punitive methods of social control. The slender thread that links these two very different arguments rests on the elimination of punishment by implicitly recommending a better alternative.

The idea that wrongdoers should not be punished but should be forgiven their wrongs may seem to be sheer lunacy. However desirable it may be for God to forgive us our sins, if society were to forgive us our crimes we would only bring upon ourselves yet more victimization. I need not dwell further on this line of objection; it is obviously what any politician or editorial writer would urge against the idea were anyone to be so naive or foolish as to broach it seriously in the first place. However, I would draw attention to two points, one of which is in its favor.

Against the idea of introducing general forgiveness, instead of punishment, for crimes, there are two facts: (a) Only the victim is truly in a position to forgive the person who has victimized him or her--and this simply cannot be done or will not be forthcoming for the worst crimes. Moreover, (b) the victim's forgiveness, without prior repentance by the criminal, seems odd or even absurd and impossible. But as things seem to stand in our world, only a small fraction of offenders are likely to repent. Quite apart from whatever effect a policy of forgiveness might have on the crime rate, these two considerations suffice to show that it is virtually impossible to hope to replace the practice of punishment with a policy of forgiveness.

In favor of forgiveness, however, there is this to be said. For parents dealing with their children, for adults in a neighborhood dealing with the children of their fellow-residents, and even in some cases of stranger-to-stranger criminal encounters, it may be possible for forgiveness to play a useful role. By forgiveness, I do not mean a victim's indifference to his victimization, nor do I mean pardoning by the authority nor any condoning of the crime. Each of the three postures or attitudes deserves to be considered in certain cases, and one or another may well be the best course of action under the circumstances. But not one of them is the same as forgiveness and should not be confused with it.

I stress a possibly expanded role for forgiveness because our morality does not consider an unforgiving nature to be a morally neutral character trait; it is rather a moral defect, albeit not as grave a defect as many others. I also believe that our society needs to give more thought to forgiveness in light of the relative small amount of harm done in some offenses, the absence of truly malicious motivation in some offenders, and above all the prospects of bringing about a reconciliation between the offender and the victim. Nevertheless, I do agree that, however plausible it might theoretically be to extend forgiveness to the fullest extent, it would be both impossible in fact and unwise in prospect to think we had made a general improvement in our moral economy if we abandoned punishment entirely.

The other alternative to be considered here is to subject convicted offenders to some sort of non-punitive policy, treatment, or method. So far as I can see, this can take at best only one form, and even this is doubtful. During the past decade, there has been considerable talk about alternatives to prison; "Tear Down the Walls" has become a battle cry for this movement. But no advocate of radical repudiation of prison has, to my knowledge, also favored, foregoing both all control over convicted offenders, and all liability to such control on the part of persons whose violation of the law makes them eligible for it. Unless both control and liability are abandoned, we have not completely eliminated punishment. At most, we would have moved away from harsh and destructive punishments and toward more lenient or productive modes of punishment. Whether one favors medical or psychological treatment, offender restitution to society and to the victims, or half-way houses, one still upholds coercive control over convicted offenders along with liability to such control; the police and the courts are still needed to establish who among the accused are eligible for such treatment or programs. At best, therefore, we can regard these alternatives as quasi-punitive regimens, since their aim is not to impose a harsh environment on convicted offenders but to produce some good either in the offenders or for others by means of the offenders' actions.

I have argued for the view that reform, restitution, and other alternatives to imprisonment are not true alternatives to punishment because its distinctively coercive aspects remain in place. (This is also evident from the fact that the threat of imprisonment is typically used to support treatment and restitution insofar as non-compliance with restitution requirements is likely to put the offender into prison.)

Is there, then, any truly non-punitive alternative to punitive types of punishment? As far as I know, the only possibility is denunciation, verbal castigation. The idea was sketched briefly a few years ago by Hyman Gross in his valuable treatise, A Theory of Criminal Justice. He called it a system of "emphatic condemnation," and spelled it out as follows:

> Suppose a public registry of convictions were established, and with suitable publicity and solemnity entries were made of each crime and its perpetrator....For many...persons, public humiliation and loss of reputation would result from their registration, and might even equal in condemnation what they would suffer by imprisonment. (p. 406)

We might imagine any of several variations on such a scheme, ranging from mandatory publication of the names of all such offenders in the daily newspapers, to subjecting the male-factors to a judge's lengthy denunciatory and admonitory speeches in the courtroom with duration depending on the gravity of the crimes committed.

Leaving aside the adequacy with which such methods might affect the future conduct of these offenders or reduce (or, more likely, increase) the incidence of crime, we need to determine whether emphatic denunciation qualifies as a true alternative to punishment. The argument for it seems to rest entirely on the idea that the disabling and deprivatory effects of punishments are not produced, nor are they intended to be produced, by such non-punitive methods. If--as Hobbes, Bentham, and most of their successors thought--a punishment is a punishment only if it causes "pain" or some other manifest deprivation, then, it is doubtful whether emphatic denunciation is a punishment. On the other hand, however, there is the argument that judicial denunciation is a coercively enforced practice. It is a <u>sentence</u>, and as such, it <u>is</u> a punishment, regardless of what we choose to call it and however mild, tolerable, of even desirable it may be.

It is not easy to resolve this dispute. We might say that the policy of emphatic condemnation or denunciation presents a true borderline case coming as close as anything can to constituting a non-punitive practice while retaining all or almost all the features of punitive policies.

If you are willing to grant this much, then you can go on to ask whether it is not only possible, but also desirable, to eliminate punishment in favor of this non-punitive alternative. Probably most of those who contemplate it are inclined to deny both the possibility and desirability of such a non-punitive policy. Why, they would ask, would it be rational to supplant punishment by emphatic denunciation if it has already been conceded (as I have done earlier in this discussion) that (a) just laws exist, (b) it is permissible to use coercive force and the threat thereof to reduce non-compliance with such laws, and (c) the use of such force does in fact contribute toward the reduction of non-compliance. While much can be said for the non-punitive practice of denunciation (in conjunction, no doubt, with suitable explanations and admonitions) as a form of moral education, it seems singularly unconvincing to argue in favor of dealing with some offenders--hardened recidivists, especially convicted adult offenders guilty of the worst crimes against the person--by such relatively lenient methods.

So far, we have explored a series of alternative schemes in the hope that each one, taken in isolation, might serve as a basis for eliminating punishment. But none of these methods will bear such weight.

The opponents of punishment need not despair entirely. Even if none of these considerations alone suffices to eliminate punishment, it may well be that some combination of them will work. I find this an unlikely possibility. While it may be true, and I believe it is, that the extent of punishment in society can be reduced through several of the strategies outlined so far, the practice of punishment itself cannot be--and should not be-- entirely eliminated. The same can be said about imprisonment: Its role can be reduced, but it cannot be eliminated as long as it is the sole effective general method of incapacitation short of unacceptably barbaric practices such as maiming and death.

My conclusion, then, is that we cannot eliminate punishment; and if we do so, it is at our moral peril. To be more precise, either it is impossible to eliminate all vestiges of punishment, including the liability thereto, or it is inadvisable because the alternatives are morally worse than the manifestations of punishment.

Now that I have reached my conclusion, you may be equally ready to reach yours, to the effect that, just as you feared, I have done nothing more than reinvent the wheel. I have, that is, done no more than show us what everyone already knew and what no one challenged, viz, that we cannot get along in the world without punishment. Not quite. Before we can be certain that punishment is justified, we have to be sure that the particular kind of punishment is justified for the offense at issue; and we have to be guaranteed that society can insure, within fair limits, that the guilty get all and only what they deserve. And we cannot do that merely by showing that we are unable to adopt policies that would effectively eliminate punishment. Instead, we have to proceed with a new set of arguments and theories to show, as I have indicated, (a) what punishment offenders deserve, given their offenses, and (b) that we can in fact generally give them what they deserve. Nothing I have said so far gives us any reasonable assurance that both of these can be determined.

This is not the occasion to pursue this new and large topic. It is perhaps enough to have seen, as I think we have, that understanding the ideal and the actual role of punishment in our lives, and in any just society, is an enormously complex task that calls on all our talents as jurists, psychologists, educators, public-spirited citizens, moral theorists, and conceptual analysts. I have hopefully made some contribution to that understanding.

NOTES

1.   Hyman Gross, <u>A Theory of Criminal Justice</u> (New York: Oxford University Press, 1979).

Part IV: U.S. Foreign and National Security Policy:

The American Democracy in the Global Community

A. The Executive Branch:

U.S. Foreign and National Security Policy

Chair: Duncan Clarke. The American University

Presentation by: Sven Groennings, Director, Fund the for
Improvement of Post-secondary Education

Respondents: Richard T. Arndt, U.S. Information Agency
Robert Beckman, School of International Service,
The American Univeristy
Charles W. Maynes, Editor, Foreign Policy

Rapporteur: Joseph G. Bock, School of International Service,
The American University

THE EXECUTIVE BRANCH

AND

U.S. FOREIGN AND NATIONAL SECURITY POLICY

Joseph Bock

An "International Education Triad"

Sven Groenning's presentation focuses on the complementary roles of the federal government and universities in international education. According to Groennings, the question of whether the federal government and the nation's institutions of higher learning should be partners in international education was "settled affirmatively long ago." This relationship developed during the postwar period when the United States assumed a "world leadership role"--a role for which military capabilities, by themselves, were judged to be inadequate. With the coming of the nuclear age, the United States rapidly developed both its military and communications technologies. Yet if communications technologies improved more rapidly than our knowledge of other countries, misperceptions could result. These might endanger national security by fostering myopic public opinion, ill-informed foreign policy decisions, and, ultimately, an over-reliance on the military.

Groennings argues that this federal government-university relationship in international education is mutually beneficial: Without federal support, universities would be unlikely to provide area studies programs to educate specialists about little-known, but strategically important, geographical regions. And international education is an intrinsic part of the university's mission, since its function is to "probe and teach about the universe of phenomena and ideas."

The future prospects for this government-university relationship in international education are bright, according to Groennings, who maintains that "international education is one of the current areas of major innovative vision and thrust of the nation's campuses." To support this claim, he cites growing university curricula in international economics and business; a move from written to oral competency in foreign language instruction; and an increase in international affairs courses for secondary school teachers and liberal arts students. On the other hand, there are signs that this relationship may be threatened by contemporary developments. For instance, Groennings points out, junior faculty have less international experience than their predecessors, and many are reluctant to participate in international exchange programs due to financial considerations and the sacrifice involved for working spouses.

Groennings offers a parallel (for heuristic purposes) between the strategic nuclear triad and the "triad of programs involving educators." Groenning's juxtaposition of U.S. air-launched, sea-based, and ground-based strategic weapons systems with three core education programs--language and area studies, international exchange (the Fulbright Program), and technical and development assistance[1]--is intended to highlight different "triad missions." Whereas the nuclear triad deters through fear, the international education triad "builds knowledge, contacts, respect, admiration, and sympathy." His argument is that the education triad, like the nuclear triad, should be seen as an integral part of national security policy.

An understanding of this proposed triad in national security terms requires an international, not national, perspective. Only one of the three programs within the triad--language and area studies--is designed to improve the expertise necessary for U.S. citizens to assume diplomatic and other foreign affairs responsibilities. This program was originated in 1958 to develop "trained manpower of sufficient quality and quantity to meet the national defense needs of the United States."[2] But, whereas this "first leg" of the international education triad was clearly developed as a national program, the "second leg"--the Fulbright Program--has been international since its inception. The United States is neither the sole[3] supporter of nor the only host government in the Program. Likewise, the "third leg" of the triad--technical and development assistance--has had an international focus. Its mission has been to strengthen the ability of U.S. agricultural universities to help the rural poor of developing countries. Each leg of this international education triad, then, has a different emphasis. Yet all legs relate to national security insofar as skilled diplomats, increased scientific knowledge, and diminished world poverty reduce the probability of war.

Perhaps the greatest utility of a presentation depicting these three educational programs as a triad is that it illuminates how they complement one another, although in practice there is a lack of program integration. For instance, as Groennings points out, there continues to be a shortage of technically skilled personnel who also have language and area studies preparation.

Groennings charges the federal government with responsibility for this lack of program coordination. He argues that whereas universities are inclined to "view the various aspects of international education as one administrative domain," the federal government "divides its jurisdictions across different congressional committees and administrative agencies." So, for each program, questions should be asked about: (1) How one program can support the other and (2) What would be the appropriate timing of program emphasis based on the recognition that skill development is cumulative? In addition, Groennings's program-specific questions have two recurring themes: the difficulty of prioritizing geographical foci and the lack of tangible indicators by which to measure program effectiveness.

In summary, Groennings argues that integration of these three programs must be fostered. In so doing, the mutually beneficial federal government-university relationship will better prepare us for a "world of change" and will more effectively build "positive, longterm relationships" among nations. Only if this relationship is cultivated will there be a "second triad" to provide for the national security by enhancing understanding, rather than fostering fear, between nations. And, finally, he emphasized that there are many questions yet unanswered.

Panel Discussion

The panel discussants were uneasy with the suggested conceptual interrelationship between the three educational programs and the strategic nuclear triad. Throughout the discussion, it was emphasized that it is extremely difficult to identify the precise relationship between international education programs and national security. Nonetheless, the "softness" of the subject matter did not mean that it was unimportant. Moreover, there has been virtually no research on the relationship between these education programs and the promotion of U.S. national security interests.

Groennings's juxtaposition of two triads also provoked a discussion about the potential danger of seeking funds for international education programs by cloaking them in "militaristic" terms. For instance, one comment was that "selling the right program with the wrong language can affect its self-definition, not to mention its perception abroad." Hence, the panel identified a problematic aspect of the joint federal government-university role in international education. On the one hand, the more persuasive educators can be about the ways in which their programs enhance the national security, the more funding they are liable to receive. On the other hand, defining such programs in terms of national security increases the likelihood that they will be misunderstood by participating foreign countries.

A great deal more research in this broad area is necessary. Absent such research, these education programs are funded on the basis of executive and legislative intuitive judgements, prodded by bureaucratic advocacy. Presently, advocates of international education programs have only national security arguments with which to garner support, for they lack a solid research base on which to argue that education enhances peace.

Although little research exists on the impact of these programs, the panel nonetheless offered its own judgments about them. These judgments were virtually unanimous:

* The lack of coordination among international education programs, and between these programs and other elements of foreign policy, is part of a larger problem-- the lack of integration in U.S. national security policy in general. Neither the international education programs nor national security policy have clear objectives or comprehensive planning. This can, and does, lead to an over-reliance on military solutions to foreign policy problems.

* The relationship between the federal government and universities in funding and implementing international education programs, though mutually beneficial, has been less cooperative than it could be. Groennings's portrayal of this relationship was, perhaps, somewhat overly optimistic.

* The United States continues to have difficulty in training and selecting a cadre of foreign area specialists. There is neither an identifiable body of training curricula nor a refined procedure by which diplomats are selected.

* There seems to be a trend toward "parochialism" in U.S. society. This might lead to protectionism and to a more isolationist foreign policy. Although this tendency would be difficult to measure, there is undoubtedly a strong need for international education programs to cultivate an awareness of the growing interdependencies of the modern world.

* Public confidence in government has declined.

Policy Prescriptions

On the basis of the problems identified by the panel, the following present policy prescriptions for the federal government and universities:

* As with foreign policy in general, the three legs of the international education triad--the international exchange program, technical and development assistance, and foreign language and area studies programs--should be more vigorously coordinated so

-184-

that they better complement one another. For this purpose, a high-level coordinating committee should be established within the Department of Education.

* Research on the relationship between international education programs and national security should be funded by the government, but conducted by a commission whose members do not have a self-interest in the results. This research should focus on how international education programs affect public attitudes about foreign countries and how those attitudes might affect U.S. decision-makers. And, if possible, it should compare the perceptions of international education with those who have a substantial background in such education.

* A joint attempt by the State Department and universities should be made to identify a core curriculum for diplomatic training. The foreign service entrance exam should at least test this body of knowledge. One university organization which the State Department could consult is the Association of Professional Schools in International Affairs (APSIA).

* The Department of Education should seriously consider making it mandatory that accredited colleges and universities include courses in international affairs and that teacher certification be partly contingent on having taken such courses.

* In order to restore public confidence in government, comprehensive foreign policy planning will be necessary. Only with such planning will it be possible to offer diplomatic solutions to international political problems while reserving the military instrument of policy exclusively as the last resort.

NOTES

1. These programs are administered, respectively, by universities, the United States Information Agency (USIA), and the Agency for International Development (AID) and the Peace Corps.

2. The original bill, Title VI of the National Defense Education Act, was modified in 1980 under Title VI of the Higher Education Act.

3. Groennings pointed out that 28 countries share the cost of the program and that now close to 120 countries participate in the exchange of scholars.

THE AMERICAN DEMOCRACY IN THE GLOBAL COMMUNITY:

THE SECOND TRIAD[1]

Sven Groennings

One of the characteristics of the American democracy in the world community is that it speaks with many voices, not all of which emanate from Congress. Executive agencies implement policy not by bureaucratic action alone, but also by cooperative arrangements with the private sector, which is a deep reserve of American ingenuity. I will focus on the linkages between federal government and university roles in international education in light of national security considerations.

The issue of whether the federal government and institutions of higher education should be partners in international education was settled affirmatively long ago. There has been a significant and multi-dimensional postwar departure from the past, with new federal-university partnerships in scientific research and in access to postsecondary education. The programmatic dimensions of the relationship have been repeatedly renewed by Congressional reauthorization, with the support of the national security and higher education communities. Most of the time the key issues have concerned broad refinements, shifting emphases within categories, and the reconciliation of differences in federal and university perspectives.

The need for federal programs flowed from the extraordinarily changed situation following World War II; the assumption of an American world leadership role; the development of global confrontation and ideological competition; the creation of new nation-states in the wake of decolonization; the growing importance of international economic relationships; the advent of instantaneous mass communications and public diplomacy; the increasing complexity of relationships with other countries. These were changes of new dimensions, and they were dangerous. They brought challenges in the realms of ideas and relationships. As a result, national security would require more than military capability, which alone could not build the desired peace and whose use would be a last resort.

We evolved a deterrence theory and capability based on a triad of nuclear delivery systems: land-based, sea-based and airborne. But international understanding also had to be improved; communication had become rapid while knowledge remained shallow. And misperception could be harmful; it was a factor in the outbreak of World War I, Hitler's assumptions, the Japanese decision at Pearl Harbor, and there were signs that it might cause trouble in Asia, the Middle East, Latin America, indeed globally.

To meet new national interests, the federal government created a triad of programs involving educators: the Fulbright Program of international exchange to build knowledge, understanding, and professional and institutional linkages, now administered by the U.S. Information Agency; technical and development assistance programs, administered by the Agency for International Development (AID) and the Peace Corps; and the campus-based foreign language and area study programs, authorized first under Title VI of the National Defense Education Act (NDEA) and now under Title VI of the Higher Education Act and administered by the Department of Education, to develop U.S. expertise in world affairs.

As the first triad aims at deterrence, this second triad aims at improving our foreign relations by deepening our understanding of others and establishing cooperative and friendly relations with other nations. These two triads are postwar structures, but there are precedents. Theodore Roosevelt established our first international exchange program, the Boxer Indemnity Fund, with China. In his inaugural address, in the spirit of the "good neighbor," Herbert Hoover called for international exchange; and Franklin Roosevelt began a program in Latin America, bringing the young Nelson Rockefeller to Washington to head it.

The major structures of international exchange followed the war, with new initiatives or programmatic emphases by both Republican and Democratic Presidents. The Truman Administration launched the Point Four Program for technical assistance, the Fulbright Program, which originally operated on surplus currencies, and authorized federal funds to implement the Smith-Mundt Act. The Eisenhower Administration developed the NDEA, beginning the Title VI programs. The Kennedy era added the Peace Corps and the Fulbright-Hays Act, which expanded the Fulbright Program. Lyndon Johnson initiated the ill-fated International Education Act, which died during the Vietnam era, but was nonetheless an initiative. The Nixon-Ford years witnessed improvements in the Fulbright Program's management and the designation of Title XII universities associated with the new Board for International Food and Agricultural Development. President Carter established the National Commission on Foreign Language and International Studies and restructured the U.S. Information Agency to include educational affairs. The Reagan Administration has created the International Youth Exchange Initiative.

The rhetoric has changed from time to time. In the exchange field, for example, the context changed from "good eighbor" to "cold war crusade" to "interdependence." But nternational education was always considered <u>de facto</u> an mportant foreign policy instrument. The exchange programs, or example, are viewed as adding credence to our policy of uilding peace while serving to project the image of an open ociety which includes not only governmental contacts, but also irect people-to-people contacts. These programs are thus the ther half of our national security picture, the second triad imed at establishing a foundation for peace.

The University as Partner

This broad policy context, which emphasized international elationships, called for the involvement of the universities. Any artnerships, of course, would have to meet not only federal eeds, but also the university's own concerns for autonomy and cademic values.

There were bases for a natural partnership--international nvolvement is basic to the very idea of a university. A niversity must reach out to the rest of the world, because its unction is to probe and teach about the universe of phenomena nd ideas. Indeed, America's universities have had worldwide nfluence in the development of knowledge and curricula. They ave served as models of educational opportunity and excellence. They have been a magnet to foreigners, some 350,000 of whom re studying in the United States now. Since 1949 more than wo million students from developing countries have studied ere, and currently nearly half the students in the world who re studying outside their own country are studying in the U.S.

This interchange has of course, been a two-way street. The ery idea of the American research university followed the German model. Many of our universities' Nobel Prize winners ame from abroad to join our faculties. Some of our brightest cademics and public servants were Rhodes Scholars, including Senator Fulbright, whose inspiration for the American exchange rogram stemmed from that experience. The numerous ntellectuals who fled to this country from Nazi Germany gave ew directions to our disciplines.

From a national well as a university perspective, the values epresented by our institutions are fundamentally important: reedom of thought, of inquiry, of communication and of ssociation. They symbolize the universal interest in human ights. No other American institutions convey these values more ffectively, and none are more closely linked to foreign spirations for a better life.

The American university, however, was not very nternational in either focus or population before World War II. It has needed to expand its international scope, just as the American government has had to do so. While the University has independently proceeded in this direction, the federal government has helped it to develop its specialized capabilities, including many that would be absent without federal support, such as Soviet Asian language capabilities.

Universities continue to seek federal support for such specialized fields of activity. The broadest new proposal is from Michael Sovern, President of Columbia University, whose W. Averell Harriman Institute for Advanced Study of the Soviet Union was recently endowed by a handsome gift. Sovern devoted his entire 1982-1983 President's Annual Report to international studies at Columbia and in the nation. He states that "America should call upon her great universities in far greater measure to help advance world security and understanding" and calls for the establishment of a National Endowment for International Studies.[2]

Paradigm Shift and Paradox

The universities are encountering harder times today than in the recent past. In these years of financial difficulties, are the campuses turning inward? Does international education have any momentum? Here we encounter both paradigm shift and paradox. On one level--from my position with the Fund for the Improvement of Postsecondary Education--it is evident that international education is an area of major innovative vision and thrust on the nation's campuses. There are four major and broadly encompassing beachheads of change:

* First, the universities, prodded by the new accreditation standards of the American Academy of Collegiate Schools of Business, are beginning--albeit slowly--to move toward expanding the understanding of business students. This includes teaching about international economics, finance, marketing and export administration, as well as worldwide business conditions and possibilities, viewed in the light of politics, labor movements, and cultures. There is an increasing number of models of curricular development, which will help to prepare the U.S. for increased corporate participation in export-related activity. This in turn will hopefully lead to a reduction in the country's enormous and growing trade deficits.

* Second, whereas our foreign language learning has been tied to written and literary traditions, oral proficiency testing is on the near horizon, as are language study for special uses, like business, and the utilization of new learning technologies. The thrust is toward practical communicative competence. People will be learning a foreign language as a skill, with the measurement of achievement moving from a criterion based on semesters

assed to one determined by proficiency. Predictably, the
stablishment of such a system will have catalytic effects on
urricular development, evaluation, and on the design of
eaching materials. Moreover, this development may spur new
ssessment approaches in other fields.

* Third, while not one precollegiate teacher in twenty has
aken any international, comparative, or inter-cultural courses
n route to certification, the purpose of education is increasingly
understood to be the preparation of students to cope in today's
world. Little can be more predictable than the rapidly growing
mpact of the rest of the world on today's teenagers, who will be
nly in their early thirties as we enter the next century.
everal leading schools of education are consequently developing
lans to increase the international content of teacher education.

* Fourth, whereas the liberal arts curriculum traditionally
as offered courses in international affairs, curricula are now
ncorporating international education more than ever before. The
remise is that developments beyond our borders will affect most
merican lives and that global perspectives are needed. It is
pparent that internationalization is attractive to students
ecause it enhances the relevance of education to their lives. It
s appealing to the faculty as it revitalizes their courses. And
nstitutions welcome internationalization because it provides
urricular coherence, a larger sense of direction, and a potential
nkage between the liberal arts colleges and the professional
chools.

These changes add up to a broad agenda for development
nd to a paradigmatic change for international education: toward
verall utility and general education, beyond elitism and the
roduction of experts. But paradoxically, there are signs in
ur colleges and universities that the junior faculty will have
ess international experience than does the generation it will be
eplacing. The overseas experiences, which in large part
parked campus developments, are no longer so common.
oundations send fewer people abroad. Junior faculty members
re reluctant to become Fulbright scholars or to work abroad
hen this entails sacrifices for working spouses; and there is
eal concern that the positions of those absent and untenured
ight be especially insecure in a tight and economizing academic
arket. Perhaps there is less fervor among the junior faculty
han among those who sought to build a different, better world
fter World War II. There is hard evidence, for example, that
he cadre of university scientists who were involved in AID's
evelopment programs in the 1950s and 1960s is approaching
etirement age and is not being replaced. So there are signs of
eparochialization at the very time our society is moving
orward.

THE TRIAD

In the context of the changing American university, we come to the triad of federal programs at the nexus of foreign affairs and education: foreign language and area studies; international exchange; and technical and developmental assistance. The elements of the triad have distinct structures and histories, yet at their best they are mutually reinforcing and can contribute to the advancement of education and our foreign affairs capabilities. Although the issues involved are different, they are all essentially generic and therefore enduring. In each case they are the kind of implementational issues associated with the Executive agencies more than with the Congress.

Title VI

The core of any university's capability for service to the foreign affairs community is the expertise of its faculty, particularly in foreign language area studies. The original Title VI premise, as stated in 1958, is that the nation needs "trained manpower of sufficient quality and quantity to meet the national defense needs of the United States." [3]

Title VI provides support for approximately 90 centers, funded and renewed on a competitive basis within a budget framework of arount $20 million in most recent years. The majority of the centers focus on world areas. While the centers are predominantly supported by the universities, not the federal government, it was typically the federal spark--and that of the foundations--that led to their establishment. Federal support has provided status, the margin of excellence, and the drawing power for other funding, while the Foreign Language and Area Studies (FLAS) fellowships have attracted the top students.

The typical student today, after his or her undergraduate years, gains foreign language competence and experience overseas, and undertakes an interdisciplinary program at the center while earning a Ph.D. in an academic discipline. The graduates are employed mainly by the foreign affairs community, the national security agencies, international broadcasting services, business, and by the universities, where they undertake analytic work, teach, and are available for consultation. Frequently, when dramatic events occur abroad, the centers' personnel are called upon to provide background information to the press, educational institutions, and to the government.

Title VI is the only Department of Education program having a direct and Congressionally-defined national security rationale. In 1980 the Congress moved the authorization from the National Defense Education Act to the Higher Education Act. In doing so, while removing "defense" from the title, Congress reaffirmed the national security rationale; but it also indicated that it was time for the international dimension to be viewed as an integral part of federal higher education legislation rather than as an autonomous Act. It also added Part B, a small dollar-for-dollar matching program to help prepare people for export-related activities. Title VI has consequently offered a bright prospect for creativity and reinvigoration of programs traditionally separated on campuses, bringing international economic and business perspectives into juxtaposition with the old NDEA programs. It has added an economic rationale to that of national security, and the program has gained a broader constituency and purpose.

As one looks back across the years, one finds the issues within the Title VI category fundamentally the same. These are:

* How many people are needed in which categories? For federal needs or broader needs? What, other than the previous year's base, will serve as a basis for calculation? How does one define geographic sufficiency?

* What particular competencies are needed, for what purposes, and at what levels--foreign language; country or topical expertise; practical competencies such as those related to exporting? Combined competencies? Given that there will be attrition of skills, how do we maintain and upgrade the skills of trained people? Is part of the problem how to match their skills to relevant employment?

* What should be the division of emphasis between foreign language and area studies? Between sharp, in-depth focus versus breadth? Between support for the center and for student fellowships; and between predoctoral and postdoctoral fellows? Between national versus regional centers; and between supporting flagship institutions and encouraging the participation of other postsecondary institutions?

* To what extent should Title VI centers undertake outreach, diffusing international knowledge? What about citizen or layman competencies--the need for informed citizens? Everyone in society should have such exposure; should the federal government facilitate this and, if so, how?

International Exchange

Whereas the campus-based Title VI programs focus on international issues and the promotion of needed competencies, the Fulbright Program is in a sense far broader, having expanded to include 120 countries and spanning the full range of academic disciplines. It is an instrument of our public diplomacy and indeed of the diplomacy of the participating countries. It has enabled more than 50,000 Americans to study and teach abroad and more than 97,000 foreigners to study and teach in this country. It now involves 5,000 American and foreign citizens annually, in all categories of exchange.

The Fulbright Program is the largest of USIA's educational and cultural exchange programs. Two-thirds of USIA's budget, nearly $93 million in FY-1984, supports the Fulbright Program. Most of the remainder supports international visitor programs, performances, and lectures.

In diplomacy, international exchange promotes understanding. It was important after World War II to reach out to wartime enemies as well as allies--including German youth. As in the case of "ping-pong" diplomacy with China, exchange sometimes preceded diplomatic relations and serves as a communications link even when there are no formal diplomatic relations. Finland's President Kekkonen praised the Fulbright Program for its contributions to his country's renewal after the War. Third World countries welcome the Program's potential for developing capabilities and contacts. It seems that nearly all countries seek the status associated with the Fulbright Program and would consider it a diplomatic affront if they were dropped. The age of interdependence, in which more decisions will be made internationally within more substantive areas, provides a revitalized rational for exchange--creating trust and cooperation among those who directly or indirectly will shape future decisions. This rationale has been reinforced by the worldwide revolution in access to higher education -- while postsecondary enrollment within the United States has doubled in the last fifteen years, it has expanded even more rapidly in many other countries, profoundly changing the nature of communications in those countries.

The Fulbright Program is important because it represents high quality communication: in-depth, personal, involving dialogue, objective, a builder of expertise and longterm professional and institutional relationships. It underscores mutuality: we teach and we learn, and of course we are more credible in our own classrooms when we actually have seen. It sacrifices no values associated with the university, while it enlarges the institutional capability and scope of the university. We gain knowledge, and not only about other societies. For example, not long ago two-thirds of the world's scientific programs were conducted in America; now, two-thirds are abroad. On a worldwide scale there has never been an exchange program more helpful than the Fulbright Program in promoting accurate perception, analysis, and education.

In 43 participating countries, responsibility for program operations belongs to binational commissions established by executive agreements between the United States and the host country. These commissions also provide counseling services to students interested in studying in the United States. Twenty-eight countries share the Program's cost, together contributing some $10 million plus indirect subsidies. Our Board of Foreign Scholarships (BFS) establishes the broad policy guidelines. Under contract with USIA, several private organizations serve as implementing agencies and select the exchanges. These organizations include, among others, the Institute of International Education; the Council for International Exchange of Scholars, which is affiliated with the American Council on Education; for the Soviet Union and Eastern European countries, the International Research and Exchanges Board of the American Council of Learned Societies; and the Hubert H. Humphrey North-South Fellowship Program for mid-career professionals from developing countries.

The strength of support for the program was demonstrated when a 66% reduction in educational and cultural exchanges was proposed for FY-1982. Senate testimony, including that of former Fulbrighter Dr. Hildegard Hamm-Bruecher, State Secretary of the German Foreign Ministry, resulted in the Pell Amendment to USIA's FY-1983 authorization. This legislation doubled, through annual increases, the budget for exchanges. There is clearly a continuing commitment to educational and cultural exchange programs, all of which--including Fulbright Awards--come under the same legislative appropriation.

A new initiative has been proposed. In its report to President Reagan, the National Bipartisan Commission on Central America, chaired by Henry Kissinger, recommended the creation of a national scholarship program to bring as many as 10,000 students from Caribbean and Latin American countries to the U.S. in order to help counter Soviet and Cuban influence in this region. Questions of whether the program should be reciprocal and/or entirely at the university level are under consideration.

Finally, there are some recurrent issues in international exchange which in all likelihood will also surface in the future:

* What should be the relationship of educational and cultural programs to broader foreign policy considerations? Should the programs constitute an element of stability or of diplomatic leadership? Can constituency support and effectiveness be maintained if the programs are viewed as politicized?

* Do we consider ourselves as competing with the Soviet Union, which now funds nearly as many exchanges with Latin

America alone as we do with the entire world? How do we add to the calculation the overwhelming proportion of foreign students in this country without federal support?

* How should we determine the relative emphasis upon the various components of educational and cultural programs or various audiences? For example, what emphasis should be placed on exchange as opposed to establishing institutions like the American Studies Center in Warsaw? On cultural performances as opposed to fine arts exhibits? On short-term topical lecturers rather than scholars in residence?

* Which geographic areas and countries should receive what kinds of programs? Should overall program resources be realigned to reflect the growing importance of developing countries? How can the latter be accomplished, given our relationships with the many "developed" countries where we share binational commissions? Conversly, how can we avoid program cuts that do not deeply affect developing countries? How do we decide to establish "a presence" rather than "a concentration" in a particular country? What weight do we place upon securing appointments for social scientists in Eastern Europe and what trade-offs are to be negotiated? What emphasis should be placed upon academic exchange as opposed to exchange of other professionals, such as journalists or emerging political leaders, who are eligible for the International Visitors Program?

* What should be the mix of American faculty and students going abroad and foreign scholars coming to the United States? How can any particular country attract the best candidates and assure program prestige?

* At what levels should academic appointments be made-- including what proportions of senior lecturers, research scholars, doctoral candidates, and teachers? How does one make these judgments in light of maintaining program quality and prestige? What stipends are required to attract appropriate candidates?

* How can the Fulbright experience be made optimal for the scholar and most effective for the program? Should scholars be made available to a region or to a single university? What should be the length of stay? How do we overcome foreign language deficiencies among applicarts, U.S. and foreign, so that we can more satisfactorily match candidates with requests by countries for people in certain fields?

* How can the federal government best complement private sector programs, especially in youth exchange?

* How is program effectiveness to be evaluated?

* Can we devise new methods of assuring financial support, such as economic development[4] soft currency loan repayments or private sector overseas funds?

Development Assistance

The third element of the triad is development assistance, involving the universities in contractual relationships to undertake projects in developing countries for AID.

Activities began after President Truman in his inaugural address promised to share technological knowledge with developing nations. John Hannah, then President of the National Association of State Universities and Land-Grant Colleges, said his institutions would help this effort. These universities spearheaded our own agricultural development, and they have remained the primary AID contract universities.

The early focus was on foreign institutional capabilities, the best-known example of which was India. In 1949, India's University Education Commission recommended the establishment of a new system of rural universities which would provide education aimed at production, a major conceptual departure from tradition. In a twenty year period six American universities, coordinated through a Council of United States Universities for Rural Development in India and collaborating with the Ford and Rockefeller Foundations, helped to establish the first nine agricultural universities in India. The American universities contributed 700 man years by 300 staff members, and received more than 1,000 Indian faculty members and graduate students on their U.S. campuses. In India, they aided in the development of new varieties of rice, wheat, and cotton, and helped many new programs.

The Vietnam experience contributed to a reconceptualization of foreign exchange. In 1973 Congress provided the "New Directions" mandate, directed at the very poorest regions and emphasizing crop production and resources productivity. The new plan withdrew support for building dams, roads, institutions, and for developing human capital and indigenous institutional capacity--the activities best suited to university action.

The "New Directions" mandate produced a reaction. A major upgrading of the university role began in 1975 with the addition of Title XII, "Famine Relief and Freedom from Hunger," to the Foreign Assistance Act of 1961. Title XII pulls together many of the university-related components of AID's programs. It is popular with the universities because of its conceptual and operational changes: It engages them in baseline studies of host country capacities and needs, so that assignments can be analyzed in light of the complete develpment of educational and human resources. It also involves pre-selection of the implementing university, which then designs the project collaboratively with the host country. The Act provides assistance to our universities in expanding their international research and institutional capacities as part of development assistance in agriculture. The program includes subsidies for small and minority institutions so that AID can draw upon a broader range of resources; and it funds longterm cooperative research between American and foreign institutions on food production, distribution, storage, marketing and consumption. A very active Board for International Food and Agricultural Development (BIFAD) advises AID's Director.

The fact remains, however, that the universities have a limited capability to respond to AID program needs. As well as structural barriers, there are shortages of technical skills and in language and area studies preparation, which are university shortcomings in the partnership. Most of the enduring issues are partnership considerations:

* The key question deals with how this country can more systematically mobilize U.S. agricultural universities on behalf of the rural poor in developing countries?

* What can AID--which sometimes has to operate in the context of a volatile official relationship between the U.S. and particular countries--do to increase and strengthen incentives for deeper commitment and more systematic involvement by universities? Can AID make longterm commitments to projects and offer sufficient financial compensation for career detours and the lack of glamour in some posts?

* How and to what degree should AID emphasize the institution-building programs and baseline studies that are most attractive for university participation?

* What can the universities do to make overseas activity an integral part of university life, work, and responsibilities? More specifically, what can the universities do to ease the internal constraints on participation caused by their own appointment, promotion, and tenure policies? How will they evaluate performance in an international setting for promotion and tenure purposes?

* How can the universities make available the number of personnel needed for overseas assignments while maintaining the quality of their on-campus teaching staff?

* What can be done to overcome deficiencies in the agricultural universities' ability to respond to AID program needs? Problems include inadequacies in foreign language skills, the lack of area and cultural understanding, the lag in updating and revitalizing professional preparation programs on third world development.

 * There is also a state government issue: To what extent should and can the international aspect of public service be a function of state land-grant universities?

 * How can we assure the stability of the AID-university relationship, given the basic problem of reconciling AID "country plan" objectives with a university's own concerns? To what extent should faculty experts be involved in project design and modification?

 * As some countries begin to need collaborative relationships more than unilateral aid, how can AID respond? What mechanisms for continuing relationsips might be developed with AID "graduate" countries no longer receiving aid, such as Brazil, Mexico, Venezuela, Nigeria, Taiwan, and Korea? Can experts from their universities and ours work jointly on problems in other countries? Can we cooperate with other providers of aid?

Triad Dimensions

AID programs receive the largest appropriations of any federal-university international programs, adding up to some $250 million per year within Title XII and perhaps as much as $100 million in other AID areas. The triad as a whole involves at least $400 million annually.

While my framework is limited to the "Big Three" sectors of the federal-university international relationship, there are several other federal programs that include international education and involve or influence universities. The staff of the Foreign Service Institute and the Defense Language Institute are part of the professional international studies community and have greatly influenced the study of foreign languages and proficiency assessment.

There is also the National Science Foundation Act, which involves approximately 100 universities in foreign interchange. And there is the $108 million budget for the Peace Corps, whose 100,000 volunteers have spent more than 65,000 classroom work years in developing countries. The Peace Corps is not particularly involved with universities, although some training occurs on campuses.

Finally, there are the two massive learning programs associated with the military: the International Military Education and Training Program, which since 1950 has provided training for more than 500,000 foreign military personnel in the U.S. and abroad; and in-service (non-ROTC) tuition assistance programs affecting 650,000 enrollments in several hundred colleges and universities here and overseas.

Congruence of Direction

Universities are more inclined than the federal government to view the various aspects of international education as one administrative domain, whereas for reasons of history and policy the federal government divides its jurisdiction into different Congressional committees and administrative agencies. Nevertheless, it has become desirable on campuses to have a central and holistic view of the triad elements, as well as of study-abroad programs, overseas fundraising, and arrangements for foreign students, whose presence in this country raises still other issues of federal policy. Also, international programs increasingly encompass component departments and colleges: business schools, schools of education, and colleges of arts and sciences, agriculture, and health, among others. Universities now commonly discuss the appointment of deans or vice presidents for international affairs to serve as a focus for the commitment, energies, and priorities of the institutions.

The international dimension on campuses will expand with the growth of technology, which already has made the world "smaller." It is in technology that economic growth is most prominent and international competition the greatest. It may well be this international development that will enable us to bridge two cultures, the scientific/technological and the liberal arts.

The federal involvement with the academic community in the international domain will continue, to the extent that earlier assumptions continue to be considered valid considerations. In summary, these have been:

First, that foreign policy concerns are of fundamental and growing importance and involve increasingly complex relationships with other countries.

Second, that our national security requires special expertise.

Third, that our foreign policy objectives will include building respect, trust, and enduring cooperative relationships; and that achievement of these objectives will require in-depth international communications as part of our public diplomacy; and

Fourth, that educational institutions play a crucially important role, not only in preparing this country for a world of change, but also in communicating with the rest of the world and generating the kinds of positive, longterm relationships that are part of our foreign policy objectives.

No issue is likely to be more important in the next few decades than national security. We can expect to face two kinds of questions: How to assure deterrence and how to improve our foreign relations. While each area has its triad, it is in the latter that the university can have a very positive impact on the world.

NOTES

1.   Originally published as a part of the ITT Key Issues Lecture Series in International Education: The Unfinished Agenda, editors William C. Olson and Llewellyn Howell. Copyright 1984 by White River Press, Inc.

2.   Michael Sovern, The Annual Report of the President, 1982-1983 (New York: Columbia University, 1983).

3.   U.S. Congress, The National Defense Education Act of 1958 (Washington, D.C.: U.S. Government Printing Office, 1958), 25.

4.   The National Advisory Board on International Education Programs, which is a creation of Title VI and is chaired by University of South Carolina President James Holderman, has issued a report, Critical Needs in International Education (1983). The report calls for a national fund which should receive "part of the reflow of funds generated by the overseas sale of U.S. government military and other properties, and by interest payments on overseas technical assistance loans." Foreign currencies earned from U.S. surplus agricultural sales abroad have been used to support international exchange for many years, but little remains of this source of funds.

Part IV: U.S. Foreign and National Security Policy:

The American Democracy in the Global Community

B. The Legislative Branch:

U.S. Foreign and National Security Policy

Chair: Stephen D. Cohen, The American University

Presentation by: Honorable Gale McGee, President,
                                Gale McGee Associates

Respondents: Willard Berry, Executive Director,
                                   Coalition for Employment through Exports
                                Stanley Heginbotham,
                                   Congressional Research Service
                                William C. Olson, The American University

Rapporteur: Ernest Plock, School of International
                                   Service, The American University

THE LEGISLATIVE BRANCH:

U.S. FOREIGN AND NATIONAL SECURITY POLICY

Ernest D. Plock

In introducing the central issues and arguments of the discussions on the legislative branch and foreign policy, it should first be emphasized that sharp divisions of opinion over what constituted a Congressional deficiency were exceptions to the rule. Even the most vocal defenders of the Congress's role in the foreign policy process readily acknowledged Congressional practices ill-suited to effective diplomacy, such as prolonged deliberation and frequent publicity on matters that demand extreme discretion. Similarly, those who questioned the wisdom of expanded foreign policy prerogatives for the two Houses of Congress rarely asserted that the Executive branch had no part in the failures to reconcile the often competing objectives of coherent foreign policymaking and the expression of the popular will.

However, there were major divergences in opinion when the panel addressed questions regarding the seriousness of Congress's deficiencies, which considerations demand the most immediate attention, and the realistic prospects for change. It is interesting that no discussant contemplated a constitutional alteration of the executive-legislative relationship in the interests of foreign policy unity, an idea advanced by some who see merit in a parliamentary form of government. Such a solution was rejected both because it was not considered to be in the realm of possibility, and because the nature of our democracy includes a system of checks and balances. Since it was agreed that Congress should continue to reflect the pluralistic element in foreign policy, the group's main priority was to target problems amenable to correction within the present institutional framework.

A second broad conceptual premise of the legislative panel was the implicit understanding that it would serve little purpose to quantify the Congressional role in foreign policy or to approach the question of whether the two houses should have "more" or "less" authority in this arena. Attention was drawn instead to legislative standards of performance and expertise, as well as to the integration of Congress into the decision-making cycle.

Confidence in Government

To the extent that the issue of confidence in government was addressed by the panel, it consisted mainly of the recognition that public disillusionment with the quality of leadership, along with sharp popular divisions over the foreign policy goals after the 1960s, were directly responsible for the breakdown of the foreign policy consensus within the Congress.

All participants agreed that the question of public confidence in government was in fact a "two-way street;" while voters had an obligation to scrutinize their Representatives' actions and programs, the individual Congressman or Congresswoman had a duty to educate constituents, particularly on the most crucial foreign policy issues.

The news media were soundly criticized as inhibiting effective communication between Representatives and their constituents. For example, broad support for American measures abroad was undermined through the ubiquitousness of the television camera. Even more damaging has been the style of news coverage of legislators' programs and its effect on methods of communication. Members of Congress are not only obliged to pay undue attention to the press for electoral reasons, but are also quickly conditioned to simplify issues or programs in a manner tailored to the "fifteen second television clip." As former House Foreign Affairs Committee member William Maillard expressed it, the media "present conclusions without information." The pressures to convey an "image" rather than a more complicated, often ambiguous, portrayal of a problem thus lends itself to a parochial treatment of complex realities.

Consensus and Diagreement

This general recognition of a constant tension between the goal of competence in foreign policy, on one hand, and electability, on the other, prevented participants from straying too far from former Senator Gale McGee's proposition that rules could be "tightened up" but not drastically altered. There was little questioning of Congressional weaknesses in the following areas: the increase in committees and subcommittees, the clogging of the legislative agenda, frequent tardiness in the Congress's responses to events, and the disappearance of voting discipline in the two Houses.

Significantly, splits on issues along party lines were not considered to be one of the most serious obstacles to responsible Congressional behavior. (The problems of Democratic President Jimmy Carter working with both a House and Senate under Democratic control were held to be revealing in this respect.) Rather, Congress's cumbersome decisional machinery, the separate and often colliding aims of the executive and legislative branches, and what McGee termed the "unleaderable" nature of the Senate proved to be central in the debate. It was generally agreed that even radical party polarization could be overcome, as it was during the early part of President Johnson's tenure, with judicious Presidential intervention to secure agreement with key senior members of Congress. Such intervention obviates the need to line up dozens of legislators separately to achieve a successful floor vote.

The panel devoted as much time to the problem of joint consultation as to any other single concern. Participants shared the view that there had been a demonstrable deterioration of consultation in recent years. One discussant concluded that with the ascent of the "imperial Presidency," successive administrations staked out the foreign policy area as the Executive's domain, jealously defending Presidential prerogatives. The questioning of this authority by a more assertive Congress in the 1970s then became the basis for our present foreign affairs "adversary process." A former Congressional staffer discussed the necessity for the Congress itself to initiate talks with the Executive and for the President to adopt a more forthcoming attitude toward talks. The view of a former senior State Department official, on the other hand, was that although administrations needed to become more aware of the two Houses' right to consultation, the dictates of national security in foreign policy demanded discretion by the Congress and understanding of the reasons why the President may not always provide complete information on given questions.

Finally, participants noted the expansion of Congressional staff and focused on the problem of inexperienced Senators, 55 of whom were still serving their first term in 1982. The increased number of staff members creates its own demand for heightened activity, resulting in waves of proposed legislation on the Congressional docket. Criticisms were nevertheless tempered by the observation that large staffs were the only way Congress could maintain a level of expertise that would allow it to oversee the vast and myriad Executive programs.

The overall consensus of the group was quite substantial. Divisions occurred most frequently on the matter of Congress's competence and record of performance relative to the Executive branch.

The presence of former officials from both the executive and legislative branches ensured that neither was exempt from criticisms of imperfections. When the parochial character of the two Houses received attention, for example, a former Senate legislative aide pointed out the disinclination of recent Presidents to read "outside" information and thus to undertake a more critical examination of policies. While the growth of professional staff was several times deplored as leading to legislative logjams, one participant defended the development as a means to strengthening Congress's expertise. And participants who perceived excessive Presidential secrecy on foreign policy vis-a-vis the Congress were given compelling reasons for the frequent impossibility of information disclosure, particularly in view of the potentially dangerous leaks and the necessity to preserve the integrity of ongoing international negotiations.

Recommendations

The panel's ideas and suggestions were both specific and general in nature. First, in an effort to resolve the often confounding question of who speaks for Congress, Gale McGee called for the formation of a "Congressional crisis standby group on instant call for emergency situations." Such a committee would be bipartisan and composed of members of the Foreign Relations, Armed Services, and Appropriations Committees. A second suggestion was that coordination of longterm foreign policy between the two branches of government would be served if the Congress reduced the number of subcommittees to a more manageable level. This would provide a means to simplifying the channels of executive-legislative communication, would curtail excessive Congressional deliberation, and would facilitate prompt responses to international developments.

A third proposal was that the Senate Rules Committee correct the jurisdictional overlaps which presently allow a number of committees to require executive department heads to testify before them. As a result, Cabinet officials cannot be released to tackle problems elsewhere.

Finally, the question of legislative voting cohesiveness led to the advocacy of one informal practice. Gale McGee advises that the staggered term should be utilized to minimize the influence of parochial interests, which exert pressure on Representatives, especially near election times. He thus contended that once key senior members of Congress came out in support of major foreign policy issues, one could more easily rely upon those representatives who did not immediately face re-election. The collective interest could be reaffirmed in the absence of overwhelming constituent pressure, and abrupt shifts in Congress's voting patterns might be avoided. This perception also formed the basis for the suggestion that the House electoral system be reformed as well--Representatives could concentrate more on legislative programs if there were an extension of the two-year term. But it was pointed out that the breakdown of the earlier national foreign policy consensus and the volatile nature of public opinion would continue to encumber attempts toward Congressional voting consistency.

If Senator McGee's suggestions had as their goal making Congress less unwieldy internally and clarifying its communication contacts with the White House, Stanley Heginbotham aimed at preserving the Congress's essential character, accepting its role, and implementing changes that, in correcting one deficiency, do not produce the reverse problem. The necessity to "co-opt" Congress into the system was thereby recognized, in addition to the provisos that it be permitted to augment its professional staff as well as fully utilize its information support services. Improving rules and the Congressional oversight function, a purpose supported by many in the room, should nevertheless not have as a consequence the "bureaucratization" of the Congress. Heginbotham thus opposed enhancing the two houses' professionalism at the expense of eliminating their public accountability and was joined in this position by Willard Berry. The former also recommended that past members of Congress actively "identify and publicize norms for reasonable foreign policy behavior in Congress."

Because of the prominence of executive-legislative consultation as an issue, participants advocated that Presidents show more sensitivity to Congress's right to be consulted. The panel voiced its support for Congressional efforts to demand more germaneness in the introduction of legislation and for stricter rules governing floor debate. The proliferation of bills and the lax rules on floor debates, as well as the growing trend toward "Congress by commmittee," were most often identified as constraints on a timely response to issues and events.

Actual changes in the functioning of Congress depend in large measure on the independent conclusions of individual Representatives. Certain incremental shifts in informal practices during the 1960s and 1970s were cited by different discussants as obstructing urgent action or desired unity. Implicit in the group's call for remedies was the idea that Members of Congress should consider the advantages of past standards, two of which were responsibility to one's party and the authority of committee chairpersons over subcommittee chairpersons and their staffs. But in the case of all suggestions, one was obliged to face two important realities: (1) The decisions of Congress could not be upheld if societal preferences at large ran athwart of them, and (2) as former Congressman Charles Whalen contended, the influence of interest groups on public policy has in many cases grown and remains a potential hazard as long as access to elected officials is constitutionally protected.

The most important lesson to be learned from the interaction of panelists and conversants may therefore be that responsible Congressional activity is predicated on further education of the American public and an improvement of "two-way" communication channels, so that constituents can formulate and express a coherent standard of expectation for elected representatives.

Implications for Government and Education

The legislative panel's recommendations for a smoother functioning of Congressional foreign policymaking recognized that present practices must be improved, not eliminated, and implied that earlier abandoned methods of consensus might be attempted anew. The candid remarks by former Members of Congress on Capitol Hill staff assistants strengthened the impression that the two Houses would be well served by listening to Congressional representatives no longer in power; such persons have the advantage of some detachment from current partisan quarrels and possess a considerable institutional memory. The present Congress's use of former Representatives in an advisory capacity would offer the opportunity not only to upgrade Congressional standards of expertise, but perhaps also to alter some media practices that misrepresent Members' messages to constituents and the broader public.

The panel also raised several fascinating issues for study by the academic community. While practically all participants shared the belief that American foreign policy displayed a much stronger bipartisan tradition prior to the Vietnam War era, their enumeration of factors contributing to a loss of cohesiveness invited questions: What were the preconditions for a bipartisan foreign policy? Was the widely-accepted notion of a common set of beliefs regarding the ends of foreign policy (e.g., containment of the Soviet Union, resistance to political factions in Third World countries) the key to executive-legislative harmony; or were simplified Congressional party and committee practices the glue for creating foreign affairs unity?

Universities might shed light on present difficulties by introducing courses and encouraging research that compare the Presidential-Congressional relationship in these earlier years prior to the Vietnam war with the watershed epoch during and after President Johnson's political decline. In an effort to understand the reasons for contemporary foreign affairs disputes between the two branches of government, such a curriculum could proceed with an eye to investigating other developments that may also bear on the bipartisanship problem: changes in the Congressional committee system, the relative distribution of authority between committees and subcommittees, party discipline, individual legislators' familiarity with foreign countries, a growing "imperial" approach to foreign policy by Presidents, voting cohesiveness, etc.

With such an orientation in university curricula, one could hope to resolve the question of whether it is the "macro"--the degree of public consensus on foreign policy--or the "micro"-- the technical performance of Congress's policy machinery--that has most heavily conditioned the course of executive-legislative foreign policy coordination. If thorough research demonstrated that the former is the case, Members of Congress would then know to devote more time to educating the public as well as to contributing to popular consensus. If the latter were confirmed, Congressional efforts would best be directed toward revising rules and perhaps reincorporating procedures in effect during periods of close cooperation between the Administrations and the Congress.

Finally, the frequently decisive influence of American policy on international developments increases the obligation of U.S. legislators to appreciate the consequences of policy decisions. The panel repeatedly emphasized the inappropriateness of the classical distinction between domestic and foreign policy: Politics irrefutably extend "beyond the water's edge." Equally inescapable is the fact that U.S. actions are perceived differently in nations that are the object of those decisions, as confirmed by both the Iranian Revolution and recent American missile deployments in Western Europe.

Another important implication of these discussions was the necessity for Congress to focus on foreign governments' responses to Congressional bills, resolutions, and positions. The recurrent zigzags in Congressional votes on foreign policy have been unsettling or confusing to allies a well as adversaries. The Congress would therefore be advised to draw upon its information support services, such as the Congressional Research Service and Congressional Information Service, to calculate probable foreign reaction to adopted measures. In short, there is a considerable need for Congress to assume collective responsibility vis-a-vis affected international parties as well as toward its domestic base of support.

The President and the Senate[1]

Gale McGee

"Europe's distress spelled America's success"--my history professor at Chicago always started his courses in diplomatic history with this quotation.[2]

The strife in Europe had afforded diplomatic openings, which the United States had exploited thoroughly during its first century and a half. While World War I became a catalyst, the Americans had first enjoyed the luxury of hesitation and delay while the powers in Europe were slowly bleeding to death. In the ranks of the victorious allies, the United States for the first time in its history became one of the major world powers, consigned to the responsibilities of peacemaking.

In a sense, World War II began as a repeat performance. Once again the American people hesitated, procastinated, and delayed--spared by the hardship in Europe from having to make the tough decision on war or peace. It took the Japanese at Pearl Harbor to shock the badly divided American public into closing ranks once again. The Second World War destroyed the luxury of choosing between two sides in world politics. The United States had to sort out, with little delay, its priorities and options.

At the very outset, the American system of responsibility for making foreign policy had to be questioned. Under the Constitution, policy was vested predominantly in the President; the Senate gave advice and consent, and ratified treaties, and the two Houses of Congress reserved the power jointly to declare war. But will this system meet the foreign policy needs of the remainder of this century and beyond? We meet here at The American University to examine the policy requisites for our country in the context of the global community during the next fifty years. I propose to analyze in particular those factors relating to the respective roles of the President and the Senate in U.S. foreign policy.

What Pearl Harbor had been to the previously isolationist generations at the 1930s and the 1940s, the victory ending World War II was for the American people as they assumed for the first time their responsibilities as a world power. A notable series of events descended upon them in rapid succession. First, there was the creation of the United Nations, an international body that would seek to correct or adjust the limitations of the old League of Nations. The hopeful dreams of its founders were modified to accommodate the two giants of the world, the Union of Soviet Socialist Republics and the United States of America. Nevertheless, as fifty-one nations signed the charter, they also agreed to base the U.N. in New York City--a contrast to the "neutral" ground that provided headquarters for the old League of Nations in Geneva. The ink was hardly dry on the U.N. Charter, however, when the strains between the U.S. and the U.S.S.R. threatened the peace.

Thus, the United States had a curious, if brief, experience with its idyllic hopes for a world at peace. An American military mobilization that numbered more than twelve million by the end of the war was immediately demobilized; the country that had escaped the devastation heaped upon Britain, Germany, and Japan offered massive economic assistance not only to its allies but to the vanquished as well. But the Soviets declined these offers; even unofficial proposals to share a short-lived monopoly on atomic know-how were greeted with "nyet." From the Truman Doctrine of 1947 that sealed off Turkey from Soviet tampering, the Berlin Airlift in 1948, the China White Paper of 1949, the war in Korea in 1950, to Cuba in 1962, and ending finally by the mid-sixties in Vietnam, the strains of "cold war" severely taxed diplomatic relations between the two great powers. As Winston Churchill reputedly noted during the Berlin Airlift crisis, "If you Americans had acted this time as you did after the First World War, Russia would be on the Atlantic Coast of Europe tonight."

By the mid-sixties, cold war diplomacy had become commonplace--two Berlins, two Germanys, two Europes, two Koreas, two Chinas, and then two Vietnams epitomized a divided world. Shortly after his own traumatic diplomatic experiences during the Cuban Crisis in 1962, Ambassador Adlai Stevenson summarized his discouragement: "One world was our dream. but two worlds are better than no worlds."

In a sense, the bipartisanship so characteristic of the period following World War II reflected Stevenson's "two-worlds" rationalization. Its strength rested upon the common experiences of an entire generation of Americans who had shared a worldwide "two front war" and had waged a tough series of wars. That bipartisan generation managed successfully to bridge the rising differences between the President of the United States and the Congress, particularly in foreign policy.

Two events--Vietnam and Watergate--exposed potentially grave weaknesses in our foreign policy structure as well as in policy procedures. The national trauma of both events shattered much of the spirit of the bipartisanship; in particular, the roles of the President and the Senate were called into question. The core of our problem has been expressed by Warren Christopher, Deputy Secretary of State during the Carter Administration. He has written that, "Our basic need is to reconcile the imperatives of democracy at home with the demands of leadership in the world.[3]

Many distinguished and experienced Americans are devoting a substantial amount of time to this question of reconciliation. Some have already concluded that another form of government such as a parliamentary system, may be required. Others contend that we need basic structural changes, which would require constitutional amendments such as limiting the President to a single six-year term, or extending House terms to three or four years, or restricting Senators to two terms, or forming an international union among the Atlantic democracies. But there are also many scholars (including the writer) who tremble at the thought of tampering with the Constitution on such matters, fearing that it could lead to a serious unraveling of the constitutional fabric. Others point to the flourishing "single-issue" groups, each with their own vision of constitutional conventions and a "new" system which would appear to be laden with similar problems.

Having served both on the White House staff and in Congress, I believe it is not too late to adjust the present mechanism from within, both at the Presidential level as well as that of the Senate, while still preserving the principle of the separation of powers deeply implanted in the Constitution. But if we are to succeed in changing our system from within, it is important that we not be tempted to view foreign policy responsibility in nostalgic terms of 1950s doctrine. The world around us has changed in so many substantive ways since the bipartisanship of the Eisenhower years that to look backward now could seriously jeopardize our efforts to cope with the foreign policy requirements in the remainder of this century. Four developments illustrate this point:

(1) The successful launching of Sputnik by the Soviets in 1957. For a dozen years after World War II, the atomic factor remained of peripheral interest due to the monopoly enjoyed by the United States. With the launching of Sputnik, the "moment of change" arrived. There began a competition of nuclear development between the Soviet Union and the U.S., and Americans started to look for a place to hide from "the Bomb" and the threat of nuclear war.

(2) The decline of bipartisanship. By the mid-sixties the World War II generation was growing old, tired, and declining in numbers. They were soon displaced by "The Me Generation." Individual priorities changed, while politics became a "dirty business" and government was a common enemy.

(3) The Third World. The number of U.N. countries grew to 157, more than triple the United Nations' original size. But the numbers were less important than the new perceptions of these younger nations.

In many cases, the United States had been instrumental in pressuring the colonial powers of Europe to initiate steps toward granting independence to their former colonial outposts. A number of the governments in turn had looked to the American Declaration of Independence as a model for their own. By the mid-1960s, however, the second generation of Third World leaders was already taking control from their own "Founding Fathers," frequently by violent means. In some cases they moved to separate themselves even further from the old colonial nations of the first half of the twentieth century, as well as from the United States in particular.

By his second term President Eisenhower had sensed the implications of this change. He was concerned that the escalating desires and expectations of the Third World would become a far more explosive factor in world politics than the earlier international Communist Party activities of the 1930s-1950s period. The President warned that unless, or until, the widening gap between the very richest nations and the poorest was meaningfully reduced, there could be no peace. World events have proven him to be right.

(4) The news media. Television and other communications technology have converted news-gathering into "instant news." This develpment has been mind-boggling. For example, at the beginning of the nineteenth century, President Thomas Jefferson wrote to his friend John Adams that the government was exploring new opportunities with France; but in regard to Spain, he added, "We haven't heard from Pickering [the U.S. Ambassador] in many months, so we conclude that matters are settling down in Madrid." What contrast with the "instant news" of today. Decision-making in national and international politics has been seriously complicated by the new dimensions of communications, such as media sensationalism, journalists' instant judgments, and the greater media emphasis on what goes wrong rather than on what goes right.

With these factors in mind, the evaluation of our procedures for shaping foreign policy responsibility remains complicated at best, and at worst impossible to resolve. As Alexis de Tocqueville wrote in the early 1800s: "I do not hesitate to say it is especially in the conduct of foreign relations that democracies appear to be decidedly inferior to other governments." Over a century and a half later Walter Lippmann, in a luncheon conversation with this writer, expressed deep concern over the state of public opinion. An impassioned opinion, he suggested, imposes "a compulsion to make mistakes," as a consequence of which, members of the U.S. Senate had been reduced to insecure and intimidated men. And former Senator J. William Fulbright, former Chairman of the Senate Foreign Relations Committee, wrote nearly two centuries after Tocqueville's observation "I confess to increasingly serious misgivings about the ability of the Congress to play a constructive role in our foreign relations."[4]

The Problems in Foreign Policy Procedures

The Founding Fathers, reflecting their sorry experiences as members of thirteen sovereignties, sought to vest foreign policy responsibilities in a single source: the office of the President of the United States. The United States Senate was given the role of authority to advise and consent. Much of the controversy over responsibilities for foreign policy has centered on this role. The President, it is asserted, too often merely notifies, failing to seek advice and consent.

The President, on the other hand, is concerned about classified materials or subtle diplomatic entanglements that might unnecessarily strain relations with another government. While individual Senators would appreciate these concerns for the majority of foreign policy affairs, there are still certain diplomatic agreements that warrant the input, scrutiny, and decision to dissent or modify by the Senators.

If the advise and consent process is to succeed, it requires the strongest good faith on both sides. The first rule for the President and his advisers is never--but never--attempt to deceive the Congress in an effort to avoid controversy. The outcome is always disaster, plus an intensified suspicion of the Chief Executive by the legislative branch that will carry over into unrelated matters.

Where sensitive materials or diplomatic politics are involved, the Senate and the White House have often worked out a formula for dealing with a small group of Senators--those who are senior in experience, bipartisan groups, etc. And this Congressional group in turn keeps other colleagues advised, as required.

There is one remaining area that strains Congressional/ Executive relations: The War Powers Act continues to fester amid the political rivalries in the White House and Congress. Enacted in 1973, the Act was motivated primarily by reactions to President Richard Nixon's desire to extend the Vietnam conflict into the neighboring reaches of Cambodia.

The Senate's track record on deciding foreign policy matters was developed between the First World War and the Second. The modest dimensions of that conflict--the limited time consumed and human and material costs--would not ordinarily have signaled serious repercussions. Although only six senators voted against the World War II declaration in 1917, the Senate quickly unravelled the fabric of the Versailles Peace Conference. They not only rejected the Peace Treaty, but blocked U.S. entry into the newly formed League of Nations. Worse still, by the 1930s our nation had divided itself into "Isolationists" and "Internationalists" and the Senate enacted the Neutrality Acts. While the thrust of this particular legislation was to prevent World War I, it seriously hobbled U.S. government efforts to cope with the Nazi threat. Had it not been for the Japanese attack on Pearl Harbor, the consequences of the neutrality laws could have been even more disastrous. The War Powers Act debates of 1973 in the Senate seemed to point backward: to the desire of many senators to prevent U.S. intervention in armed conflict, in this case Vietnam.

After a decade of living under the Act, there remain misgivings about the Act's ability to help efforts toward wise policymaking. There have been some helpful modifications to the War Powers legislation, but the increasingly sophisticated dimensions of war, plus the shrinking of time and space through technology, leave in question the wisdom of the Act. New political and technological complexities require even greater initiatives by the President if we are to avoid yet another war. It is one thing to advise and consent, but it is quite another to hobble the presidency in a time of crisis. Shortcomings in the White House are not corrected by transferring them to one hundred self-proclaimed secretaries of state in the Senate.

Strained relations with the Congress are not the only area of Executive problems. There are also recurring hostilities between the Secretary of State, who acts as the President's cabinet chief of foreign affairs, and the President's National Security Council chief. While this issue did not arise during the Kennedy-Johnson years, it became conspicuous and embarrassing for Presidents Richard Nixon and Jimmy Carter. The struggle between Secretary of State William Rogers and Nixon's National Security Council Chief Henry A. Kissinger was a notable case in point. This antagonism was allowed to proceed much too far (and too long). Rogers was forced out and Kissinger became Secretary of State. But the conflict should not have been allowed to happen in the first place. The Secretary of State is responsible to the President; the National Security director is only the President's private adviser. The latter is not subject to Senate approval and thus should be confined to the role of private counselor to the President. Kissinger violated this limitation by "going public"--holding press conferences, appearing on media shows, and the like.

Similarly, President Carter's National Security chief, Zbigniew Brzezinski, soon opened a barrage of verbiage challenging Secretary of State Cyrus P. Vance. The verbal bombardment continued until Vance resigned his post late in the Carter term. As a result, much unnecessary confusion was injected into foreign policy problems during the Carter Administration.

Under the Reagan Administration, there has been no sign of actual hostilities, although they threatened to break out early. Former Reagan Secretary of State Alexander Haig wrote recently about the efforts of the President's Security Council Advisor, Richard Allen, to challenge him in the post. Other members of the Reagan White House staff were apparently also involved in forcing Haig's resignation and replacing him with George Shultz.

The Reagan Administration has sought to clear up this matter. In an address to the Former Members of Congress organization in the Spring of 1984, the President's National Security Advisor, Robert (Bud) McFarlane, made a strong statement of the President's intent to preserve the office of Secretary of State as the responsible authority on foreign affairs and diplomacy. The National Security Advisor was to remain the President's private counselor, but was to avoid public policy announcements and/or clashes with the Secretary of State.

Suggestions for Change

First of all, the Senate has to establish certain senators as its "leaders." There has recently been a demise of leadership in that body. One of the explanations given for this "unleaderability," as Senate Majority Leader Howard Baker calls it, is that the Senate may have "over-reformed" itself after Watergate and Vietnam. A commonly heard complaint on the Senate floor concerns the overstaffing of subcommittees in particular. Subcommittees have proliferated to the point where there are not enough Senators to serve effectively on the numerous subcommittees. (Some Senators are on as many as sixteen or seventeen of them.) While staffers have multiplied, substance and depth have thinned considerably. For example, the number of legislative bills has skyrocketed, with a resultant glut on the Senate calendar. While there have always been many innocuous or otherwise unimportant bills to be considered, the increased volume of minutiae has cluttered the legislative process.

Another factor contributing to the Senate malaise has been the high rate of turnover, bringing in more than the usual number of new Senators. By 1982, for example, there were fifty-five Senators serving their first term! Lack of experience and a less-developed sense of history would have to account for some of the "unleaderability" of the upper body.

The television camera presents a third complication for Senate procedures. TV coverage has extended the legislative processes, particularly committee procedures. The number of speeches by committee members rises in direct proportion to the presence of television cameras. Moreover, the current practice of televising many committee hearings and meetings compounds the problem. While politics, it has been said, is the art of compromise, on camera it is another matter. With constituents--or worse, lobbyists who contribute financially to the individual member--filling the hearing room, it becomes unrealistic to expect a particular Senator (or Senators) to compromise their _public_ commitments while their public watches them on the TV screen. The committee member often has to make one speech for the "folks out there." Then the committee meets to do battle in private, working out acceptable compromises. Once the basic agreement is worked out, they "go public" one more time merely to confirm what has been achieved off camera.

There is one more adjustment in the Senate system that should be undertaken without delay, namely, greater attention to the reason for the staggered, six-year terms of Senators. At the founding of the republic, Senators were given six-year terms, with one-third voted into office every two years. The purpose was clear: With longer terms they would be protected against the day-to-day whims of the populace in general; and with only one-third of the senators running for office every two years, the remaining two-thirds would act as the steadying hand on the rudder of the ship of state. In recent years at least, this concept has been neglected, and some would argue it may have been destroyed. It has certainly been neglected. But it can hopefully still be restored. Because of its place as one of the foundations of our political system, its revival would serve as a strong legislative base for refurbishing the Senate's constitutional role in foreign policy.

Four sectors of the United States Senate should focus on the procedural problems in foreign policy formulation: the Senate leadership, the Senate Rules Committee, the party caucuses, and the individual Senators themselves.

The first priority is that the Senate recover and reestablish its own "leaderability." Both institutional proceedings as well as "Senatorial courtesies" need refurbishing. The present-day Republican and the Democratic leadership is held by experienced Senators whose sense of history is an invaluable asset for a new beginning. In addition, each understands the many interlacings that hold "The Club" together; they are skilled partisans as well as expert practitioners in bipartisanship. Their combined experience is irreplaceable in restoring the Senate to a more significant and responsible role in its advise and consent capacities.

The Rules Committee is now reportedly working on procedural guidelines for the future. A reduction in the number of committees and subcommittees should be high on their list. New priorities should include control and disciplinary procedures for filibusters, particularly for the pre-filibuster tactics recently in evidence.

The party caucuses have already been brought in to work on these procedural problems. They could well be a natural vehicle for discussing the dimensions of the staggered term options that now face the Senate. But in the final analysis it is the individual Senators who have to resolve these procedural problems. Their dilemma is that they increasingly lean toward the whims of public opinion, especially in matters of national and international importance. Too many legislators seem overly eager to find issues that are popular at home rather than to delve into areas of critical importance to the entire country. As Edmund Burke warned, "Your representative owes you, not his industry alone, but his judgment, and he betrays, instead of serving you, if he sacrifices it to your opinion."

Every member of the present U.S. Senate ought to rally around an effort to raise the level of public understanding of a Senator's special role as a representative of the nation. The distinction between the responsiblities of a member of the House and those of a member of the Senate has to be repeatedly articulated.

Two large segments of our society have to close ranks behind the Senators and assume a strong leadership role in world affairs. They are the universities and schools, and national organizations and public opinion oriented groups outside of government and academia.

College and university programs in government, politics, and history have multiplied, particularly in enrollments. Some critics continue to suggest, however, that numerous campuses have forfeited excellence in their appeal for large enrollments. But many fine programs remain. The American University, Georgetown University, George Washington University, Howard University and the Universities of Maryland and Virginia all contribute a wealth of materials as well as an abundance of academic and personal excellence. Extending these capabilities to the rest of the country, there is a potential reservoir of present and future Senators. Increasing numbers of Senators have been identified with academic roots, Ph.D.'s, Rhodes scholars, and the like.

Despite this education, there remains a growing tendency among the new Senators to surrender to popular demands--to be followers rather than leaders in foreign policy. Greater academic emphasis on the national interest priorities of the Senate would increase the odds of having better qualified Senate candidacies. But until our educational system incorporates into its teaching the staggered terms concept and national interest priorities, the quality of Senators will not be sufficiently raised.

National organizations, such as the League of Women Voters and the two major political parties, need to focus their programs more on the integrity and capability of the Senate candidates and to insist that they address the national interests before the local or pedestrian ones. "Agreement" with the Senator ought to be secondary to "respect" for him.

Finally, there is the urgent need to teach the purpose of the staggered terms at the most elementary education levels. While most young students know about the bilateral legislative system, few, if any, are aware of the Senator's responsibilities as representative of the national interest. This would require special preparation for elementary and secondary school teachers and a re-examination of the adequacy of explanations provided by textbooks. A part of the problem here is not the failure by textbooks or teachers to mention the formal institutional purposes of the House and Senate, but rather the need to devote substantially more time to this study in order to counteract the detrimental effects of "quickie" news and TV cliches.

Thus, in the longer run of the next fifty years, there has to be an improvement in public understanding of the U.S. government and its role in the world. And in the shorter run, the Congress and the President must--without further delay--put their respective houses in order. In the Congress, it will require restoring the attributes of leaderability while preparing to lead public opinion and motivate constituencies to respect the responsibilities of leadership. For the President, it requires genuine consultation with the Congress and more control over the Executive's responsibilities for policy procedures and announcements. And for the public at large, it requires the greatest understanding and support for the separate demands of national and international policy objectives. The requirements of a representative democracy at home must be distinguished from the demands of world leadership abroad.

NOTES

1.   Originally published as a part of the ITT Key Issues Lecture Series in International Education: The Unfinished Agenda, editors William C. Olson and Llewellyn D. Howell. Copyright 1984 by White River Press, Inc.

2.   J. Fred Rippy, America and the Strife of Europe, University of Chicago Press, 1938.

3.   Warren Christopher, "Ceasefire Between the Branches: A Compact in Foreign Affairs," Foreign Affairs (Summer 1982).

4.   J. William Fulbright, "The Legislator as Educator," Foreign Affairs 57 (Spring 1979): 719.

Conclusion:

The Role of the Federal Government: The Next Fifty Years

Introduction of Speaker: Milton Greenberg, Provost,
                                  The American University

Speaker: Honorable Elliot L. Richardson

THE ROLE OF GOVERNMENT

IN THE UNITED STATES:

THE NEXT FIFTY YEARS

Elliot L. Richardson

When I was first invited to speak about the role of the federal government in the next 50 years, I reflected on the life of Arthur Flemming who, having started out as Director of the School of Public Affairs 50 years ago, saw first hand, through positions of major responsibility, the process of change. Certainly we can gain no better feel for the processes that will affect the shape of the future, than by trying to understand the ways in which they have shaped events during the past 50 years. In that time, Arthur Flemming has embodied what Star Wars fans refer to as "The Force." On first meeting him, most people would not instantly think of him as a strong, aggressive character. On the contrary. But in analyzing his role, the phrase is not inapplicable: He has been patient, persistent, endowed with character, courage, and vision. He has developed the strength and reserve necessary to exert a lasting influence.

Once, when I was serving as his Assistant Secretary for Labor Relations, he spoke to the President about an area of great concern to us at the time--the role of the federal government in support of higher education. He used the strongest expletive during the course of the conversation that I had ever heard from him: "Damn." A man who can deal with sharp disappointment in this restrained manner also possesses the strength and dignity to exert a steady, cumulative influence on people.

My own entry into public administration occurred 40 years ago, when I became a legislative assistant to the senior Senator of Massachusetts, Leverett Saltonstall. From that point on, I could see that the practice of public administration could, roughly speaking, be divided into three kinds of approach. First, there was the "seat of the pants" approach--acting by instinct. At its best, it reflected a high degree of experienced savvy and was very effective. Second, there was "exhaustive analysis," requiring cogent, practical rationalizations of the implications posed by various possible options. Finally, there was a third, equally significant, style of public administration--decisive ignorance. Indeed, people have on occasion confused that style of administration with leadership. It does have at least one asset: It conveys a sense of total confidence, albeit confidence that would have been unimaginable had the administrator better understood what was involved.

Transcending each of these styles of administration was the approach that I associate with Arthur Flemming, during both the Eisenhower Administration and the Nixon/Ford years. It is called "informed judgment"--judgments made in a manner that addresses the unfolding pressures of external events. One of the most integral elements of such judgment is the understanding of timing, without which the administrator's actions may be too little or too late.

In analyzing the processes that have brought about the changes in the government's role, I will not try to deal with substantive areas except to say in passing that certain opportunities will, over the next 50 years, come to be regarded as inalienable rights. These include, for example, health care and further education. We already understand that fairness requires access to these benefits. The government's response to this awareness has thus far been somewhat fragmentary, but discernable in its support for health care and its underwriting of higher education. As medical care becomes more capable of dealing with illnesses and suffering that were once thought untreatable, it becomes unconscionable to withhold that quality of treatment from anyone. Similarly, as education grows increasingly necessary to cope in a complex technological age, the opportunity for access to such education must come to be regarded in the same light as the opportunity for access to a high school education was viewed 50 years ago.

The role of government will also have to expand to deal with the complex manifestations of our tampering with the environment. This has already been one of the most dramatic areas of growth, particularly in the past 20 years.

During the period when I served under Arthur Flemming at Health, Education, and Welfare (HEW), the Robert A. Taft Sanitary Engineering Center in Cincinnati was part of a program of federal assistance for the construction of waste treatment center plants, an early form of federal involvement in the problems of environmental protection. But the Eisenhower Administration said it felt it had to eliminate the program, a recommendation initiated by the so-called "Federal State Action Committee." I went before the Senate Committee on Public Works in support of a recommendation to turn the waste treatment construction program back to the states in return for a share of the telephone tax. I will never forget what Senator Robert Kerr, Chairman of the committee, said to me: "Young man, you sound like a young lawyer sent to court with a hopeless case. It's quite clear that you've done as well as anybody could with it, but there was no way you could win. I suggest that you go back to the other end of the avenue, and remind those who sent you here of that inscription at the base of the monument to those who fell at Thermopylae. You recall it says, 'Stranger who passes by, go ye and tell the Spartans that we lie here obedient to their command.'"

As in the area of environmental protection, we are bound to see an inexorable increase in the complexity of government processes and in the relationship between the government and the individual. That which is true of environmental pollution--it results from a number of separately growing exponential trends--is also true of complexity. That is, it is a product of population growth, environmental pollution, the expanding transportation and distribution system, and the growth of disposable income. As per capita disposable income increases, so too does the opportunity to choose from among different kinds of products. That, of course, requires more varied materials, more sources, more complex transportation systems, and so on.

Insufficient emphasis is placed upon such complex phenomena when addressing, for example, the evolution of the presidency's role over the past 50 years. Perhaps the single most sensational manifestation of this phenomenon is the increase of congressional staff, as related to the proliferation of subcommittees, which are in turn a response to complex realities of dealing with information in the computer age. To a significant degree, the second phenomenon, the technological one, can help us to manage the first. Technology can bring considerable improvement not only in our general forecast capability, but also in our ability to discern and predict the consequences of alternative government policies and alternative forms of government intervention. In the next 50 years, we will establish better, more consistent data. We will develop a more sensitive awareness of what kinds of data are relevant for purposes of improving our forecast capabilities. We will better comprehend the physical and ecological phenomena that need to be taken into account in our global, regional, and local analyses.

In short, we will be alerted sooner and more accurately to problems that are going to need to be addressed. In order to deal with these problems of the future, we will need a relatively long lead time, which will result from our improved forecast capabilities. These capacities will also help us to avoid the indefinite accumulation of government intervention, which depends on the determination to preserve the largest possible role for individual freedom of choice.

It becomes all the more important, therefore, to seek to ensure that government intervention is as precise as possible and causes minimal disruption. What we need in order to preserve the maximum degree of individual freedom of choice is to learn how to use government with the kind of precision necessary to achieve a given public objective, but without causing gratuitous consequences.

A second requirement, or opportunity, associated with a better understanding of our system, is recognition of the qualitative element of choice. The National Income Account, upon which we now rely for many of our public policy choices, does, to be sure, represent an extraodinary achievement. The problem is that there is no way of factoring the gains in clean air and clean water, for example, into the Gross National Product.

This Administration came in under the mistaken impression that people would rather keep money in their pocket through tax cuts than pay for the means necessary to achieve cleaner air and water. In fact, it was well understood by the American people that clean air and clean water were good, desirable, worth paying for, and could only be obtained through allowing government to have sufficient resources with which to build requisite systems and take adequate measures. But until we have ways to factor qualitative benefits and assets into resource allocation, the process of choice itself will be distorted.

People must change the criteria on which they base their choices. They have to determine the ways in which unquantifiable benefits, such as a healthy environment, figure into the GNP and, more generally, the measurement of success. If a whole society believes that its success is measured by the annual GNP growth, it is likely to dedicate its effort and resources to that result. That is the way this society views success. But quite clearly, that is not going to be an adequate measure of success for the next 50 years.

Another requirement for coping with future and present complexity is a better means of dealing with disputed issues in the fields of science and technology. We have achieved a measure of success. For example, the system of National Accounts is for all practical purposes removed from political controversy. It would be unthinkable to conduct a national campaign, while having to ward off suspicion regarding the legitimacy of the unemployment figures, GNP, or inflation figures. The fact that these numbers are accepted is a tremendous accomplishment and an enormous contribution to democratic processes. We need to deal with issues like nuclear power, for instance, in a manner which creates a comparable degree of confidence in the scientific and technical judgments fundamental to ultimate political choices.

In conclusion, we are approaching a fork in the road. One route is increasing reliance on expertise and, hence, expert authority. What lies this way is a benign authoritarianism, perhaps, to the extent that the experts are dedicated to the public interest; but it is nevertheless a society in which citizens have abdicated their responsibilities. Down the other path is a continual, conscious effort to offset the consequences of complexity and technological change in order to preserve a role for the individual. It is important that we follow the second road, but that is possible only through a conscious and sustained effort to preserve opportunities for individuals.

The processes discussed in this paper can contribute to the potential for intelligent political choice. Clearly the importance of exposing and gaining acceptance for confident adjudication of technical and scientific issues is that we the people can thereby better understand the risks and elements of uncertainty that we are being asked to accept, as well as knowing about factors that are relatively certain.

The role of the federal government in the next 50 years is going to depend to a large degree on the extent to which we remain committed to a society where participation in ultimate choices is an end in itself. What is significant about our past history is not that better choices were made through public involvement, but rather that we live in a country where the individual matters, where each voice counts. It is this opportunity that must be preserved, despite the complexity and impacts of technological change. If th's is achieved, we can say that, whatever the role of the federal government in dealing with problems generated by change, it will at least be a role that was conceived for it from the very beginning.

Appendix I

List of Contributors To This Volume.

Hugo Adam Bedau is Austin Fletcher Professor of Philosophy and director of the Center for the Study of Decision Making at Tufts University. His Ph.D. in Philosophy is from Harvard, and he has taught at Dartmouth, Princeton, and Reed before coming to Tufts in 1966. His principal fields of interest are social, legal, and political philosophy. He was a Liberal Arts Fellow at Harvard Law School (1961-62). He is the editor of Civil Disobedience: Theory and Practice (1969), Justice and Equality (1971), and The Death Penalty in America, now in its third edition (1982). He co-authored Victimless Crimes: Two Views (1974), and has written chapters in more than two dozen books, as well as many essays and reviews.

Joseph G. Bock is a Ph.D. candidate at the School of International Service, The American University. He graduated from the University of Missouri--Columbia summa cum laude with a B.S.W in 1980 and with a M.S.W. from that institution one year later. His specialties are economic development, U.S. responses to insurgency movements in Third World countries, and arms control.

Richard Bolling served as Congressman from the Kansas City area of Missouri from 1949 to 1982. Long-term chair of the House of Representative's Rules Committee, Representative Bolling is most known for his interest and leadership in Congressional reform and his work on education and civil rights legislation. A graduate of the University of the South, he is the author of House Out of Order, Power in the House, and America's Competitive Edge. He is currently Goldstein Professor of Public Policy at Washington College (Maryland).

Robert P. Boynton is a Professor of Government and Public Administration and the Director of the Center for Technology and Administration at The American University. He holds a B.A. degree from Calvin College in History, and M.A. and Ph.D. degrees in Political Science from the University of Michigan. His fields of specialty are organization and management theory, management technologies, development administration, and urban management. His current research interests focus on the cross-cultural transfer of western management technologies.

Marilyn C. Bracken is the Vice President for Product Testing and Liability of the Environmental Testing and

Certification Corporation, Edison, New Jersey. She received a B.S. in Chemistry from Carnegie Mellon University and a M.A. and Ph.D. in Public Administration: Technology of Management from The American University. Dr. Bracken is a specialist in domestic and international regulatory activities dealing with chemicals and consumer products, the development and implementation of toxic substances monitoring, and information management programs and policies. She previously served as Deputy Assistant Administrator and Associate Assistant Administrator in the Office of Pesticides and Toxic Substances of the U.S. Environmental Protection Agency. Dr. Bracken has published widely, served on numerous official committees, and received a number of honors including the Presidential Rank Award, Meritorious Executive, and the Distinguished Alumna Award of The American University.

Robert E. Cleary is Dean of the College of Public and International Affairs and Professor of Government and Public Administration at The American University. He holds a Ph.D. from Rutgers--the State University of New Jersey. He is the 1984-85 president of the National Association of Schools of Public Affairs and Administration, and a past president of the Society for College and University Planning. The first executive secretary of the Harry S. Truman Foundation, he has also served as Provost and as acting President of The American University. His scholarly interest focuses on the politics and administration of higher education.

James J. Fyfe is an Associate Professor of Justice at The American University, and a senior fellow of the Police Foundation. A New York City police officer for sixteen years, he holds a B.S. from John Jay College of Criminal Justice, City University of New York, and M.S. and Ph.D. degrees from the School of Criminal Justice, State University of New York at Albany. He has published and lectured widely on a variety of police related issues and, in 1979, his research on police deadly force was honored by the American Society for Public Administration as the year's outstanding national contribution to criminal justice administration.

Sven Groennings is the Director, Fund for the Improvement of Postsecondary Education, U.S. Department of Education. Holder of a Ph.D. from Stanford, he has taught at Indiana University, and worked for the U.S. House of Representatives, the Department of State in the Bureau of European Affairs and the Bureau of Educational and Cultural Affairs, and the U.S. Senate. He is the author or editor of three books: The Study of Coalition Behavior; Scandinavia in Social Science Literature; and To Be A Congressman: The Promise and the Power. A career focused on both foreign affairs and education leads him to speak and write frequently on international education.

Michael G. Hansen is an Assistant Professor and Director of the Key Executive Program in the School of Government and Public Administration at The American University. Research interests include implementation analysis of government programs, bureaucratic politics, and organizational learning. Dr. Hansen received his M.A. from the University of Illinois and his Ph.D. from the University of Southern California. He is currently co-authoring a textbook on public management to be published by Wadsworth, and editing a book on executive development to be published by Jossey-Bass.

Richard G. Higgins Jr. is an Assistant Professor of Government and Public Administration at The American University. He received both a Ph.D. and a M.P.A. from the Maxwell School, Syracuse University. His teaching and research interests include public budgeting and financial management, state and local government, intergovernmental relations, and general public management. Topics of recent publications include integrated financial management, and the state and local government response to federal aid reductions.

Martha Keys served in the U.S. House of Representatives during the 94th and 95th Congresses. She was Special Advisor to the Secretary of HEW, Assistant Secretary of Education, and later appointed to the National Commission on Social Security Reform which made recommendations for changes in the law to the President and the Congress in 1983. She is currently a consultant, teacher, and speaker. She holds a Bachelor of Arts degree from the University of Missouri.

Nanette S. Levinson is an Assistant Professor and the Director of the Advanced Technology Management Program in The Center for Technology and Administration at The American University. She received her Ed.M. and Ed.D. from Harvard University. Dr. Levinson has written extensively in the areas of information transfer and research utilization. Her current research interests focus on science policy issues involving interorganizational perspectives and the utilization of new information technologies in management processes.

Howard E. McCurdy is a Professor of Government and Public Administration in the College of Public and International Affairs at The American University. From 1976 to 1981 he served as Director of the University's Public Administration Program. His practical experience includes terms of service with the U.S. Office of Management and Budget, the National Wildlife Federation, the staff of the Washington State Legislature, and a study with the Kenya National Parks. He has written a textbook on public administration and a major bibliographic guide to the field, and his articles have appeared in Public Administration Review, Policy Studies Journal, The Bureaucrat, Journal of

Contemporary Business, _Urban Land_, and _Psychology Today_. He received his M.S. degree from the University of Washington and his Ph.D. from Cornell University.

Gale W. McGee is President of Gale W. McGee Associates . A three-term United States Senator from Wyoming (1958-1977), he was a member of three standing committees--Appropriations, Foreign Relations, and Chairman of Post Office and Civil Service. He helped establish and served as first chairman of the African Subcommittee. His ambassadorial service, under Presidents Carter and Reagan, as Ambassador to the Organization of American States, influenced opening Gale W. McGee Associates, an international consulting firm emphasizing the western hemisphere and international relations. He taught at the Universities of Notre Dame, Iowa State, and Wyoming as well as at several secondary institutions. Dr. McGee earned his bachelor's degree at Nebraska State College, his M.A. at the University of Colorado, and his Ph.D. at the University of Chicago, where he wrote his dissertation on the Monroe Doctrine.

Chester Newland is a Professor of Public Administration at the University of Southern California in Sacramento and in Washington, D.C. A graduate of North Texas State University, he holds a Ph.D. from the University of Kansas. He is a past president of the American Society for Public Administration, and in 1984 he was appointed editor-in-chief of the _Public Administration Review_. He was the initial director of the Lyndon B. Johnson Library and was twice director of the Federal Executive Institute. He is an honorary member of the International City Management Association and a member of the National Academy of Public Administration.

Ernest D. **Plock** received his Ph.D. in International Studies from The American University's School of International Service, where he also instructed several World Politics classes and lectured in courses focusing on the Western intellectual tradition. Dr. Plock's research and study interests include the domestic and foreign policies of European states, with a special emphasis on East-West German relations and international trade issues. He is presently an information and intelligence management specialist with the U.S. Department of Commerce's International Trade Administration.

Nelson W. Polsby is a Professor of Political Science at the University of California, Berkeley. He received his A.B. from a Johns Hopkins University and a Ph.D. from Yale University. His latest books are _Consequences of Party Reform_ (Oxford, 1983) and _Political Innovation in America_ (Yale, 1984).

Elliot L. Richardson is the senior resident partner in the Washington office of Milbank, Tweed, Hadley, and McCloy. He is former Ambassador to the United Kingdom and to the Law of the Sea Conference, and former Secretary of Defense, Secretary of Commerce, Secretary of Health, Education and Welfare, Attorney General, and Undersecretary of State. A graduate of Harvard College and Harvard Law School, he is the author of The Creative Balance--Government, Politics, and the Individual in America's Third Century.

Bernard H. Ross is the Director of Public Administration Programs and a Professor of Government and Public Administration at The American University. Dr. Ross earned a B.S. in Economics at the Wharton School, University of Pennsylvania and a M.A. and Ph.D. in Government from New York University. He has authored and/or co-authored Urban Management, Business Regulation and Government Decision Making and Urban Politics.

Ronald I. Weiner is a Professor of Justice and Social Welfare in The American Unviersity School of Justice. His areas of expertise are law and mental health, forensic criminology, and organizational behavior. He received his Doctorate in Social Welfare from the University of Maryland. He is a nationally recognized consultant in Criminal Justice with the National Institute of Justice and has served as consultant to a number of private firms as well. His current research interests include an exploratory study of the psychological effects of deadly force incidents on police officers.

James Q. Wilson is the Shattuck Professor of Government at Harvard University and a Professor of Management and Public Affairs at the University of California at Los Angeles. He is chairman of the Board of the Police Foundation and the author of Thinking About Crime (revised edition), Varieties of Police Behavior, and a forthcoming work with Richard J. Herrnstein, Crime and Human Nature. He is also the editor of Crime and Public Policy.

Appendix II

March 1984 Conference

Program

THE AMERICAN UNIVERSITY

Public Affairs — 50:

SERVING the PUBLIC in the AMERICAN DEMOCRACY

Celebrating the FIFTIETH ANNIVERSARY of
THE COLLEGE OF PUBLIC AND INTERNATIONAL AFFAIRS
The American University

THE ROLE OF THE GOVERNMENT IN THE UNITED STATES:
THE NEXT FIFTY YEARS

Dates: March 2-3, 1984
Place: The American University Campus
Host: College of Public and International Affairs,
Dr. Robert E. Cleary, Dean

MARCH 2nd

9:30 a.m.	PLENARY SESSION: Role of Federal Government: The Next Fifty Years	**Kay Spiritual Life Center**
	Welcoming remarks and introduction of speaker: Dr. Richard Berendzen, President, The American University	
	Speaker: Honorable Elliot L. Richardson	
10:30 a.m.	Refreshments	**Ward Lobby**
10:45 a.m.	Federal, State, Local Relations: The Next Fifty Years	**Ward II**

Chair: Honorable Elmer B. Staats

Panel Members:
Mr. Wayne F. Anderson, Secretary of Administration and
Finance, Commonwealth of Virginia
Mr. Manuel Deese, City Manager, Richmond, Virginia
Dr. Parris Glendening, County Executive, Prince Georges
County, Maryland
Mr. John J. Gunther, Executive Director, U.S. Conference of
Mayors

Rapporteur: Dr. Bernard Ross, The American University

12:30 p.m.   LUNCHEON for conference participants at the **Mary Graydon Center**
of The American University

MARCH 2nd

2:00 p.m.   Four Concurrent tracks on:
Role of Government: Next Fifty Years

I.   THE PUBLIC SECTOR:
Responsibility and Accountability

A. Confidence in Government   **Ward 317**

Chair: Honorable John W. Macy, Jr.

Presentation by: Dr. Chester Newland, George Mason University

Respondents:
Dr. Charles Levine, The Brookings Institution
Dr. Patricia Florestano, University of Maryland
Dr. Lee Fritschler, The Brookings Institution
Dr. Dwight Waldo, Emeritus, Syracuse University

Rapporteur: Dr. Howard McCurdy, The American University

B. Promoting the General Welfare   **Ward 319**

Chair: Dean Dorothy B. James, The American University

Presentation by: Dr. Nelson Polsby, University of California
at Berkeley

Respondents:
Hon. Stuart E. Eizenstat, Powell, Goldstein, Frazer and Murphy
Hon. John A. Svahn, The White House

Rapporteur: Dr. Michael Hansen, The American University

II. SCIENCE, TECHNOLOGY, AND GOVERNMENT:
Harnessing the Technological Revolution for the Public Good

A. Science, Technology, and International Competition   **Ward II**

Chair: Dr. Louis G. Tornatzky, National Science Foundation

Presentations By:
Hon. Daniel Lungren, U.S. House of Representatives
Dr. Bruce Merrifield, Assistant Secretary, U.S. Department
of Commerce
Dr. Walter Plosila, Deputy Secretary for Technology and Policy
Development, Commonwealth of Pennsylvania
Mr. Ronnie Straw, Communication Workers of America

Respondent: Dr. Robert Stern, Institute of Public Administration

Rapporteur: Dr. Nanette Levinson, The American University

B. Science, Technology, and Government: Regulation of Private Enterprise
(Three specialized panels will address this general topic.)

First Panel: Implications of Regulation in Controlling Adverse **Ward 318**
Impact of Scientific and Technological Innovation

Chair: Dr. William D. Rowe, The American University

Presentations by:
  Dr. William Cavanaugh, President, American Society for
    Testing and Materials
  Mr. Jim J. Tozzi, Director, Multi-National Business Services, Inc.
  Dr. Leon Weinberger, President, Leon Weinberger Associates

Rapporteur: Dr. Marilyn Bracken, Vice President, Environment
  Testing and Certification Corporation

At 3:30 p.m. a Second Panel will discuss The Impact of Standards **Ward 318**
and Regulation on Technological Innovation.

Chair: Dr. William D. Rowe, The American University.

Presentations by:
  Dr. Charles Elkins, Director, Office of Policy Evaluation,
    Environmental Protection Agency
  Dr. Henry Piehler, Carnegie-Mellon University
  Dr. Hilliard Roderick, former Director, Environmental Program,
    Organization for Economic Cooperation and Development

Rapporteur: Dr. Marilyn Bracken

III. SOCIAL JUSTICE
  Beyond Criminal Justice
  (Two specialized panels will address this general topic.)

First Panel: Integrity in Justice Institutions (all afternoon Friday) **Ward 112**

Chair: Dean Rita Simon, The American University

Presentations by:
  Mr. Edward Codelia, Associate Director, The Prison Fellowship
  Dr. Patrick V. Murphy, President, Police Foundation
  Dr. James Q. Wilson, Harvard University

Rapporteur: Dr. James J. Fyfe, The American University .

MARCH 2nd

IV. U.S. FOREIGN AND NATIONAL SECURITY POLICY:
The American Democracy in the Global Community

New Lecture
A. The Executive Branch: U.S. Foreign and National Security Policy   **Hall Rm 102**

    Chair: Dr. Duncan Clarke, The American University

    Presentation by: Dr. Sven Groennings, Director, Fund for the
    Improvement of Post-secondary Education

    Respondents:
      Mr. Robert Beckman, School of International Service,
      The American University
      Mr. Philip Odeen, Coopers and Lybrand
      Mr. I.M. Destler, Carnegie Endowment for International Peace

    Rapporteur: Mr. Joseph G. Bock, School of International Service,
    The American University

B. The Legislative Branch: U.S. Foreign and National Security Policy   **Ward 3**

    Chair: Dr. Stephen D. Cohen, The American University

    Presentation by: Honorable Gale McGee, President, Gale McGee
    Associates; former U.S. Senator, Ambassador to Organization
    of American States

    Respondents:
      Mr. Willard Berry, Executive Director, Coalition for
      Employment through Exports
      Dr. Stanley Heginbotham, Congressional Research Service
      Dean William C. Olson, The American University

    Rapporteur: Mr. Ernest Plock, School of International Service,
    The American University

5:45 p.m.   Reception in the **Lobby of the Ward Circle Building**, The American
University

6:30 p.m.   DINNER for conference participants at the **Mary Graydon Center**

MARCH 3rd

9:30 a.m.   PLENARY SESSION: **Kay Spiritual**
Role of Federal Government: The Next Fifty Years   **Life Center**

         Introduction of Speaker:
            Dr. Milton Greenberg, Provost, The American University

         Speaker: Honorable Richard Bolling

                                                               Kay Center
10:30 a.m.   Refreshments   **Lower Level**

MARCH 3rd

10:45 a.m.   Panels continue discussion with same membership, coming to conclusions and identifying areas of consensus and disagreement, unless new panels are noted here:

The Third Panel on Science, Technology, and Government will discuss Alternatives, Supplements, and Institutional Arrangements for Efficient Regulation.   **Ward 318**

   Chair: Dr. William D. Rowe, The American University

   Panel Members:
   Dr. Neil Kerwin, The American University
   Dr. Henry Piehler, Carnegie-Mellon University
   Dr. Hilliard Roderick

   Rapporteur: Dr. Marilyn Bracken

                                                                            New Lecture
The Second Panel on Justice will discuss Punishment in a Just Society.   **Hall Rm 105**

   Chair: Dr. Jeffrey Reiman, The American University

   Presentation by: Dr. Hugo A. Bedau, Tufts University

   Respondent: Dr. William Hemple, U.S. Probation Office, U.S. District Court for D.C.

   Rapporteur: Dr. Ronald Weiner, The American University

12:30 p.m.   LUNCHEON for conference participants at the **Mary Graydon Center**

   Presiding:
   Dr. Robert E. Cleary, Dean, College of Public and International Affairs, The American University
   Mr. J. Jackson Walter, President, National Academy of Public Administration

   Recognition of Dr. Arthur S. Flemming, Dean, School of Public Affairs, The American University, 1934-1939

   Co-sponsored by the National Academy of Public Administration

1:45 p.m.   Panels report conclusions; general discussion   **Kay Spiritual**
                                                                        Life Center

4:00 p.m.   *Closing Remarks:* Convocation makes a commitment to publish a report and to explore the implications regarding the future needs of government and the curricula of universities.

PUBLIC AFFAIRS — 50

Program Changes

Rep. Bolling will speak at 9:30 a.m. on March 2nd; Ambassador Richardson will speak at 9:30 a.m. on March 3rd.

Mr. Mark E. Keane, former Executive Director of the International City Management Association, will be replacing Mr. John Gunther on the "Federal, State, and Local Relations" panel.

Dr. John Holmfeld, Committee on Science and Technology, U.S. House of Representatives, will be replacing the Hon. Daniel Lungren on the panel "Science, Technology, and International Competition."

Mr. Charles W. Maynes, Editor of Foreign Policy, and Richard T. Arndt of USIA will replace I.M. Destler and Philip Odeen on the panel "The Executive Branch: U.S. Foreign and National Security Policy."

Dr. Hilliard Roderick is unable to participate on the "Science, Technology, and Government" panel.

Appendix III

March 1984 Conference Participants

PUBLIC AFFAIRS-50 CONFERENCE

List of Participants

P.B. Akridge, IBM Corporation

Anita Alpern, School of Government and Public Administration, The American University

Wayne F. Anderson, Secretary of State and Finance, Commonwealth of Virginia

Dr. Richard T. Arndt, United States Information Agency

Dr. Nancy S. Barrett, Professor of Economics, The American University

Lucius D. Battle, School of Advanced International Studies, Johns Hopkins University

Walter E. Beach, The Brookings Institution

Robert Beckman, School of International Service, The American University

Hugo A. Bedau, Professor of Philosophy, Tufts University

David Bell, Division of Occupational Safety and Health, U.S. Department of Labor

Dr. Richard Berendzen, President, The American University

Willard M. Berry, Executive Director, Coalition for Employment through Exports

Charles Bingman, National Academy of Public Administration

Gen. George S. Blanchard, McLean, Virginia

Ralph Bledsoe, Special Assistant, The White House

Joseph G. Bock, School of International Service, The American University

Andrew Boesel, National Association of Schools of Public Affairs and Administration

Richard Bolling, former Congressman from Missouri

Dr. Marilyn Bracken, Vice President, Environmental Testing and Certification Corporation

Dr. Walter Broadnax, Professor of Business and Public Administration, Harvard University

Dr. William Cavanaugh, President, American Society for Testing and Materials

Patrick Choate, TRW

Warren Cikins, The Brookings Institution

Dr. Charles Clapp, Executive Director, U.S. Postal Rate Commission

Dr. Duncan L. Clarke, School of International Service, The American University

Dr. John Clarke, AMTRAK

Dr. Robert E. Cleary, Dean, College of Public and International Affairs, The American University
Edward Codelia, The Prison Fellowship
Dr. Stephen D. Cohen, School of International Service, The American University
Ralph Cole, Washington Academy of Sciences
Ellen Collier, Congressional Research Service, Library of Congress
Murray Comarow, School of Government and Public Administration, The American University
Dr. Anthony Cox, Embassy of the United Kingdom
Elizabeth Crimi, School of Justice, The American University
Dr. Robert Curvin, Dean, Graduate School of Management, New School for Social Research
Dr. Robert S. Cutler, National Science Foundation
Dr. Roger Davidson, Congressional Research Service, Library of Congress
Alan Dean, National Academy of Pubic Adminstration
Manuel Deese, City Manager, Richmond, Virginia
Dr. Earl H. DeLong, Dean Emeritus, School of Government and Public Adminstration, The American University
Dr. Stephen Ebbin, Institute of International Education
Stuart Eizenstat, Powell, Goldstein, Frazer, and Murphy
Charles Elkins, Environmental Protection Agency
Darlene Fisher, National Science Foundation
Dr. Arthur S. Flemming, Executive Director, National Coalition for Quality Integrated Education
Dr. Patricia Florestano, Institute for Government Service, University of Maryland
Dr. H. George Fredrickson, President, Eastern Washington State University
Dr. A. Lee Fritschler, The Brookings Institution
Dr. Osmund Fundingslund, General Accounting Office
Dr. James J. Fyfe, School of Justice, The American University
Dr. Zewde Gabre-Sellassie, Office of the Secretary General, The United Nations
Eilene Galloway, Washington, D.C.
Dr. Parris Glendening, County Executive, Prince Georges County, Maryland
Dr. Milton Greenberg, Provost, The American University
Dr. Ernest S. Griffith, Dean Emeritus, School of International Service, The American University
Dr. Sven Groennings, Director, Fund for Improvement of Postsecondary Education
Dr. Charles Hamilton, Professor of Government, Columbia University
Dr. Susan W. Hammond, School of Government and Public Administration, The American University
Dr. Michael Hansen, School of Government and Public Administration, The American University
Dr. Lowell Hattery, Mt. Airy, Maryland

Harry S. Havens, Assistant Comptroller General, General Accounting Office
Barbara Hawk, Institute for Government Service, University of Maryland
Davis Hays, Arlington, Virginia
Dr. Stanley Heginbotham, Congressional Research Service, Library of Congress
Dr. Walter Held, McLean, Virginia
Dr. William Hemple, Probation Office, U.S. District Court for the District of Columbia
Lynn Herring, Chief, United States Park Police
Dr. Richard Higgins, School of Government and Public Administration, The American University
Dr. Thomas Hogan, National Science Foundation
Dr. John Holmfeld, Committee on Science and Technology, U.S. House of Representatives
Phillip S. Hughes, Undersecretary, The Smithsonian Institution
George Ingle, Chemical Manufacturers Association
Judge William A. Irwin, U.S. Department of the Interior
Dr. Dorothy B. James, Dean, School of Government and Public Administration, The American University
Kenan P. Jarboe, Assistant Professor of Technology and Planning, University of Maryland
Mark E. Keane, former Executive Director, International City Managers Association
Dr. Neil Kerwin, School of Government and Public Administration, The American University
Martha Keys, U.S. Association of Former Members of Congress
Dr. George LaNoue, Professor Political Science, University of Maryland, Baltimore County
Dr. Samuel Lawrence, National Oceanic and Atmospheric Administration
Dr. William LeoGrande, School of Government and Public Administration, The American University
Dr. Charles Levine, The Brookings Institution
Dr. Marsha Levine, American Enterprise Institute
Dr. Nanette S. Levinson, Center for Technology and Administration, The American University
Marion Logue, Archivist, The American University
Hugh Loweth, Office of Management and Budget
John W. Macy Jr., Chairman, National Citizens Committee for Food and Shelter
Charles Maechling Jr., Carnegie Endowment for International Peace
William S. Maillard, former Congressman from California
Dr. Thomas E. Mann, Executive Director, American Political Science Association
Dr. Milton C. Mapes, Executive Director, National Peace Academy Campaign
Robbin S. Marks, Silver Spring, Maryland
Charles W. Maynes, Editor, Foreign Policy

Dr. Howard E. McCurdy, School of Government and Public Administration, The American Unviersity
Dr. Gale McGee, President, Gale McGee Associates
Dr. Bruce Merrifield, Assistant Secretary, U.S. Department of Commerce
Michael Michaelis, President, Partners in Enterprise
Patrick V. Murphy, President, The Police Foundation
Richard A. Myren, School of Justice, The American University
Dr. Mark Nadel, General Accounting Office
Dr. Chester A. Newland, Professor of Public Administration, George Mason University
Robert Nicholas, Committee on Science and Technology, U.S. House of Representatives
Robert Norris, Vice Provost, The American University
Thomas Novotny, Editor, The Bureaucrat
Kirk O'Donnell, Office of the Speaker, U.S. House of Representatives
Walter Oleszek, Congressional Research Service, Library of Congress
Dr. William C. Olson, Dean, School of International Service, The American University
Dr. Henry Piehler, Carnegie-Mellon University
Dr. Howard Pittman, McLean, Virginia
Ernest D. Plock, School of International Service, The American University
Dr. Walter Plosila, Deputy Secretary, Department of Commerce, Commonwealth of Pennsylvania
Dr. Nelson Polsby, Professor of Political Science, University of California, Berkeley
Dr. Jeffrey Reiman, School of Justice, The American University
Elliot L. Richardson, Milbank, Tweed, Hadley, and McCloy
Dr. Anthony Robbins, Committee on Energy and Commerce, U.S. House of Representatives
Dr. Nina M. Roscher, Vice Provost, The American University
Bernard Rosen, School of Government and Public Administration, The American University
Dr. Allan Rosenbaum, Institute for Policy Analysis and Research, University of Maryland, Baltimore County
Marc Rosenberg, National Coalition for Science and Technology
Dr. Bernard H. Ross, School of Government and Public Administration, The American University
Dr. William D. Rowe, Center for Technology and Administration, The American University
Elaine Ryan, GTE Telenet Communications
Dr. Isabel Sawhill, The Urban Institute
Judith Schneider, Congressional Research Service, Library of Congress
Richard L. Seggel, National Academy of Sciences
Gary Senese, General Electric Information Services Company
Dr. Michael Shapiro, U.S. Environmental Protection Agency

Dr. Rita J. Simon, Dean, School of Justice, The American University
Daniel Skoler, Social Security Administration
Dr. Gordon Smith, Fairchild Space Company
Sidney Sober, School of International Service, The American University
Dr. Howard Sorrows, National Bureau of Standards
Dr. Elmer B. Staats, President, The Truman Foundation
Dr. David Stanley, Vienna, Virginia
Dr. Donald Stone, Adjunct Professor of Management, Carnegie-Mellon University
Ronnie J. Straw, Communication Workers of America
John A. Svahn, Assistant to the President, The White House
James W. Symington, Smathers, Symington, and Herlong
Philip T. Thorson, Glen Echo Heights, Maryland
Dr. Kenneth Tolo, Associate Vice President for Academic Affairs, University of Texas at Austin
Dr. Louis Tornatzky, National Science Foundation
Jim Tozzi, Director, Multi-National Business Services
John Travis, U.S. Probation Office
John Tuthill, President, Salzburg Seminars in American Studies
Dr. Richard W. Van Wagenen, Washington, D.C.
Dr. Dwight Waldo, Professor Emeritus, Syracuse University
J. Jackson Walter, President, National Academy of Public Administration
Dr. Leon Weinberger, Leon Weinberger Associates
Dr. Ronald I. Weiner, School of Justice, The American University
Dr. Madeline Weiss, Bethesda, Maryland
Charles W. Whalen Jr., former Congressman from Ohio
Joseph Wholey, Professor of Public Administration, University of Southern California
Dr. Francis O. Wilcox, Director General, The Atlantic Council of the United States
Dr. James Q. Wilson, Shattuck Professor of Government, Harvard University
Jerry Wilson, Peoples Drug Stores
Ron Wilson, McLean, Virginia
Mary Woodworth, VITRO Laboratories
Dr. John D. Young, Center for Technology and Administration, The American University
John H. Young, Reston, Virginia